Prakash Bansod

Publisher: MITE Inc., Mississauga, Ontario, Canada

First Edition (2016)

www.canadianvisitor.com

Acknowledgements

Many thanks to the following reviewers whose comments and feedback helped to improve this book:

Kalyan Harpalani, Mississauga, Ontario, Canada
Marya Kumar, New Delhi, India
Seema Mahdavi, East Lansing, Michigan, USA
Raj Marwa, Toronto, Canada
Paresh Mehta, Puné, India
Larrick Pinto, Mississauga, Ontario, Canada
Gosia Siuda, Mississauga, Canada
Sylvan Valladares, Mississauga, Canada

Dedication

To grandchildren everywhere.
"May their world be safer and cleaner"

"An eye for an eye will leave everyone blind!"
Mahatma Gandhi

Disclaimer

This novel is a work of fiction in the mystery and adventure genre. All characters, in this book, are fictitious. Any similarity to an actual person with a similar name, physical appearance, character or manner of speaking, is a coincidence. Most institutions such as schools, school boards, government agencies and political parties are also fictitious.

Intellectual Property Rights

The author, Prakash Bansod, owns the publishing rights and copyright to this book regardless of the type of publishing medium. This includes conventional print, eBooks, Internet based sources, video, audio reproductions and film scripts based on this book.

ISBN eBook: 978-0-9939847-0-9
ISBN Soft Cover: 978-0-9939847-1-6

Contents

Prologue

Mr. Alfred Pinto, India's Defence Minister, planned on reducing his country's conventional armed forces to an internal security and anti-terrorist organization. Mr. Pinto's political party, the Asian Global Alliance, AGA, only had a slim majority in the Indian Parliament. It was somewhat left of centre in its thinking but was backed by Industrialists. AGA's mandate was to spend less on defence and more on infrastructure, farm subsidies, healthcare, education, water management and green energy projects. However, there were two other rival right wing political parties. Neither differed much at least on their policies on national defence. Their strategy was to dominate the region and maintain nuclear strike capability. India's multi-billion dollar defence budget was the apple in the eye of arms manufacturers worldwide. The arms dealers were also interested in this opportunity. The right-wing political parties received contributions, including personal kickbacks, from arms dealers. Most Indians still lived below the poverty line, regardless of the party in power.

Ever since the Kyoto Conference on Climate Change, the G8 countries had tried to persuade the developing world to do their part in Green House Gas (GHG) emissions reduction. However, the developing nations were reluctant to comply. They reasoned that the developed world still produced a significant portion of the global GHG emissions and it made sense that they should lead by example. Although many had committed to ambitious targets, most signatories had only made little of no advances in emissions reduction.

The proliferation of nuclear weapons also caused concern. Once again, there was a call for the developed countries to lead by example and reduce their nuclear arsenal. There was an impasse on both fronts for many years; GHG reduction and nuclear disarmament. Fortunately, for the AGA party, all this changed dramatically during the election year. The leader of a famous British rock group, Tryst With Destiny (TWD), was a well-respected philanthropist called Mano. He proposed that an international consortium be created to encourage the decommissioning of nuclear weapons in the developing world. For each nuclear weapon decommissioned, the consortium would invest in infrastructure, education and carbon abatement projects.

The tide turned in favour of Mano's idea when the AGA agreed to cooperate. The notion of the Indian sub-continent secure and free of nuclear weapons created an attractive vision of a large stable and democratic country of entrepreneurs, ready to do business. About 50 billion dollars were pledged through international Crowd Funding efforts for the project within a month of Mono's proposal. Subsequently, Mono created a non-profit foundation called the Carbon Abatement and Nuclear

Disarmament Organization (CANDO). CANDO would administer the funding and select vendors to carry out proposed projects. The UN's committees on Climate Change and Nuclear Disarmament enthusiastically endorsed Mano's proposal. AGA's initiatives on defence cuts prompted the UN to suggest India as a test bed for CANDO. The UN appointed Mano to act as a mediator. He was tasked to broker a unified CANDO deal with the Indian Government.

The AGA party brass welcomed Mano's ideas in principle. In practice however, they had a hard time selling the idea. The two right wing parties, in the coalition, would have nothing to do with it. They argued that the lack of a nuclear strike capability would leave the country vulnerable to nuclear blackmail.

As the AGA started serious discussion with CANDO, the hitherto civilized debate got ugly. The arms deals were worth billions of dollars. The diversion of funds would end the lucrative arms business. The arms dealers were prepared to fight to the finish. Terrorism irrupted first in India and then spread to countries that supported CANDO's goals.

This book is about a victim of terrorism. There is a curious thing about terrorists and their victims. They rarely know one another and yet, one can become like the other.

Chapter 1: For the Love of Chikki

A common misconception is that the Himalayas have acted in the defence of India since recorded history. Their foreboding stature apparently deterred foreign invaders. It turns out that most invaders, starting with the Greeks to modern times have entered India through some pass in that mountain range. It could be that a successful passage through the formidable Himalayas lulled these visitors into a false sense of accomplishment. They let their guard down and ventured further into the subcontinent. When they did venture further south, they inevitably came upon the Deccan Plateau amidst the Sayadhri mountain range. From the coastal lowlands, abutting the Indian Ocean, the terrain climbs to an elevation of about 2000 feet where it meets the serene plains of the Deccan Plateau. There was no easy passage through this Maratha Kingdom. The Moguls and later the British learnt this to their expense when they struggled against the guerrilla tactics of the Peshwa Dynasty. The Peshwa were unbeatable in the mountainous regions of the Sayadhri at least until the arrival of Lord Arthur Wellesley. He subdued the Marathas by attacking from the South. This tactics bypassed the hideous guerrilla mountain warfare that had bogged down northern intruders for years.

It was often assumed that the superior British military tactics were based on lessons learnt during the European wars. Lord Wellesley, later as the Duke of Wellington, vanquished the Napoleonic armies at Waterloo. The Duke gave credit to the military tactics he developed while battling the Marathas. A lasting homage to his exploits in this region is a mountain peak named after him called Duke's Nose. Now in the 21st Century, it is a popular picnic and hiking tourist destination.

The descendents of these noble warriors now live in a region that has developed into a prosperous business zone. It is strategically located between the commercial centre of Mumbai and the ancient university city of Puné. Earlier, in order to get to Puné, one needed to negotiate treacherous winding ghats. These ghats had numerous hairpin bends with only two lanes. This dangerous route winds through the scenic splendour of the Sayadhri forests and waterfalls. Here, tigers once roamed before they were hunted to the brink of extinction. At the end of the uphill journey is the town of Lonavala. Mumbaikars often seek refuge in Lonavala, on weekends, to avoid the humidity and congestion.

Recent infrastructure upgrades required the construction of a new highway. This highway cuts through the mountain with a series of tunnels. Although this saved an hour of travel time to Puné, it bypassed the town completely. Much to the chagrin of the commercial community, this caused a considerable loss of business. The rail link from Mumbai carves an equally scenic route aboard the Deccan Queen. The electric train service has been in operation for over 80 years. The Queen stops at Lonavala, travelling in either direction, in order to add an engine or remove one as required. The stop is for five minutes but all pandemonium breaks loose as the train enters the station. Young hawkers, brandishing their Indian Railway licenses, do brisk business selling boxes of the world famous Lonavala Chikki.

The best Chikki comes from Lonavala. Its history parallels the development of regional road and rail infrastructure. There was a need for an inexpensive energy rich food supplement for workers. It consists of layers of nuts of a single type, or a mixed variety bonded together by a hard sweet resin. The resin is made from a closely guarded secret recipe. It has evolved and now comes in a number of colours, shapes and ingredients, including sugar free types. Some passengers lean through windows and others step on to the platform. They struggle with a choice of Chikki in order to comply with the numerous requests from family, friends and business associates.

Mr. Madanlal was a prominent Chikki merchant in Lonavala. His family had been making Chikki for generations. They claimed to be one of the original suppliers to Indian Railways. Along with the numerous vendors, he lamented the loss of the road business. He survived, like others, who were still in business, by selling online. The hard sugary resin and nuts require no preservatives and this makes it ideal for long distance transport. He first sold Chikki across India and then to the vast Indian diaspora worldwide.

It was April, and the start of the tourist season. The academic year for most institutions of learning only lasts up to the month of April. Beyond this, the heat is unbearable. Scholars, teachers and the rest need a respite from the relentless humidity of Mumbai until the monsoons arrive in June and July. The lush Mango groves, in the coastal plains of Konkan and Sayadhri valley, beckon. At this time of year they are laden with the prized golden king of fruit – the Alphonso mango. It takes on a characteristic gold green tinge and begs to be picked.

The mango harvest coincided with the tourist season. Regardless of their problems, the consortium of Chikki manufacturers looked forward with great excitement to a special day. It concerned the arrival of the Mumbai School Board's bus on their annual picnic. A teacher started this tradition decades ago as a reward for her best students. The prospect of "all you can eat Chikki" motivated some to academic excellence. The School Board later extended this opportunity to all schools. Schools could send one nominee on the trip. The participants' accomplishments were impressive. They consisted of winners of spelling bee competitions, elocution contest stars, top scorers in public exams, top wicket takers and run makers in cricket, chess champions, distinguished volunteers and so on; very simply the brightest and the best.

Madanlal's company was always involved in some capacity, but this year was very special. It was the trip's 25th anniversary. He reflected on the years that had gone by. Decades ago, a rickety old bus would bring the students up from Mumbai. It would barely make it up the ghats and on more than one occasion, it had broken down and almost ruined the trip. The girls and boys sat in different areas of the bus. The only entertainment was an approved list of school songs. Everyone wore school uniforms. The girls wore their shiny long black coconut oiled hair in one or two platted strands with bowed ribbons at the ends. As years went by, everything got slicker and more relaxed. The young scholars now arrive in a posh luxury air-conditioned bus with video screens and outlets for their devices. The girls are smartly turned out, never wear their uniforms, and troop out sporting the latest Bollywood fashions. Some wear blond streaks through their hair and are usually texting on cell phones. Others stare ahead as if in a stupor while listening to their MP3 players. The boys are more boisterous than ever and some have already formed liaisons with the girls.

Mr. Madanlal did not let all this modernity distract him. He knew that despite those external impressions, they were just as sharp if not sharper than ever before. Since he was the spokesman for the Lonavala Chikki Association, he often had to face a barrage of questions that got tougher and more candid by the year.

"Does the Association enforce child labour laws?" one girl asked. Another was concern with recycling, and yet another wanted to know more about the online business, and if the Lonavala Chikki Website had secured a high spot on the Internet search engines. Last year there was a question about what the Association was doing to reduce its collective Carbon Foot Print. Madanlal had a special surprise for the kids. The bus arrived on time and 32 bright eyed students filed out along with four staff and the driver; 37 visitors altogether.

The entire business community came out to greet and welcome the young tourists. The tour commenced with a walk around Mr. Madanlal's factory. They were shown the various stages of Chikki manufacture and packaging. As they exited, Mr. Madanlal pointed with pride to his surprise; a new array of solar panels. He hoped to solicit some compliments from his visitors. To his disappointment, he was greeted with unimpressed set of blank stares.

A student broke the awkward silence and asked, "Where is your wind turbine? In this mountainous region you must have a high average wind velocity. You could generate enough power for all the factories."

Poor Madanlal looked around helplessly and was lost for words. Another member of the reception committee came to his rescue. He claimed that they were planning this in the near future. Next, the party went to a banquet hall of a local hotel where every factory owners' wares were on exhibit. Each student was presented with a generous assortment of Chikki in a special 25th year commemorative package. The next phase of their trip was a picnic and hiking in the vicinity of Duke's Nose, about 15 km away.

The bus was soon on its way towards Duke's Nose. The business community returned to work, and the crowds began to disperse. About 15 minutes later, a distant explosion was heard that was powerful enough to rattle windows and utensils in Lonavala. The thunderclap echoed across the Sayadhri mountain range and valleys. Madanlal looked around curiously at his staff but none had an explanation. He ran outside only to see other businesspersons were emerging into the street with anxious faces. Then, someone pointed in the direction of Duke's Nose. An ominous mushroom shaped black plume rose in the distance.

Madanlal had a bad feeling about this and yelled to his son to get the company van from the back of the factory. It was being prepared for a shipment of fresh Chikki to retail outlets in Puné, 65 km away. Madanlal got into the passenger seat, and they drove furiously to the Duke's Nose resort area. Soon they could see orange flames in the distance. As they approached within hundred metres, they could see the bus or what was left of it. An explosion had split it into two, with the rear portion still in flames. Madanlal asked his son to call for help on his cell phone while he ran towards the burning debris. Apart from cracking flames, there was a deadly silence. A stench of burning flesh and gasoline filled the air. As he approached, he saw bodies, and body parts strewn in random everywhere. He looked desperately in all directions to find some one he could help. Just then, he heard a whimpering sound from behind a bush.

"Pani (water), Pani ..." cried the feeble voice in Marathi. It was the young wind turbine "expert". Madanlal knelt beside the boy and noticed his legs were missing. Madanlal called out to his son to fetch some bottled water from the van.

"The Police and ambulances are on their way," said Madanlal's son. He hurried to his father's side with a case of water bottles in his hand. He was just in time to see his father pass his hand over the dead boy's eyes, shutting them for all eternity. He also witnessed for the first time, his father, a stoic, well-respected leader of the community, weeping uncontrollably.

"Papa, did the bus hit something?" asked the young man.

"No, no, no! ... This ... this is no accident. This shaitan came to us from Mumbai. There must have been a bomb on the bus. But, why ... why kill my smart, beautiful children? For years, they visited us. We fed them, cared for them and gave them a good time. Why? … Why would anyone want to harm them?" cried Madanlal looking around at the deadly silence that engulfed Mumbai's brightest and best, now lying in pieces, in a nondescript field, in the shadow of Duke's Nose.

Chapter 2: An Awakening

In Puné, the morning of the Lonavala Bombing, was hot and sultry. The power had gone off during the night. It had lost the battle of supply and demand. Air conditioners and overnight shifts in local industry had taken their toll. Jeevan Gill awoke to a strange sound that drifted up to his make shift balcony bed, on the first floor of his apartment building. It was neither the noisy Puné Municipal Transport buses nor the clamour and chatter due to the early rush hour pedestrians on the sidewalk below, that awoke him. He had learned to tune these things out and sleep right through them. A man was singing. His rich baritone voice appeared to lift itself above all else and waft tantalizingly into Jeevan's balcony. Jeevan sat up and peered sleepily over the railings.

A holy man dressed with nothing more than a loincloth and a thick beaded necklace around his neck lay on his back on the sidewalk and sang an ancient poem. Patterns in ash covered his naked torso and forehead. A busy stream of people, hurrying to work, divided past him and occasionally threw some coins into a battered hollowed out gourd, carried by a young saffron robed assistant. The bard sung a verse and propelled himself forward by rolling a few turns over his stomach and back before coming to rest. He would then start to sing yet another verse. He had a long way to go to the temple, on the top of the hill. This was the famous Jungle Emperor Road. Through the passage of time, it had seen revolutions, freedom fighting demonstrations, assassinations and floods. The deity had witnessed it all.

Jeevan, a project manager for Roshni Sound and Light International, RSLI, had grandiose plans to translate scholarly Sanskrit text. He planned to bring the vast array of mythological figures, deities, demons, lovers, conquers and the vanquished to life in film and TV cartoon characters. This at least was his official daytime job. He was, in real life, an intelligence officer on a top-secret mission in Puné. No one apart from the powers that be in New Delhi knew of his mission.

The holy man's verse challenged Jeevan's high school Sanskrit. He recognized the section from the famous scene of a conqueror who had won a battle, on the Indo-Gangetic planes that had changed the course of history, but he appeared to have lost his soul. The conqueror surveyed the death and destruction around him where legions were put to the sword in a gluttony of revenge, but for what! He now meditated on the futility of war. An eye for an eye, kill or be killed, dig two graves before you seek revenge. What was the point of it all? Jeevan allowed himself the luxury of questioning if this was the only way. He shook his head and smiled at his own naivety and thought, perhaps there was no other way.

In terms of the events as they were to unfold, Jeevan would remember that striking scene. He wondered if the message was for him or was he to convey it to some one else. Jeevan stood at the balcony and listened intently to the sage's singing, and as the duo continued to make their torturous journey uphill, he reached for his wallet on the dresser and selected a generous note. He crumbled it into a ball and called out to the gourd-carrying assistant. The startled young man rushed forward to catch the paper ball in his gourd, much to the amusement of the passing throng. Hardly had the money passed through Jeevan's hands when he felt a strange sense of guilt. What was he doing? Why did he act so impulsively? Did the sage's singing inspire him to be generous? It was none of these things. As he prepared for work, it came to him. He saw himself observing a historical conspiracy. Humans will sin, some more than others but there would always be some pious individuals who would volunteer to atone for the world's sins. They would die on a cross, be burnt at the stake, be imprisoned for decades, or even grovel in the dirt and sing classical verse, and just for few Rupees this would ensure our salvation.

Jeevan was on his own mission to save the world from the powers of darkness but content to being an unsung hero. Global terrorism must be stamped out, he reminded himself, but for him this war must be won at home.

The sage's early morning wake up call had bought him an extra 15 minutes. His maid was in and well into making his lunch, which would be delivered to him later that day by the dubha wallah. She persuaded him to eat a more substantial breakfast instead of his usual coriander tea. He cast his eye a newspaper but skipped to the business section. He read an interesting article on Carbon Trading and its relation to the Kyoto Agreement. A think tank proposed a brilliant idea. Some nations that produced below their quota in emissions could sell these savings or Carbon Credits. The Carbon satiated countries could buy themselves some redemption and move closer to being compliant. Jeevan smiled to himself when he saw an analogy between this and the sinners, and salvation providers concept that had crossed his mind earlier.

Jeevan tucked into the spicy omelette that the maid had served up for him. He diced his fresh toast, speared the delicious omelette and inadvertently switched on the TV. It happened to be tuned to the news channel. The current dose of terrorist carnage immediately jumped out at him. It seemed to say, 'There is no avoiding this; you might as well look at it now.' However, today's news, because of the loss of children, was particularly gruesome. It made him lose his appetite for the haut cuisine. The grim news ruined his plans for the day.

The Mumbai press were present in force. TV vans with roof top mounted antennae crowded the narrow streets. A distraught Madanlal, with is back to his Chikki factory, faced a barrage of questions. As the details of the carnage emerged, it made Jeevan's blood boil. This was not Srinagar or a distant border outpost anymore. The terrorists had struck close to home; right in his backyard. This time they murdered innocent children. It was a shocking escalation. He called into RSLI and left a message to say that he needed to resolve some urgent family issues. He would be away for a few days. He could not attend to his undercover day job while priorities as an intelligence officer took over. He ruled out a trip to Lonavala. It would have blown his cover. He was on the phone to ensure that the local constabulary cordoned off the area. They did not touch anything until a forensics team arrived to conduct their investigation.

A few days turned into a week. The forensics team drove up from Mumbai, which is North of Lonavala. They took the same route as the school bus and went to work looking for any remnants of the bomb and its triggering mechanism. When they found what they wanted they contacted Jeevan who then returned to RSLI.

Gohkale Industrial Park was situated on the edge of the sprawling Fergusson College campus. There were many new buildings in the enclave, including new venture projects. Fergusson College, which was affiliated to Puné University, had developed lucrative Information Technology (IT), pharmaceutical, and biotechnology interests. A 25 square kilometre high security fence enclosed the entire gated industrial community.

The entrance to the enclave was a short driveway that came off Fergusson Road. At the end of it was a checkpoint complete with a barrier that was usually up. The resident Gurkha kept a watchful eye on pedestrians and vehicular traffic. He raised a forbidding arm if he did not recognize anyone or if they were not wearing ID. The Gurkha amused the workers by turning out in a variety of garbs. Sometimes he wore khaki shorts, sporting the traditional curved short bladed kukri and olive toupee. Occasionally he would wear his full battle fatigues, jack-boots, flak jacket, helmet, with embedded wireless, and an Uzi sub-machine gun at hand. Whenever the gun and flak jacket came out, the barrier was usually down, much to the annoyance of the inmates of Gohkale Park. The Gurkha would salute the passengers of an occasional limousine that would drive by with a flourish in proportion to the value of the previous year's Devali baksheesh. Whenever Jeevan Gill rode by on his carefully restored Triumph 500 Speed Twin, the Gurkha would jump smartly to attention and salute. If a weapon were at hand, he would shoulder it and slap the frame smartly with his right hand.

Nobody questioned the additional security, and nobody knew who paid for it. All this security appeared about the time RSLI moved into an unassuming white ivy covered, two storied building, with a huge satellite antenna on its roof. The ground floor had large open windows that showed the RSLI staff hard at work. They looked like retired college professors. They arrived every morning on bicycle or scooter with the exception of their boss, Professor Paranjpé. His niece, Padma, drove him to work in a Tata Nano. Today, Prof. Paranjpé appeared to be arguing with his niece as they entered the building together.

"Uncle, Samir and I want to keep our wedding simple. There is no need to go into all that expense...," said Padma.

"Nonsense!" interrupted Prof. Paranjpé, "No niece of mine is going to have a 'simple wedding'. Your late father, God bless his soul, would never forgive me if I didn't do the best I could for you."

"But how are we going to pay for all this, " persisted Padma when he interrupted again, "You and your Aunty (his wife) should just worry about the guest list and make sure that fiancé of yours returns from the States in time for the wedding." The conversation ended abruptly, as the pair entered the office.

After a brief round of greetings, with the six researchers and translators in the open working area, Prof. Paranjpé went to his office. He sat and stared pensively at papers strewn at random across his desk. A deep sense of remorse overcame him as it always did when Padma's wedding came up. Various options, from pawning his wife's jewellery to re-mortgaging their modest house, were being considered. However, it was not just the wedding; a mediating "third party" approached him with a proposal for a "settlement". Nobody used the illegal D word or its equivalent in any Indian language anymore. The young man's foreign training and job in the US had raised his price.

If he could have put the clock back on his life, he would never have been involved with the Deccan Mandate. As a carefree undergraduate, he searched for a cause. They recruited him. Originally, the Deccan Mandate was merely a right wing nationalistic non-violent association that spoke out against any Indian separatist movements. Whether it was Kashmir, Nagaland, Khalistan or Tamil Nadu, these anti-separatists, had a finger in every pie. Their modus operandi was to discredit Federal politicians, taking part in peace negotiations. They did this by using the social media to expose corrupt practices, nepotism, publish compromising evidence of extra-marital liaisons etc.

The impoverished masses of India, the largest group of semi-literate people in the world, saw no use for defence expenditure. They demanded a radical change in spending priorities. In order to thwart this popular movement, Deccan Mandate changed from an intellectual think tank to something much more ominous. Arms dealers had a stake in fuelling the flames of animosity between the Government and separatist groups. They took a serious interest in the Deccan Mandate and funded it substantially. A number of unsavoury characters replaced the upper echelons of the association. They were only interested in making as much money as possible by satisfying the needs of arms dealers. The arms dealers in turn acted as intermediaries for a huge multi-billion dollar arms supply chain. As long as orders for munitions, jet fighters, tanks, destroyers, submarines, and the occasional aircraft carrier kept coming in, nobody cared to question the financial transactions between arms dealers and Deccan Mandate.

As money poured in, there appeared to be a split in the Deccan Mandate. An aggressive element emerged, which thought nothing of kidnappings and assassinations as a means to an end. The moderate elements put some distance between themselves and its ultra right wing faction. They were forced to go underground when most member countries in the UN labelled them as a terrorist group.

Prof. Paranjpé was a brilliant academic, with several international peer reviewed publications to his credit. He specialized in the modern interpretation of Indian Philosophy. He rose through the ranks and soon became the principal of Fergusson College. It was one of the finest post secondary educational institutions in the region. However, when he applied for the Vice Chancellor's position at Puné University, his opponents produced a police background check that revealed his youthful connection to the Deccan Mandate. The local newspapers alleged links between Paranjpé and every political assassination in the previous 10 years. To avoid further scandal, the University administration persuaded him not only to withdraw his application but also to take an early retirement from Fergusson.

An organization called Dhaku, described as an association of professional assassins, operated unseen in the background. They had been in the assassination business for generations. They were apolitical, discreet, mysterious, and rarely missed a target. They operated from safe houses in Maharashtra and were headquartered in Puné city. For a price, a political opponent could be made to disappear or a similar fate could await a rival corporate executive. These "disappearances" were usually high profile with broad community repercussions. Jealous lovers, wives or husbands, and malicious uncles with an eye on a relative's estate, did not interest Dhaku. There was a quaint sense of professional pride practised by them. Law enforcement was frustrated in their pursuit of Dhaku. The capture of any member and his/her subsequent prosecution could draw out decades of connected situations. This could tarnish the good name and implicate many businesses. The resignations and or arrests of the area's most influential citizens would cause unthinkable turmoil. It was best to leave those skeletons in the closets across the land. The Dhaku acted swiftly, discreetly and left no trace. Local police followed up and arrested the usual suspects. After months or years of unsuccessful investigations, the files were closed and everyone would move on. They could do nothing against these silent killers from a mythical society.

Over the decades, the media had aggravated the situation by building on the Dhaku folklore. However, they were always careful not even to hint at the name of a suspect. Even Bollywood stayed clear of any plots that mentioned the Dhaku for fear of deadly reprisals. They could get no actor to play the role of a Dhaku operative. Generations of kids on the subcontinent, were persuaded to eat their meals, do their homework, go to bed or stop being naughty. If they did not obey, the ultimate threat was issued that the Dhaku would be called to get them. The Dhaku belonged to a timeless clan of professional criminals for whom there was no known beginning and no end. They were a pervasive dark society that resurfaced from time to time. Much like a virus, that stays dormant for years and then emerges mysteriously.

The winds of prosperity blew across the Indian sub-continent. No amount of terrorism was going to stop the good times that were forecasted. The electorate demanded cuts in defence spending, investment in infrastructure and social programs. There were plans to work towards a nuclear free zone in South Asia. To solve the regions chronic territorial disputes, dual citizenship, common currency, and united armed forces were being considered. Not far along lay the possibility of an Asian Union. This would connect most South Asian countries in a tariff free trading block.

The Deccan Mandate watched with grave concern as these events unfolded. Their sponsors stood to lose billions of US dollars in international arms deals. Something drastic needed to be done to stop this cosiness. They focused on spectacular assassinations or threats against any public figure, politician or otherwise, who supported a peaceful resolution of the Kashmir dispute. The Federal intelligence agency known as the Research and Analysis Group, R.A.G., fought a campaign against the Deccan Mandate with limited success. However, what emerged shocked them. The Deccan Mandate out-sourced, its assassination business to Dhaku.

Not content to spend the rest of his life in obscurity, Prof. Paranjpé decided to retaliate and spent a year researching a book on the Deccan Mandate, its origins and its connection to the mysterious Dhaku. However, no publisher would have anything to do with it fearing retaliation by the Dhaku. Paranjpé himself got an ominous telephone call threatening him with dire consequences, if he were to publish. One day he received a mysterious call from someone who spoke English with a Punjabi accent and introduced himself as Mr. Jeevan Gill.

"Prof. Paranjpé, I am sorry to disturb you Sir. I represent a large publishing consortium in New Delhi that is interested in utilizing your services as a consultant."

"Consultant? In what capacity?" asked Prof. Paranjpé suspiciously.

"Oh, they want you to translate and re-interpret the entire works of the Mahabharata so as to make it more amenable to adaptation by the film and animated cartoon industry. These characters need to be brought to life in a modern setting and made more attractive to children by the use of cartoon characters."

Paranjpé winced at the thought of working with the film industry. The voice was most persuasive particularly when it mentioned the size of the budget. Paranjpé agreed to meet Mr. Gill at a location in Gokhale Park. That was the start of what was to become the Mahabharata Project at RSLI.

Chapter 3: An Unholy Alliance

Prof. Paranjpé's reminiscing was interrupted by Padma who entered with his morning tea and a copy of Sakaal, the local Marathi newspaper.
"Uncle, Jeevan wants to have a word," she said ushering in Jeevan with a broad smile and obviously pretentious bow to acknowledge their benefactor. Jeevan's tall well built fame momentarily blocked the view through the door. The clean-shaven Sikh nodded and shut the door as Padma departed. He sat in front of Prof. Paranjpé. Prof. Paranjpé hated these closed-door sessions. The conversations always seemed to drift to discussions on the Deccan Mandate, and that made him uneasy. He waited uneasily to find out the reason for Jeevan's visit.
"Good Morning Professor," greeted Jeevan Gill. Prof. Paranjpé smiled sheepishly but avoided eye contact.
"Hello, Mr. Gill, It's good to see you back. I take it that your family crisis has been resolved and things are back to normal?" Prof. Paranjpé asked.
"Not quiet but I'll get to that soon. How's Padma's wedding plans coming along, Professor?"
"Okay, I suppose but for all these money problems," he said shaking his head in despair.
"Even in this day and age," he continued, "the boy's side is still demanding a settlement."
"Ah yes Professor, isn't it a shame? How much are they asking?"
"Fifty lakhs! And all in US dollars," blurted the professor before he could check himself.
"Wow! It's gone up since my day," said Jeevan frivolously.
"How is your family in Delhi?" asked Paranjpé, hoping to change the subject.
"They are fine, thanks. We were planning to move house to Poona, err… I mean Puné," replied Jeevan, reverting to the nationalistic version of the famous city's name.
"We don't want to upset our Deccan Mandate friends, do we?" continued Jeevan with a smile, "Unfortunately all our plans are now on hold since I have applied for a foreign assignment to UK or North America in order to market the Mahabharata Project. But that's not the only reason I came to see you."
"Oh I am sorry to hear that you may be leaving. How will we manage without you Mr. Gill? What's up anyway?" asked the Professor.
"Don't worry, Delhi will be sending a replacement. Well, it's a long story but I don't want to take up any more of your time."
"No, no, it's okay, please," said Paranjpé with polite curiosity.

"I suppose you have heard of that carnage in Lonavala, with those school children and their teachers that were blown up in a school bus? They were all out on a picnic organized by the school board. Regrettably, our sponsor's young relatives were killed on that bus and he is overwhelmed with grief. In fact his office called me from New Delhi and asked for my help. This is why I had to take a sudden leave of absence. I know that this is nothing to do with your work but it is very dear to his heart. He wants to get to the bottom of this."
"Yes, yes we should try to help," offered Prof. Paranjpé eagerly.
Jeevan raised a cautionary arm before Paranjpé made a big commitment, "Professor, it involves the Deccan Mandate. I recall the informal discussions we have had on this topic mostly centred on your book, and your frustration in having it published."
"What's the connection with Deccan Mandate?" asked Prof. Paranjpé.
"The Sponsor is an influential industrialist and has many friends in high places. It did not take him long to get the latest police report on the investigation. Everything points indirectly to the Deccan Mandate."
"Indirectly, did you say?" asked Prof. Paranjpé.
"Well," said Jeevan, choosing his words with care, "the Deccan Mandate appears to be working in collusion with another group. What do you know about something called Dhaku?"

Prof. Paranjpé looked up startled and sat up erect as though someone had walked in on a stolen mid-afternoon nap. He then smiled as if he had just figured out that Jeevan was pulling his leg.
"Oh, come on Mr. Gill! That's kids' bogeyman stuff! Don't tell me you believe in all that. It's as if Santa Clause is real," he added laughing nervously.
"Our Sponsor," said Gill in a morose tone, "would be very generous indeed if anybody could get to the bottom of this crime."

He then turned and nodded towards a credenza, which had a picture of Padma on it, receiving a prize at a college convocation. Prof. Paranjpé got the message. The Sponsor was well endowed. The entire Mahabharata project to date must have cost a small fortune and it was yet to generate any revenue, let alone break even and turn a profit. Paranjpé reflected on this but said nothing. He was getting into dangerous waters. As a Brahmin, to him, family honour was worth more than life itself. A solution for his financial predicaments had just presented itself. Paranjpé suspected a connection between Dhaku and the Deccan Mandate but was careful enough to conceal the depth of his understanding in his book. Others suspected that he knew more than he was letting on.

Jeevan Gill stood up and as he left he said, "Think about it and let me know. We need to move fast on this."

Prof. Paranjpé registered no response but stared at the blank wall. He could almost read his destiny. He would probably not die of a heart condition, cancer or old age. Nevertheless, his niece would now have the wedding she deserved.

Jeevan walked past the open office area. Dilip, a young team member approached him. He inquired if the esteemed Sponsor had read his proposal regarding new computers, broadband access and publishing software. Jeevan assured him it was approved and the equipment would be available soon. The young man retreated gracefully and spread the good news. They had huddled around one computer, with its low speed telephone modem connection, for over a year.

Jeevan got to his windowless office and locked the door behind him. He reached under his desk and pressed a concealed button. A narrow door, hidden behind an enormous batik wall hanging, slid open. Jeevan walked through the door that slid shut behind him. He entered a narrow dimly lit passage that led to a stairway to the second floor. As he walked up the final flight of stairs, he sensed the blank stare of a security camera looking directly at him. At the top of the stairs, Jeevan negotiated a retinal scan access, to enter the regional office of the Research and Analysis Group (RAG) of India's Federal Security Services.

Three members of his team were already at work. They entered through an inconspicuous but secure entrance at the back of the building. They would be seen arriving for work in the parking lot by the Professor and his RSLI staff but were never associated with Jeevan. Jeevan claimed to be an agent of a mysterious, wealthy and eccentric Sponsor with a fetish about modernizing the Mahabharata. He maintained that they were a bunch of local IT professionals. They worked on a defence contract and hence it was all "hush, hush". This rumour eventually spread through the Gohkale Park Industrial community.

"Sir, HQ are on hold for this morning's conference call," said an assistant urgently and ushered Jeevan into a videoconference room. Jeevan sat on the assigned seat facing the camera. He looked across to the a large wall mounted thin panel video screen and saw his boss, Lieutenant General Anwar Khan, conferring with his second in command and other senior staff in RAG's videoconferencing studio in New Delhi. Jeevan's assistant fidgeted with the camera settings and tapped nervously at his laptop.

"Ahh! You are now live Sir!" he finally proclaimed.

Jeevan saw himself as New Delhi would see him on a smaller monitor, and suddenly the folks on the monitor turned and appeared to be looking straight at him. The assistant raised the audio volume.

"Aahchaa, Aahchaa! Inspector Gill how good of you to finally join us," said Khan and asked, "Do you have anything meaningful to contribute this morning?"

"I've just been talking to Prof. Paranjpé," answered Gill, "As we've always suspected he may be able to help us with Dhaku. His unpublished book is quite comprehensive and tells us most of what we need to know about the Deccan Mandate. What's missing is its connection to Dhaku, the location of Dhaku cells, and their objectives."

"We know their fucking objectives!" interrupted Khan impatiently, "They want to disrupt the peace talks with the separatist groups in order to make politicians nervous and spend more money on arms deals."

"Sir, those are Deccan's objectives, I suspect Dhaku is apolitical and will undertake any political assassination it is paid to do. According to Prof. Paranjpé's unpublished book, ever since they assassinated our military attaché in Sri Lanka, the Deccan Mandate has gone underground and is as illusive as Dhaku. Whereas the Dhaku is an ancient legend, the Deccan Mandate is very real."

"All this is useless speculation." said Khan, getting more irritated, "I have waited long enough for an answer from your professor. It has taken you almost a year to set up this elaborate Puné sting operation. Events have caught up with us now with this dastardly Lonavala bombing. Clearly, the old professional assassins' code is out of the window and the Deccan Mandate has morphed into a ruthless terrorist organization. I am thinking of sending Dr. Karmarkar and his boys to talk to the professor."

The mere mention of Dr. Karmarkar's name sent a shiver down Jeevan's spine. Karmarkar was an ex-Indian army medical doctor who was caught moonlighting in a lucrative organ donor business. Not all organ donations were voluntary. To avoid a scandal, the army transferred him to RAG's Interrogation Department. Here the infamous doctor met his true calling. He developed a handbook on terrorist interrogation techniques, euphemistically called first, second and third degree "pain protocols". His technique preyed on his subjects' psychological vulnerabilities in combination with the use of hallucination causing drugs. Once he discovered the subject's phobia, he would exploit it ruthlessly.

"There is no need for using strong arm tactics on the professor," pleaded Jeevan. "Prof. Paranjpé has financial issues. All we need is money. It's less messy. Give me a month, and I will have some concrete answers." A pregnant pause followed. Jeevan waited on hold as the camera showed a test screen.

Soon Khan came on again and said, "Okay, Inspector Gill, in consultation with everyone here we have decided to give you the funds and more time. However, I am preparing Karmarkar for a trip to Puné just in case you fail, and you'll be back at a desk job. Do I make myself clear, Gill?" he asked.

"Absolutely Sir!" said Jeevan Gill with confidence.

"Oh, by the way," continued Anwar Khan, "our Mumbai anti-terrorist team did a pretty good job on the remnants of the Lonavala bomb. They managed to piece together some of the triggering mechanism and found it surprisingly sophisticated for its intended purpose. A calibrated pressure transducer drove the device. As the bus climbed through the torturous passage, from the coastal lowlands, where Mumbai is situated, up towards Lonavala, the transducer detected a change in pressure due to the change in altitude, which is about 2000 feet. With the bus parked, the device detected a consistent low pressure. This set off a timer. From that point the bus was doomed. The bomb exploded after a predetermined interval. Had the party lingered longer, it would have destroyed most of the business centre. Why would those lunatics go through all that trouble when a simple timer alone would suffice?"
Jeevan thought for a moment and then blurted out, "It could be a dress rehearsal for something more spectacular."
"Yes of course! Good thinking Gill." conceded Khan grudgingly, "But where and when is now the question."
"I will have an answer in a month," said Jeevan firmly and the meeting was adjourned.

In the days that followed, Jeevan and Prof. Paranjpé had several "closed door meetings." Even Padma hadn't a clue as to what was happening. Soon, the Prof. emerged from his office to announce that the senior translator would be running things whilst he was away doing field research.

During the next four weeks, Prof. Paranjpé hung out in his old haunts in Sangam Peth, Puné, the Deccan Mandate's unofficial headquarters. He hadn't frequented those places since his student days. He observed many changes. Fashionable bars replaced coffee shops. Non-vegetarian restaurants thrived even in the City's orthodox Brahmin district.

The professor caught up with some of his old cronies. There were backslapping and hugs, as the Deccan Mandate welcomed their prodigal son. On the surface, not much had changed. In particular, a non-violent opposition to separatists was still the predominant view. However, things had changed drastically in the administration. A radical, powerful, and ruthless mercenary group had taken over the reins. They managed to ostracize the moderates. Arms dealer money was everywhere and could be seen in the homes and foreign cars. Terrorism made good money. Every assassination, car bomb or derailed train that slowed the peace negotiations brought a fresh wave of prosperity. What is more, the collusion between the Deccan Mandate and Dhaku was closer than he had expected. Dhaku operatives were in abundance and made no effort to disguise themselves. The local law enforcement, having been paid off, kept its distance and only pleaded for discretion. Prof. Paranjpé and his informants met behind closed doors and at different residences whenever possible. However, the professor suspected that there could be a mole amongst their midst. Loyalty was rewarded, but betrayal earned a sudden disappearance courtesy of Dhaku.

The professor kept his word and duly showed up at work to meet with Jeevan Gill within a month. As he entered the general office area, the young IT enthusiast, came rushing forward and called after the professor.

"Sir! Sir! The new computers are here, and we have high-speed access to the Internet. We logged on to the British Museum Library and the Smithsonian and downloaded tons of useful documents! Do you want me to demonstrate the publishing and animation software?"

"That's good news; I expect you folks will be more productive now. I'll be back to take a closer look at all this later," he said continuing on to Jeevan's office.

Jeevan rose to shake his hand.

"Good morning Professor! I heard you have been busy in the old city rubbing shoulders with your Deccan Mandate friends," said Jeevan, motioning to a chair.

"They are not my friends," retorted the professor. "I told the same to those bureaucrats at the Puné University. They stubbornly insisted on my resignation. The Deccan Mandate is no longer what it used to be."

"So tell me, what's changed since you were an active member."

"The changes are quite serious and have taken place over three years. The Mandate has evolved from a right wing think tank into a terrorist group funded by some unscrupulous arms dealers. They now call themselves the Deccan Dhaku; a frightening coalition of an underground fascist political organization with and ancient order of professional assassins."

"You mean to say we have a fascists or Nazi like organization head quartered right here in this City, complete with its own variant of Gestapo, and no one knows about it?" asked Jeevan.

"The terrorist plans that these people have in mind will make them a house hold word in the sub-continent, let me assure you. Your reference to WWII Nazism is relevant. It turns out that the Deccan Dhaku uses a black Nazi Swastika on a saffron background as their calling card. However, note the Indo-Aryan Swastika has an anti-clockwise orientation. It is the universal symbol of peace and tranquility. The Deccan Dhaku uses a clockwise version similar to the WWII Nazi Swastika."

Jeevan listened mesmerized as the professor continued. Unbeknown to the professor, hidden video cameras relayed the meeting

to Lieutenant General Anwar Khan and staff in Delhi. They watched the interview live, with equal interest and fascination.
"Professor, you mentioned tentative plans earlier. Any idea where they will strike next?" asked Jeevan.
"Deccan's political objectives are multi-faceted," replied the professor. "Their mandate is to fan the flames of unrest wherever there are regional problems, funding anti-separatist groups in the Punjab, Nepal, Sri Lanka, Nagaland, and Kashmir. They are not interested in gaining notoriety; their goal is to destroy peace initiatives between the government and separatists, or for that matter neighbouring countries, which support them. They don't want a slow down in the arms trade."
"But you haven't answered my question!" interrupted Jeevan.
"Yes, Yes I am coming to that but I just wanted to give you the big picture," said the professor. "My information," he continued, "through the Deccan Mandate grape vine is somewhat sketchy. The alliance has plans for North America or UK; most likely the assassination of a prominent Indian politician or a peace negotiator. Deccan Dhaku is very interested in sabotaging the nuclear disarmament talks."
"Well, they are raising the stakes," reflected Jeevan.
"And finally," said the Prof. Paranjpé with an air of a narrator who had saved the best for last, "I was told that the Deccan Dhaku are now recruiting Hijaras!"

The Hijaras are Indian transvestites who usually live in communities. Hijaras are well known for their theatrical talents and abilities. They have taken cross-dressing to a fine art and are able to portray either male or female roles in an equally convincing manner. Their physique and external observable attributes are neither male nor female and herein lies the tantalizing mystic they display on stage. Hijaras are considered to bring good luck. They are perceived as pure virginal or sexless angels. Hijaras are often invited to auspicious ceremonies such as weddings to entertain guests with their songs and dances. Hence, it disturbed Jeevan that some members of this much-venerated group, debased themselves by being linked to Deccan Dhaku.

"What? You must be kidding," shouted Jeevan jumping off his chair, visibly upset. There was a prolonged silence as Prof. Paranjpé let Jeevan grasp the magnitude of the situation. He paced the floor for a few more minutes and then sat down again.

He threw his head back on his headrest, looked at the ceiling and said in a soft voice to himself, "Of course! Of course! Hijaras are born actors and masters of disguise. It all makes treacherous sense. Besides, we would not know if we were looking for a man or a woman."

After a brief pause he collected himself and continued, "Professor, sorry to keep persisting with this but could you give us a name or something tangible to go on. Your report is fascinating but we can't point a finger at anyone yet. Besides even if our influential Sponsor could persuade the Special Forces to invade a part of the Puné city, where would they go? Who would they pick up? Apart from your word, there is no evidence that this alliance even exists. Give us some concrete evidence that could convict their leaders."

"I am not a police officer!" snapped the learned Brahmin, thinking that all his work had amounted to nothing.

"Of course not Professor, your information is nevertheless invaluable. But we need to do some more work." casting a sly glance in the general direction of a security camera. "We, I mean, I have learned a lot from all this and I will shortly be conveying this to our Sponsor who will no doubt be very grateful and .... and... generous," said Jeevan struggling to be diplomatic.

"I shouldn't be doing this," said Prof. Paranjpé shaking is head, "we need to contact a Federal intelligence agency, to investigate and take over from here. If my sources are right, there could be dire international consequences and someone with prior knowledge could be held accountable."

"Now Professor," cautioned Jeevan, "I must insist on complete secrecy in this matter. Let the Sponsor deal with this through his influential contacts. Just get me a name. Please, I must have a name. Just get me a naaammme!"

A grim expression over came the professor. It was as good as a death sentence to probe any further. But Padma's wedding day was approaching and he was already in debt. He would get that damn name! Up to now, his presence in Sangam Peth had been greeted with polite curiosity. He knew he was being watched and just the other day Padma got a mysterious phone call from a woman speaking in Marathi.

"Tell your uncle to stop doing what he is doing or else there will be trouble!" and then the woman hung up.

Prof. Paranjpé stood up and looked at Jeevan with rage in his eyes. The professor said nothing, turned heel and left shutting the door quietly behind him. He was not going to lose his temper or fight with Jeevan. After all, he was a true Brahmin; a peaceful and learned Indo-Aryan! A few of his caste had sullied the Brahmin Aryan reputation, as the keepers of knowledge. He would get even. He blamed them for his ostracized solitude and his loss of the vice chancellor's post. Now just a name came between him and Padma's happiness, family honour and retribution.

Jeevan rushed upstairs to the RAG office, passing through the security zone to participate in the video conference. Lieutenant General Anwar Khan and his team seemed to be having a stormy debate. A hushed silence followed when Jeevan came online.
"Well done Gill," said Khan hesitantly, "I think we may have caught this problem just in time. We always suspected the Deccan Mandate but we took our eye off the ball and missed the subsequent developments. They seem to have evolved into a major menace. I don't however subscribe to the professor's diatribe about some foreign campaign or this cloak and dagger stuff about forming an alliance with Dhaku. In all these years a Dhaku operative has never been arrested and prosecuted."
"And I hope we never do!" interjected a team member.
Khan nodded and continued, "These gone astray Brahmins from Puné are smart, they plan, and then they act. In the past, they have never shown much taste for violence so they now out source the gory stuff to the Dhaku clan. How convenient! The best way to deal with this Ravana monster is to cut off its head."
"Unfortunately, Sir," interjected Jeevan, "as you recall, Ravana had many heads. Similarly, the Deccan Mandate is a secretive society without even a post office mailbox to its name. They could be anybody; a neighbourhood professional, a lawyer, an engineer or a nurse. This Mandate is dispersed through out the City. There is nothing tangible; they appear as shadowy figures in bars, nightclubs, temples, mosques, and churches. That's where the professor is getting his information."
"Well, that's not good enough. Have you considered the possibility that your naïve, idealistic professor may have been fed this misinformation?"
Jeevan sat in frustrated silence not knowing what to think.
"By the way, that stuff about recruiting Hijaras didn't impress us a lot either. We have long suspected that group of Deccan Mandate intellectuals were a bunch of faggots. This Hijara recruitment business might be for their private amusement."
A roar of laughter irrupted around the table and seeing the unintended mirth he had caused amongst his team, he joined their laughter too.

When the laughter subsided and a round table of further homophobic remarks finished, Khan resumed again, "Fortunately, we have some footage from security cameras in Mumbai. They show the suspicious movements of some Deccan Dhaku operatives. There is a common denominator. This gentleman," pointing a small laser pointer to a screen, "appears to be in several shots. Nobody can identify him or place him even as a guest in any Mumbai hotel. He disappears from the video records, a day before the Lonavala bombing. He's our best suspect. Perhaps the professor can wave his picture around and come up with a name."

Jeevan's assistant sent the image of the suspect to a printer in the vicinity. Jeevan picked up the photo and gazed at it for over a minute. It could have been a photograph of any typical Brahmin male from Samgam Peth, with a light brown complexion, about five feet and nine inches in height. His sharp haunting sky blue eyes appeared to look into your soul. The face mesmerized Jeevan. It was youthful or even effeminate looking. The head sported shoulder length black hair.

"I have already anticipated your need for a name. The video tape and this picture should help," said Jeevan as he took his boss's leave and signed-off.

Jeevan and the professor studied the picture and video recordings. They played it back again and again on one of the new computers when the translators, scriptwriters, and animators had left for the day. Finally, a scene showing the suspect, sipping a drink, seemed to jog the professor's memory.

He said excitedly, "I have seen this person before. I wasn't introduced to him. He was pointed out to me at a restaurant two weeks ago, in Samgam Peth, as a possible Dhaku operative. I remember only his last name, which I thought at that time, in an historical context, was interesting."

"What name were you given?" asked Jeevan.

"Godbolé, no, no it's Godsé, ...it's Godsé, I'm sure of it," replied the professor.

Later, Khan's team put this name through RAG's terrorist database and came up with nothing. A match was found however, in the airport/seaport database, for "Godsé". The name, Anil Godsé, was returned with a note indicating he had left the country, last week, on a plane bound for Toronto, Canada.

"That's good news," said Anwar Khan, "he's now somebody else's problem. Good riddance! We won't have to worry him about anymore!"

As events unfolded, Khan would regret saying this as the professor's earlier warning on a probable Deccan Dhaku foreign "hit" became prophetic.

Chapter 4: Niagara

Jeevan always dreaded the bi-weekly Friday afternoon conference calls with its mandatory attendance requirement. Khan was particularly menacing on Fridays. Everybody had to give progress reports on their Management by Objectives (MBO). Anyone falling short of their goals would find themselves victims of snide and sarcastic remarks. These were designed to humiliate them into action as well as to amuse the team. However, on this occasion, Khan seemed subdued, and everyone sensed something was afoot.

When the reporting finished, Khan said somewhat reluctantly, "I suppose there is some truth in the rumour that Deccan Dhaku are operational abroad and pose a meaningful threat to our political dignitaries on foreign visits. The Ministry of Defence, having conducted an investigation, based on Gill's earlier observations, have now arrived at the same conclusion. Good work Gill!"

"Thanks Sir", responded Jeevan.

"I have good news," continued Khan, "the overseas assignment, which you craved for so long is going to be given to you. You will take charge of the Defence Minister, Mr. Pinto's security arrangements for his trip to Canada and the UK. Your promotion has also come through. Congratulations Commander Gill!"

Khan waited for the polite applause, both at Delhi and Puné, to subside. Jeevan was beaming from ear to ear. His team at the Puné office walked around the table shook his hand and patted him on the back.

"Mr. Pinto has scheduled a meeting with NATO in Toronto and will be going to London, UK to also meet with the Carbon Abatement and Nuclear Disarmament Organization or CANDO." said Khan, and added, "You are to be with him all the time. Clearly, the Deccan Dhaku may try something nasty. Thanks to your research with Prof. Paranjpé, we were able to advise the Royal Canadian Mounted Police, (RCMP), to keep Anil Godsé under surveillance."

"What about weapons Sir?" Jeevan asked.

"You'll be allowed to carry your Glock 17 in Canada. We have a reciprocal weapons agreement with the RCMP and their undercover people in India, but not in the UK. MIQ, the British Intelligence agency, are more restrictive about arms even with their own people. Take your laptop, which is networked through our secure satellite link." Jeevan's face fell when Khan added, "This way you can keep in touch with the rest of the team and attend the Friday MBO meetings via video."

The Deccan Dhaku kept a close watch on the evolving political situation. Their arms dealers saw their business drying up in the Indian Subcontinent. They started to put a lot of pressure on the Deccan Dhaku to stop the advance of the AGA party. The Lonavala bomb was their first major terrorist act. There was much more to come.

A gleaming new Bombardier Global Express, an executive jet used by the Indian Central Government , stood on the tarmac in the special security zone at New Delhi's Indira Gandhi International airport. It had just returned from Israel, where it was fitted out with electronic counter measures, to guard against missile attacks when landing and taking-off. The cargo and passenger areas had bomb sniffing devices installed. Jeevan arrived early. He waited for the minister and his entourage to arrive and passed the time making small talk with the two pilots. They were ex air-force officers with plenty of experience with foreign assignments.

When he asked them about U.K., the Captain, Rohan Kapadia said, "I hate going to London there are so many Asians there. I don't feel I have left India!"

His co-pilot nodded in agreement.

"Thankfully, this is going to be my last Government job with its pitiful salary," said Captain Kapadia.

"How Come?" enquired Jeevan.

"Well, having fought two air wars for those buggers and subsequently put up with all their favouritism, bureaucracy, and being passed over for promotion, I decided to tender my resignation. I will be taking up a new assignment with Air Kanishka in Toronto," said Captain Kapadia.

"Air Kanishka? Oh Yes, I've heard of them. They placed a large order for the new Airbus 380s at the last Paris air-show. But won't it be a big change?" asked Jeevan.

"Yes, but I'm not complaining since I receive twice the salary in US Dollars. In a few years time I could look forward to a comfortable retirement. I am going to fly their inaugural flight from Toronto to Montreal, London and then on to Mumbai non-stop."

"What I mean to say is that there will be a meaningful technical change from flying jet fighters and executive jets to flying the A380. It is the largest passenger jet in the world," said Jeevan.

"Well, yes," said Capt. Kapadia "this has taken a year of planning. After decades of continuous service, I accumulated 8 weeks of vacation. I devoted most of this time to simulator training and actual flight training in Europe. I am ready as ever to fly the big jet."

The minister's entourage eventually arrived. Jeevan noticed a young, South-Indian face that looked familiar, but it took him some time to figure out where he had seen him. It was Mr. Thiruvengadum Krishnaswamy, a world-renowned expert in nuclear disarmament and for many years a considerable embarrassment to the former hawkish Central

Government. The AGA however, appreciated Mr. Krishnaswamy's scholarly work, enticed him away from his job as the executive director of a think tank in Bangalore, and appointed him as advisor to the Ministry of Defence.

An hour after take-off, a meal was served. Jeevan and two embedded reporters settled down to a game of bridge towards the rear of the luxurious wide bodied executive jet. Later, the curtain that separated them from the Minister and his senior staff, parted and Mr. Krishnaswamy, walked towards them with a sheaf of papers in his hand. "Er... excuse me gentlemen," he started hesitantly, "there are going to be changes in the Minister's itinerary in Toronto. After the NATO meeting he has planned a sight seeing tour to Niagara Falls. Following this, instead of taking this Global Express, he will take a commercial flight to London, England. He will participate in Air Kanishka's inaugural service from Toronto to Mumbai via Montreal and London. Our Government owns 50% of Air Kanishka, and hence Mr. Pinto has accepted their invitation to represent the Government on this historic event. They are starting a new service using an Air Bus 380 Super Jumbo aircraft, named Kashmir Princess."

He then handed Jeevan an itinerary. However, he stopped short putting anything into the reporters' out stretched hands, one from Times of India, and the other from Deccan Times.

"You two newspaper people," warned Mr. Krishnaswamy waving a finger at them, "are hereby officially informed that this information regarding the Minister's change of plans is secret and done for good reason. Remember your management has signed a proprietary information agreement. Please do not report this change. Is this understood?"

The two reporters nodded but the reporter from Deccan Times, Depak Phadké, also asked, "What travel plans are we allowed to report?"

"I understand the ban is on reporting any of the Minister's proposed travel arrangements. I think this includes his planned trip to Niagara Falls," suggested Jeevan.

"Exactly, exactly!" said Krishnaswamy squinting to read Jeevan's security badge, "Thanks, Mr. ... I mean Commander Gill."

The Minister, his entourage and Jeevan arrived in Toronto without incident. They went to their suite at the Royal York Hotel in Toronto, the site of the NATO conference.

Since Mr. Pinto's country was not a member of NATO, he did not participate officially in the day's closed-door meetings. Instead, several prearranged meetings outside conference hours or between breakout sessions were arranged in special meeting rooms. Jeevan spent countless hours sitting behind the Minister and his staff and then led the way into the corridors, to check every nook and cranny.

The RCMP had assigned two plain clothes officers. Much to Jeevan's relief, one officer, a tall blonde female, Constable Mavis Hayes, took up driving duties. Vehicles with automatic transmission never appealed to him, a confirmed biker, who liked the sound and handling of any vehicle he operated. The other officer, Superintendent Peter Passarelli worked closely with Jeevan to assist with surveillance. Defence ministers from almost every country within the NATO alliance, dropped by to offer an opinion. The Norwegians were the most enthusiastic participants. They arranged for a negotiator to coordinate appointments with other members of NATO.

The decommissioning of nuclear weapons was a complicated process. NATO insisted on stringent inspections and inventory of the entire system. This included the nuclear payload, guidance as well as the propulsion system. Moreover, they required a further breakdown of the payload's components, which contained the triggering mechanism and the fissile core.

The meetings were not going well. Every country in NATO had its own vision of how it would work, and it seemed impossible to get a consensus. What's more, other Asian countries that were part of the "Asian Nuclear Club" did not commit to the CANDO initiative, and hence India was still on a precarious unilateral disarmament path that Mr. Krishnaswamy knew would not work. The Indian delegation did not own a higher moral plane by persisting with CANDO. It is just that their political masters, the AGA party, had every thing to lose if the talks broke down because they were elected on a disarmament and swords to ploughshares mandate. Rumours of the troubled talks had reached the Subcontinent. The Indian press featured the impending failure of the negotiations. The opposition parties called on the Government to resign. Amidst all this chaos, Mr. Pinto, India's defence minister, was given his marching orders, "Do what ever it takes within reasonable limits to make it work." He promptly passed this directive to Mr. Tiruvegadam Krishnaswamy or Tiru for short.

Tiru wandered around the Royal York suite, assigned to the Indian delegation, muttering to himself. He looked a very worried man. He drank coffee incessantly from a special percolator set aside for him. He brewed his brand of South Indian coffee, which was too strong for everyone else's taste. He would sit at his laptop, and then get up and pace the floor, his head bowed, and his hands behind his back.
He had his head between his hands, and his eyes closed in deep concentration when Mr. Pinto entered the room and asked abruptly, "How's it going Tiru!"

"Why don't you take a seat Sir?" motioned Tiru to a vacant sofa.
"Oh no," said Pinto with a tone of apprehension, "this isn't good."
Tiru took a deep breath and looked at the Minister squarely in the eye, and said, "Nuclear Disarmament in its present form doesn't work. It has never worked, and it never will!"
"What?" asked the Minister as he jumped to his feet and shouted at Tiru at the top of his voice, "The Government is about to collapse, and those war mongering lunatics may take over power again. The whole region's welfare programs and infrastructure development will be set back decades. There's almost certain to be a proletarian, grass roots like Marxist revolution and the best you can come up with, after all this time, is that nuclear disarmament doesn't work!"
"No Sir, I've being saying this all along. You will see this in the papers that I have published. Ever since Mano came up with his proposal and raised billions to back it up, everyone focused on getting the money. There is a ridiculous notion that disarmament can be bought, and it is now inevitable. Many third-world countries have built nuclear bombs, the delivery systems, and guidance. The power and prestige that comes with belonging to the nuclear club is irresistible. You don't mess with a nuclear powered country even if its weapons don't have the range to reach you."
"So what alternative solution do you have?" asked the Minister in a calmer tone.
"It's not a solution but an alternative approach that addresses the reality of deterrents. To date no nuclear power will accept unilateral disarmament. It would be political suicide. The approach I would like to take is based on the premise that the possession of nuclear weapons is not in itself a threat to humanity. No responsible and sane Government will launch a nuclear strike against another nuclear armed adversary or even a non-nuclear state. The threat of retaliation by the adversary or its friends is the basis of how nuclear deterrents work. However, there is always the danger of an accidental launch or a launch due to incorrect information. The biggest threat is the falling of the nuclear weapons system into the hands of terrorists. They believe in global destruction and want to rebuild society in their preferred format. That's where the urgency really lies."
"Tiru, my friend," said the Minister rising to his feet again, placing his hand on his shoulder, "stop lecturing to me! Where's your alternative?" However, realizing that he was dealing with the most brilliant mind in his circle of advisors, he tempered his tone and continued saying, "What you say makes sense. I am curious ... very curious, with what you come up with."
Tiru looked up and gesticulated with the curved fingers of his right hand, which he held apart.

"I'm almost there Sir, almoooost there. There is just a small piece of the solution that is missing. I am close to a plan that will be acceptable to the UN, NATO, CANDO and the Indian Parliament."

The Minister paced the room for about half a minute. Then, in a more conciliatory tone, to make up for his earlier outburst, he said, "Why don't you take a break and come to the Niagara Falls with Jeevan and me. I was advised by the RCMP that I should not tour on my own. A stretched limousine has been booked. The good news is that our Norwegian friends persuaded NATO to reconvene in London. This has bought us a little more time. The London meeting with CANDO will now include a core NATO delegation. This will be our last chance to negotiate a disarmament agreement with the joint NATO/CANDO delegation. If we fail, CANDO with take its lucrative offer, worth billions of dollars, to another country."

"But Sir, we are to take the Kashmir Princess to London tomorrow night. This does not give me much time to come up with a new proposal."

"Ahhray chodhow yaar!" said Pinto slipping into Hindi, "All this can wait. We will work on it together on the flight. We have a suite on the Jumbo's upper deck. There is enough space for us there to play a cricket match. That fresh air and cold-water spray at Niagara will do you good. Please leave that damn laptop of yours behind. I want us to relax and have fun."

Tiru thought better than to argue further and agreed to go along. But no sooner had Mr. Pinto left the room than he whipped out a small tablet device. He transferred the draft proposal to it. Then he turned to Jeevan who was watching all this with interest and winked at him saying, "The Minister said that I was to leave my laptop behind did he not?" Jeevan just smiled and shook his head as he marvelled at the man's dedication.

Jeevan decided to turn in early. He anticipated a long day ahead and a transatlantic flight to follow. As he was about to nod off, his cell phone rang with the ring tone associated with RAG. He recognized the duty officer's voice as he gave his password. The officer asked Jeevan to provide his password. After this, the officer delivered a terse statement. "Commander Gill, download a top priority message."

Jeevan downloaded the message from a secured server and decoded it on his laptop. The message was from Lieutenant Gen. Anwar Khan. What he read ensured that he would not sleep much that night.

In essence, the message said that RAG determined with 90% certainty that the Deccan Dhaku planned to embarrass the Indian Government and assassinate the Defence Minister, and his peace seeking entourage. They were plotting to place a bomb aboard the Kashmir Princess. Moreover, the Deccan Times informed RAG that Mr. Phadké, the embedded reporter, did not work for them. They never applied for embedded status. Since Phadké was most likely a Deccan Dhaku operative, plans to conceal Mr. Pinto's participation in Air Kanishka's inaugural flight, had been compromised. The Air Kanishka ground staff at Toronto International Airport should be advised to manually search all baggage and shouldn't rely on X-Ray machines. They should also remove any unaccompanied baggage. The Minister and staff should fly to London on the Global Express. Finally, although RAG already contacted CISIA about the situation, Jeevan should use his contacts with the RCMP to request the detention of Messrs Godsé, and Phadké. The Indian Government will make a formal extradition request.

Since Jeevan had no contacts with CISIA, he called Superintendent Passarelli. Passarelli didn't like being bothered at that late hour but asked for the decoded email to be forwarded to him.

Jeevan next went to Minister Pinto's suite. Fortunately, he and his staff were still up. Lata Desai, his press secretary, ushered him in. The Minister and his executive assistant, Kamala Taskar were engaged in a conference call with his Ministry staff in New Delhi where a new working day dawned.

Lata and Kamala gave up senior management positions in multinational companies, just for the honour of serving in this elite ministry with its multi-billion dollar defence budget and international reach. Both women were a model of efficiency and ran the Minister's office like clockwork. They formed an impenetrable barrier for people who constantly sought favours and tried to manoeuvre a business advantage. Arms dealers disliked them and complained about the lack of access to the Minister. An unlimited privilege they enjoyed in the previous government.

Lata leaned over and whispered something in the Minister's ear, which made him, cast an annoyed glance at Jeevan. About five minutes later, he rose from the large round table with a speakerphone. He walked over to Jeevan and asked, "What's all this about some urgent top-secret message?"

Jeevan realized he was on shaky ground. The Minister's inner circle with the exception of Tiru, viewed him with much suspicion. This went back to the time when the AGA party, when in opposition, voted against the formation of RAG, and the funds that it was allocated. When they came into power, they were waiting for the right opportunity to dismantle it. Other than official NATO and CANDO meetings, whenever Jeevan was around or appeared unexpectedly, the conversation slipped into a hushed silence.

Jeevan handed him a decoded copy of the email he had received earlier.

Mr. Pinto read the note and said, “Looks like you RAG people showed poor judgment and threw caution to the wind in allowing an undocumented press agent on our flight. What else is new? Your total lack of professionalism has compromised the safety of my staff! I don’t know who to believe now.”

“Sir, with respect, could we nevertheless err on the side of caution and take the Global Express to London?”

“Absolutely not!” yelled the Minister and this brought Lata and Kamala rushing to his side. He handed Lata the note. She read it and passed it to Kamala. Lata, the older and more experienced of the two women, was dressed in a shalwar kameez and draped herself with a large hand embroidered shawl; the air-conditioning in the hotel was too cold for her. Kamala wore jeans and a sweater to keep warm in the temperate Canadian Summer. Both women stood between Jeevan and the Minister who returned to the round table to continue his conference call. Jeevan thought to himself that, short of a rugby tackle, there was now no way he could get past them to approach the Minister again.

“We have had no indication from the Ministry HQ that we need to change our travel plans. They have the best eyes and ears on the sub-continent, and if anything were amiss they would be the first to hear of it,” said Lata confidently.

Kamala added, “You must understand that Air Kanishka has been planning this inaugural flight for months. They have invested almost a billion dollars on new aircraft. The Indian Government is a major stakeholder. It would look bad if the Minister did not turn up. Besides there is going to be an inaugural ceremony and a big party in the VIP lounge with the press, tour operators, and local connecting airline staff in attendance.”

“Can I at least persuade you ladies to come with us to Niagara Falls tomorrow?” asked Jeevan looking hopefully at Kamala.

“Sorry, Jeevan,” said Kamala “besides diamonds, shopping is a girl’s best friend. Lata and I plan to spend our meagre foreign exchange allowance at the Eaton Centre. Everyone back home expects gifts when you go abroad! Then we have to leave early for the airport to make sure everything is setup in the VIP lounge.” She paused and added, with a smile, “But I’ll see you at the party when you return with the Minister won’t I Jeevan?” Jeevan looked at her for a few moments. There was a sad expression on his face. He just nodded his head, turned heal, and shut the suite door quietly behind him. Something told him he would never see that charming smile again. Lata and Kamala looked at each other in bewilderment.

Lata broke the silence by saying, “Well, this is the official line anyway, but I have a bad feeling about all this. Some months ago,

Jeevan's name popped up as the head of security for this trip. I reviewed his accomplishments and impeccable service record. The man has a distinguished career to date. There must be some truth in what he said."

"Can we not call the duty officer at the Ministry of Defence and ask him to snoop around?" asked Kamala.

"Believe me, Alfred is looking into this," replied Lata.

Mr. Pinto did check; his Ministry had already asked the Ministry of External Affairs in Canada to track and watch Anil Godsé. They were unaware of any specific threats against the Kashmir Princess. It turned out that RAG's latest findings did not reach the higher echelons of the Ministry. Someone chose to ignore their warnings due to the continued animosity and distrust between the two departments.

Jeevan went back to his room in the hotel and locked the door behind him. His job was to protect the Minister at any cost. He would do anything to stop him taking that flight. He opened his suitcase and rummaged through his clothing. He reached down and lifted his Glock handgun holster and from a pocket on the belt, he removed a magazine of rounds. He took out a Swiss army knife and worked for the next few hours, only leaving to visit a local all-night store to buy some duct tape.

Jeevan planned the Niagara trip meticulously. The itinerary was given to the Minister's staff and the RCMP escort. The party would check out of the hotel at 10:00 am and take an unmarked limousine to the Niagara Falls area. They would journey back to Mississauga's Pearson International Airport at about 4 pm, in plenty of time for the 8 pm departure. At the airport, the Air Kanishka's staff would meet the Minister and escort him to the VIP lounge.

Superintendent Passarelli and Constable Mavis Hayes arrived early to call on Jeevan. He had ordered breakfast for all in his room by pre-arrangement so as to go over the day's security arrangements.

"Good morning Jeeves," said Passarelli as he entered the room with his young assistant. The condescending nature of the corruption of his name was lost on the commander who was unfamiliar with the fictitious character of the same name.

"Thanks for your email. You are not going to like this but you need to know that Mr. Godsé was taken off surveillance a week ago and as for the other guy..." Scrolling down email on his phone, " Mr. er … Mr. Fad ... I mean Phadkee, he has already left the country on a flight bound for the Middle-East."

Jeevan looked at Passarelli in open-mouthed amazement. When he recovered his composure he blurted out, "You must be joking. These people are terrorists. They are responsible for the murder of 37

children and adults by blowing up a school bus. In spite of our warnings you just let them go!"
"Look Jeeves," said Passarelli as he poured himself coffee, "I have a hundred and one things to attend to. This trip to Niagara Falls with your boss is a major disruption to my schedule. We don't care about the problems in your little India. Ever since 9/11 and the London subway bombings, there are major security issues to deal with here. All we know, they may be refugees being persecuted for their political beliefs by your Government. We can't take sides in this third world crap. Your Ministry of Defence could not provide us with any evidence that they were terrorists. Unlike India, Canada has strict Human Rights legislation. We couldn't get a judge to allow us to extend Mr. Godsé's detention or prolong surveillance with no proof. As for this Phadkee guy, your warning came too late. He had already left Canada, before we could pick up his trail."
"But Phadké is on our no-fly list," complained Jeevan.
"Well, he's not on ours or the one that we share with the EU and the US. These are the only lists that matter!" retorted Passarelli, munching decisively into a chocolate doughnut.
He continued to say, "I have however, alerted the detachment at Pearson International to be vigilant at the Air Kanishka's boarding area. A uniformed officer will keep a lookout for any trouble."
Constable Mavis Hayes, who up to this point nibbled on a low fat bran muffin, interjected, "Gentlemen lets get back to the task at hand. We have a long day ahead, and I would like to make an early start."
The drive to the Falls area was uneventful. Constable Hayes took the wheel while Passarelli, put on his tour guide hat and explained in detail the geographic nuances of the Niagara Escarpment. He described the unique microclimate it created for the Niagara wine growing region, and that the Minister should not pass up the chance to take home the region's famous ice-wine.

Mavis parked in a special police-parking zone, which was secluded and removed from the paid public parking. As soon as they emerged from the quiet confines of the stretched black limousine, the waterfall's roar was audible.

The party, led by Passarelli, walked a short distance towards the Falls. They reached a popular tourist vantage point, which gave a panoramic view of the gigantic horseshoe shaped waterfall. They looked with awe at the cascading waters and marvelled at the mist, which rose high above the Niagara River.
"Oh, look! There are boats in the river below, and they are so close to the waterfall!" exclaimed the Minister.

"Those are tourist boats. Those boats are called Maids of the Mist. Would you like to go on them Sir?" asked Passarelli.
"Definitely, definitely! I think we should all go," said the Minister.
"Feeling up to it Tiru?" he asked.
"I am afraid of the water Sir. I can't swim. You people go along. It's fun just to watch from here," said Tiru.
"Oh what a spoil sport you are Tiru! The planet's surface is 71% water. What if you were to fall into water somewhere? You have got to learn to swim. It's like riding a bicycle," said the Minister sounding disappointed.
"I can ride a bicycle," said Tiru defensively as a point in his favour.
"That's all we need! A South Indian cycling across the Niagara Falls," said the irritated Minister.
Passarelli and Jeevan roared with laughter.
"A rather poor imitation of Marilyn Munroe, wouldn't you say Sir?" said Jeevan adding fuel to the fire.
"Oh leave him alone for heaven's sake. If he doesn't want to go, that's okay. I'll stay behind with him," said Mavis coming to Tiru's defence.
"You can wear a life jacket Sir, if that will help," offered Passarelli.
However, Tiru just shook his head like a stubborn little boy.

Passarelli went over to the kiosk and soon returned with the tickets. The next boat would leave in half and hour so the group decided to catch an early lunch. Jeevan asked Passarelli to order him a burger. He borrowed the limousine's keys and mumbled something about having forgotten his camera and hurried in the direction of the police parking area.

Jeevan returned just as the orders arrived. Tiru said he was not hungry and asked for coffee. The others enjoyed juicy beef burgers and Chilli with the exception of Mavis who tucked into a tofu salad.
"The meat you get here it is excellent," remarked Jeevan.
The Minister nodded with approval and added, "We have recently opened some fast food burger restaurants back home."
"It's made from good Canadian beef. Our kids are raised on this stuff. That's why with only a fraction of your population we've won at least a hand full of Gold medals at the last Olympics. I understand you folks haven't won much in over the last 60 years. You are better off slaughtering those cows that wonder across your streets and feeding them to your starving millions. Then may be you'll win a bronze or two medal one of these days," said the mountie smugly with a thin red trickle appearing to run down from his lip as he devoured his enormous rare steak burger.
"But we are good at other things," said Tiru defensively.
"Like what for instance?" asked Passarelli.

"Well, just remember we invented Yoga and the Karma Sutra was written by a vegetarian!" he retorted with a mischievous gleam in his eyes.
"Now here comes the *Diet for a New America* speech," moaned the Minister.
That was Tiru's cue to cease and desist from his well-worn diatribe on the fallacies of a non-vegetarian diet.
Mavis came to his defence again and said, "Wait a minute, I'd like to hear his views on diets."

This was enough for Tiru to postulate with a professorial air, "Most of North America's arable land is used to grow grain and cereal as feedstock for the cattle and poultry industry. This in turn supplies meat products for the fast food industry. This is the most inefficient way to synthesize protein. Far better to eat cereal directly as part of a healthy vegetarian diet," pointing to the marinated soya cubes in Mavis's salad. He continued saying, "Vegetarian diets avoid the steroids and antibiotics that are injected into these animals. The latter kill digestive bacteria in our gut, which could lead to obesity. Not to mention the pesticides, herbicides and nitrates from fertilizers, which get washed off farmlands and eventually get into the aquifers."

He paused for a moment to see what effect he had on his audience. Everyone, with the exception of Mavis, kept eating and paid little attention to what he was saying.
"What is more, corn and other such cereals are now diverted to produce ethanol. This forces the food prices up in developing countries," continued Tiru, while he waved an accusing finger at possibly the SUV industry. The bemused Mavis looked on.
"I hate to tell you this, but that limousine that you rode in this morning is partly fuelled by ethanol," said Passarelli wryly.
"That's always been my point. Having high environmental principles is one thing but living up to them is another," chuckled the Defence Minister.
Passarelli glanced at his watch and announced that it was time to leave for the boat ride.

Chapter 5: Nuclear Escrow

Mavis glanced at her ward and found him meditating with arms crossed about his chest, and his eyes closed. After this went on for five minutes, Mavis decided to break the awkward silence and interrupt.
"Aren't you going to have any lunch? We have an hour to kill before the others return," she asked.
Tiru awoke and sat up saying, "Aahh, good idea, good idea!"

He reached into his backpack and pulled out a stainless steel cylindrical container, the likes of which Mavis had never seen before. It had a thin steel handle, which was attached and pivoted on the upper part of the container, just below a removable lid. The circular lid was press fitted to the top of the cylinder. Tiru pried the lid off the top revealing a white curd like preparation with a number of cut vegetables mixed in it. He picked up a plastic spoon and kept his head low over the yogurt and proceeded to devour its contents quickly while making a slurping sound and rolling his head appreciatively at every spoonful that he consumed.
"Looks very appetizing," remarked the amused Mavis.
"Have some, have some please," offered Tiru as he looked up and pushed his lunch in her direction.
Mavis obligingly sampled a spoonful and said, "Tastes delicious. What are the ingredients?"
"Oh, Onions, tomatoes, cucumber, coriander leaves, and cardamom mixed in plain yogurt with a sprinkling of chilli-powder."
"I think you've added a lot of chilli-powder," said waving her hand in front of her mouth in an attempt to stifle the pungent taste.
"Please have some more," invited Tiru.
"O.K. just one spoon," said Mavis bravely.
Tiru was pleased to see his talents, culinary at least, were appreciated and said, "I don't have the right ingredients or else it would have tasted even better. You'll have to visit us in Bangalore."
"I would love to tour India, particularly South India. I have heard it is so picturesque and clean. May be on my honeymoon," she said.
"Ah, you are getting married soon," remarked Tiru.
"Well, my fiancé and I haven't set a date but we are busy buying a condominium that we hope to move into next year."
Next year? So you put down a deposit?"
"It's a condominium unit in a high rise, planned for an undeveloped area that hasn't been approved yet. We had to get a mortgage to buy the unit outright. Those who buy-in early benefit from a good deal and a preferred location in the new development."
"What if the plans don't go through, will you get your money back?" asked Tiru getting even more curious.

"Yes we will get the money back plus the interest on the mortgage," said Mavis.

"But what happens to these funds that everyone has raised while they wait for approval?"

"It's held in an Escrow Account. No one has access to it until the City gives the builder approval to go ahead with the project. Once approved, they will use the money for among other things, to buy the land, building material, insurance and labour costs," said Mavis and added "An Escrow account is legalese to describe a trust account that nobody can access until certain agreed requirements are met."

"Escrow Account… Escrow Account…" said Tiru to himself thoughtfully and looked misty eyed past Mavis into the distance towards the thundering falls for almost a full minute.

Then to her further surprise, he jumped up from his chair, threw his hands up in the air, and shouted, "Nuclear Escrow! A Nuclear Escrow account! That's what we need!… I got it! I got it! The missing piece of the puzzle!"

Then to her further embarrassment but to the tourists' amusement, seated in the patio area, he leaned forward, pinched her cheeks, and said, "Miss Mavis you are brilliant! You are simply brilliant! You helped me solve my problem."

"What problem? What are you talking about?" she asked.

However, Tiru was ecstatic. He skipped along toward the parapet and proceeded to do a strange dance, which appeared to be a fusion of the Saturday Night 70's Disco and Punjabi Bhangra. Mavis's jaw dropped at the sight of Tiru uncharacteristically beside himself, gyrating to a hidden beat and repeatedly pointing to an unseen aerial object.

With the Niagara Falls in the backdrop, he shouted, "I got it, I got It. Nuclear Escrow is the way to go, Nuclear Escrow is the way to go …"

Worse still, the other patrons got into the sprit of things by clapping in unison. This was a security nightmare. They needed to be discreet and not draw attention to themselves. Mavis, being a fresh graduate of the RCMP Training Academy, could recall nothing from her training manual that could help her to deal with this situation. With the cheering and clapping now on the increase and furthermore with casual passers by now stopping to look at the free entertainment, Mavis was filled with a new sense of urgency. To her credit, she took things into her stride and quickly put Tiru's unfinished lunch back in his backpack. She then rushed over to his side, akin to a mother chasing after a child who had left the table without finishing his meal.

She tactfully grabbed Tiru by the elbow and manoeuvred him to a side exit. This led them to a picturesque path, which overlooked the Niagara river, upstream past the thundering crest, over looking the swift current, as it sped up to its inevitable plunge over the falls. Tiru walked sheepishly beside her and occasionally muttered to himself in a language Mavis did not understand, but guessed it was one of many Indian languages. She recognized the speed and intonation as similar to that Tiru used when he spoke English.

They progressed further along the scenic lane. Mavis then turned and scolded Tiru, "What is the matter with you drawing attention to yourself? Don't you know we have a security issue at hand? Frankly Mr. Tiru, I am really very disappointed. What's more, I am alone here with no backup."

"I am sorry, Miss Mavis but you inspired a major break through." said Tiru "I don't normally behave like this..."

"I hope not, you being such an important official for the Indian Government. I would have expected something better," interrupted Mavis still annoyed and embarrassed with Tiru's epiphany.

Tiru found a bench to sit on and proceeded to finish his lunch. Mavis sat at the other end of the bench biding her time hoping that Passarelli would return and relieve her soon. She glanced at Tiru and noticed a change in his posture and demeanour. He seemed to have a confident air about him and smiled at her saying, "You helped me to find a missing piece of the puzzle that I have been struggling with for the last few days. Now I have a complete solution!"

"A complete what? I'd say you made a complete ass of yourself out there!" said Mavis still smarting from the professional embarrassment he had caused her. "Good thing I'm not in uniform or I would have arrested you for causing a disturbance," she continued to chide.

Tiru decided to accept this rebuke. He now had bigger and better things on his mind and reached into his backpack for his tablet. He then crossed his legs Yoga style on the bench, leaned forward over his feet, and started to type at a rapid pace, ignoring everything around him excepting the occasional tourist from the patio deck that would wave appreciatively at him. One even called out, "Hey, Bollywood Man!"

To Mavis's relief, the Minister's party returned from their boat tour. The Minister and Jeevan where holding large yellow disposable plastic keepsake raincoats.

"You missed an amazing trip Tiru," said the Minister.

"I hope Mr. Tiru behaved himself Mavis?" asked Passarelli as he winked at Tiru.

"Nooo Comment!" said Mavis darkly, to everyone surprise, leaving the rest to wonder what transpired between the two of them.

"I think we have time for some tea before we move off?" asked the Minister.

"Sir, I recommend making an early start to avoid local rush hour traffic. I know a place en route where we can stop," said Mavis hoping to avoid the restaurant patio.

"The limousine has a mini-bar, Sir. I don't recommend any further exposure until we enter the secure confines of the security zone at the airport," recommended Jeevan. Passarelli nodded his approval.

The Minister got into the limousine first followed by Tiru and Jeevan. However, as Passarelli attempted to join them, Tiru said abruptly to him jerking his head to the front of the vehicle, "You go and sit in front!"

Passarelli stopped and raised his surprised eyebrows.

Just then, the Minister leaned over and said diplomatically, "Please, let's just humour him."

Mavis drove the limousine towards the highway and proceeded at a high rate of speed to Toronto. The group at the back sat in stony silence until the Minister looked at Tiru and asked, "What's up Tiru?"

Jeevan, anticipating a serious announcement, pressed the partition button. The glass partition between the rear cabin and the font driver's area slid up and entombed them in a soundproof zone.

"Sir, I may have the complete solution that should be acceptable to NATO, CANDO and eventually to the Indian Parliament," said Tiru.

"The trip cured your writer's block did it?" asked the Minister cynically.

Undeterred Tiru continued, "If you recall when we last spoke, I expressed my disillusionment with the whole idea of Nuclear Disarmament. It turns out the solution was staring at us in the face all the time. One needs instead to disarm in smaller measures but with almost the same effect."

"You're talking in riddles. I'm tired so get to the point. I would rather take a short nap," snapped the Minister stifling a yawn.

Tiru continued undaunted, "Since the seventies and eighties, people overcame their concerns with the mere existence of nuclear weapons. In Russia, US, and Europe, these weapons of mass destruction constantly point at one another but not everyone is losing sleep over it. The hotline between Washington and Moscow has helped but this is an impractical solution for other countries. We now fear the proliferation of nuclear weapons. My idea is to allow countries that have nuclear weapons to keep them. However, nuclear weapons must be disassembled to such an extent that it would take at least a week to launch them."

"What's the point if they can still reassemble them and fire them off anyway?" asked the Minister losing his patience.

"Ahh," said Tiru, "that's where the new treaty comes in. I am proposing a nuclear treaty based on a 'Nuclear Escrow Account'. The signatories to the proposed Nuclear Escrow Treaty would agree to separate all the weapons' components. These include the guidance system, warhead, trigger, and the propulsion system and place them in secure, separate, but closely monitored zones, called Nuclear Escrow Zones. In these zones, nothing is allowed to physically move outside a prescribed maintenance boundary. The weapon systems will remain functional but not immediately deployable. It's not as final as nuclear disarmament but it makes it impossible to deploy a nuclear weapon at short notice. The time it would take to reassemble the disparate systems would be enough to politically diffuse a military confrontation. At least it removes the hair-trigger aspect of nuclear war. Moreover, if terrorists were to take over a Nuclear Escrow Zone, the world would have time to react and stop them with conventional weapons."

"But what's stopping any country, that signs on to this treaty, from removing each component from its Escrow Zone and reassembling the entire system? How do you plan to track the disassembled parts?" asked the Minister for once taking a serious interest.

"The individual parts will be labelled with a Radio Frequency Identifiers or RFID technology and linked to a Global Positioning System, GPS. The RFID label tells us everything about the component. The GPS unit will track its location and monitor its movement within a prescribed maintenance boundary. All this information will be beamed up to a secure satellite network. A neutral country could remotely monitor the treaty's integrity."

"My major concern is to convince Parliament to venture into this scheme unilaterally. I am not convinced they would want to take the risk," said the Minister.

"It's no secret that we have over 100 nukes. Even if we were to place 10 nukes into escrow, we still have more than enough to defend ourselves. However, this is where Mano's brilliant idea comes into play. The billions of dollars invested in India, in exchange for each nuke that gets escrowed, will be spent on job creating green energy products, stop suicides on farms, send thousands to post-secondary institutions and provide feeding programs for school kids. Minister, for once, you will have millions of happy voters. Moreover, once our nuclear adversaries see how we are benefiting, they will want to sign on to the escrow treaty rather than see their nukes rust on launch pads. I say we grab those escrow dollars before our competitors can get to it!" said Tiru gleefully.

"This could work," said the Minister, "only if escrow information is revealed to a neutral third party. This entity needs to be unbiased and trustworthy in monitoring it."

"A third party, with unquestionable integrity is the foundation on which my proposal is based. Moreover, impenetrable security is another essential ingredient required to make the system work. I don't have all the answers. We now have the basis for a proposal, which we could offer CANDO. If they accept this, our next hurdle is to debate it in Parliament before the elections," said Tiru beaming triumphantly.

"Well, write the whole thing up if that's the best you can come up with. Without their approval, we have no funding, and the entire project will be dead in the water. That will be a pity because the real and immediate threat to our way of life, and even our very existence, is a nuclear duel with our Asian nuclear adversaries and not just climate change," said the Minister.

The limousine sped along the Queen Elizabeth Way, towards Mississauga's Pearson International Airport. They had been on the highway for 25 minutes and still had a long way to go. The Minister watched the soya bean fields interspersed with cornfields rapidly slip by his window with boring consistency. This helped him to nod off to sleep.

Tiru and Jeevan, the latter now a welcome editor of the Nuclear Escrow proposal, huddled together in the other corner. Tiru had pulled out the mini-bar tray from the seat in front of him, had set up his tablet on it and was soon busy at work. They discussed and argued about technical details.

Jeevan noticed a large roadside sign that listed fines associated with the speed limit; the higher the speed infraction, the bigger the fine. As he worked out the equivalent Rupee value, to see what fraction of his weekly pay they would represent, there was a muffled bang from the rear followed by a loud continuous rumbling sound. The limousine swayed from one lane to the other as Mavis struggled to regain control.

Jeevan lowered the glass partition just in time to hear Passarelli turn around and yell, "Burst rear tire. Hang on!"

Just then, there was a sound of screeching tires behind them. A huge tractor-trailer, which drove at a steady pace in the slow lane, slammed its brakes to avoid hitting the limousine, which had drifted into its path. Mavis saw the impending danger, in her rear view mirror and allowed her slowing vehicle to drift further right, on to the hard shoulder. The tractor-trailer rumbled past them on the left. Its rear heavily loaded bogey, snaked forward due to its momentum, and scraped the concrete barrier adjacent to the fast lane. This action spun it around causing it to come to a stop with the cabin facing the wrong way but partially covering the hard shoulder. Mavis steered further right but could not avoid a glancing blow from the protruding fender. This deployed the airbags in the front and rear. The limousine was nudged into a narrow ditch where it came to a stop. Apart from some minor airbag bruising, no one was hurt.

Mavis ran back to check on the driver. He appeared to be slumped across the steering wheel. She reached for her cell phone and called for an ambulance. This soon arrived but wisely in the opposite direction since the tractor-trailer blocked all three Toronto bound lanes. Traffic started to backup behind the accident scene. The party were relieved to see the driver recover consciousness. He made his own way to the ambulance.

Passarelli urged the party to move away in case of a gasoline leak and fire. He then made several calls for a replacement vehicle to be sent. The traffic was now backed up for at least 1 kilometre. The nearest exit was 25 km away. Minutes turned to an hour and Passarelli got irritable and cursed on his cell phone. He informed them that he was assigned to diplomatic security and needed help urgently. Tiru removed his backpack from the limousine, sat with his back against the perimeter fence, and continued to work on his proposal. Eventually, Jeevan and the Minister joined him, and soon got engrossed in discussions while Tiru typed their suggestions.

Passarelli looked at the troika and shook his head and whispered to Mavis, "These Indians never stop working. No wonder they are catching up to us!"

Mavis walked to the rear of the limousine. She crouched on her haunches to look at the damaged tire. Something caught her eye. She pointed a small torch towards a hole, the size of a golf ball, on the inner sidewall.

"Peter, take a look at this," she called out to Passarelli. Passarelli crouched and looked in the direction of the beam. He could see an irregular edged hole with fragments of silver duct tape on either side of it. Mavis was about to reach under the rear fender and remove the tape fragments when Passarelli cautioned, "Leave it alone. Let's not touch anything. This is now a crime scene. Let forensics deal with this."

"Why is this a crime scene?" asked Mavis.

"Someone attached an explosive device to this tire. It's the oldest trick in the book. You tape a low ignition point explosive to a tire. After several minutes at high speed on the highway, the tire heats up and this heat ignites the explosive material that explodes with enough force to puncture the tire," explained Passarelli.

"Just check the other tires please, Mavis."

Mavis returned a few minutes later and shook her head and said, "All clear. I couldn't find anything suspicious."

"Just as I thought," said Passarelli "If they wanted to kill us, they would have blown out one of the front tires. But why would they want to leave us stranded in the middle of nowhere? Unless of course… "

"Unless what Peter?" asked Mavis anxiously.

Passarelli did not answer her but said to her firmly, "Mavis you are on perimeter security duty until our replacement vehicle arrives. Stop any civilians from approaching within 50 metres of our vehicle. If anyone persists, shoot to kill! When we get back to the office, don't talk to anyone about what you have seen. I will handle this from now on."

Mavis walked passed the tractor-trailer's wreckage, towards the line up of vehicles. She showed her RCMP badge and waved curious onlookers back to their vehicles. Another hour went by before the flashing lights of a RCMP car were seen, followed by a tow truck. They drove towards them, precariously on the hard shoulder. However, it was too late for the Minister to attend the Air Kanishka's reception or to catch the inaugural flight. He had already called the Toronto Consular General's office. He delegated him to represent the Indian Government at the reception and to apologize for his absence. The party asked to be driven to the Royal York Hotel.

Chapter 6: Kashmir Princess

Passarelli began to realize that he had made a colossal blunder in underestimating Jeevan's plea for more security for Air Kanishka. To make matters worse, the Pearson RCMP staff advised him that the newly installed X-Ray machines in the Air Kanishka's boarding area had developed a glitch. Many passengers were in a boisterous party mood. They enjoyed an open bar at the inaugural reception. They couldn't wait to get on board, where more free drinks were promised. The airline staff let the luggage through in a frantic attempt to cope with over 500 impatient passengers.

It was too late to do anything. The flight had already taken off on the first leg of its Trans-Atlantic journey to Montreal. In a last minute crisis of conscience, Passarelli called the RCMP detachment at the Pierre Trudeau International Airport, Montreal. He asked that the flight be delayed until sniffer dogs could be sent into the super Jumbo's cavernous hold. He also requested that un-boarded passengers' luggage be removed. This plea was turned down by the local RCMP constabulary. They reminded him that in order to delay an international flight they would need some evidence or at least a directive from CISIA.

Back at the York Hotel, the Minister's party resigned itself to taking the Global Express to London. They planned to have a leisurely brunch and fly out the next day. Everyone retired to their respective rooms after a long eventful day, except for Jeevan. He sat in the spacious lounge area of the suite, in front of a large screen TV and watched a live cricket test match broadcast between Australia and England.

He would flip to the BBC World News during commercials. To his surprise, Tiru wandered out of his room in his robe. He was too excited about the Nuclear Escrow idea to get any sleep. But the test match caught his interest and like Jeevan, soon got absorbed in the game.

Jeevan woke up with a start. A medium frequency repetitive beating noise had woken him. The cricket match was long over and his watch showed about 6 am local time. He had been asleep for almost 5 hours. He recognized the sound as that of a helicopter rotor. The TV was still on and showed the helicopter's shadow that appeared to be flying over a lush green landscape adjacent to a rugged coastline, with an endless sea beyond. There appeared to be a break in the transmission typical of a newscast that was not scripted but done on the spur of the moment as in an emergency.

The commentator's voice came on intermittently, "... we are flying toward a large reported oil slick and debris field. Every known commercial vessel has been diverted to the same area including the Irish

Coast Guard." Then tantalizingly the voice was cut off, and all Jeevan could see was a blue sea rushing past, and the cameraman's vain attempt to pan his camera across the foreground in the hope of capturing something of interest.

Jeevan switched from the sports network to the BBC World News channel. Once again the dispatch was caught in midstream, "… about one hour ago, local air traffic control, in Southern Ireland, announced that it lost radar contact with a commercial aircraft owned by Air Kanishka. Its last reported position was off the coast, near Cork. Fishing trawlers in that area have seen a large debris field…"

Jeevan's worst fears were realized. He stood by helplessly seeing hundreds of innocent people killed. Could he have done more? He considered going to the airport, Glock gun in hand, and taking the Air Kanishka staff hostage. He would release them on condition that all baggage is checked! What if all this were a bluff? It would have been an International embarrassment for the Government and a certain end to his career.

Jeevan held his head in despair and tried to rationalize his predicament but the souls of 539 victims cried out to him in one voice. You did your best but it was not good enough! Jeevan stood up and found the blood rushing to his head. He had an awful sinking feeling and his stomach began to cramp with anxiety. He noticed Tiru slumped over on a sofa, snoring, and occasionally mumbling to himself. Does this guy ever stop thinking? Jeevan asked himself.

He chose not to wake anyone. He needed official confirmation from Air Kanishka. Besides the Minister would bombard him with questions and he didn't have any answers.

Half an hour later, he switched to the Canadian Broadcasting Corporation's (CBC) TV channel. A spokesperson for Air Kanishka made a terse announcement at an impromptu News Conference at the Air Kanishka baggage check area at Heathrow Airport. "We have been in touch with the Irish Coast Guard. They have confirmed, based on the debris collected and the positive identification of at least two bodies recovered, that are on our passenger list, that Air Kanishka, Flight 281, Kashmir Princess has crashed into the sea off the coast of Ireland. With deepest regret we announce that there are no survivors from amongst the passengers and crew…."

Jeevan decided that it was time to alert the Minister. He knocked hard on the door and was soon greeted by the bleary-eyed Minister. "What's up Gill," he asked in an irritated tone, "I thought we were leaving in the afternoon."

"Sorry, Sir but we have an emergency," said Jeevan in a voice heavy with emotion. This caught the Minister's attention. Jeevan wiped a tear from the corner of his eye before it rolled down his cheek and cleared his throat. Still struggling to keep his composure Jeevan continued, "The Kashmir Princess has crashed off the coast of Ireland. I waited for the Air Kanishka staff to confirm this on a TV interview a few minutes ago. There are no survivors. They are now in the process of recovering bodies."

The Minister stood speechless for a moment and staggered over to the sofa, almost stumbling over Tiru's out stretched legs.

"Wake him up!" ordered the Minister.

The Minister hunched forward intently watching the CBC newscast live from a line feed off the Irish Coast. He was just in time to see a large piece of wreckage being hoisted by a crane onto the deck of a salvage vessel. It appeared to be a part of the Airbus 380's enormous tail fin. As it dangled in the air, it turned in the wind to reveal Air Kanishka's unmistakable logo, a flying Pegasus. The Minister was distracted with the thought that an Indian company needed to borrow from the Greeks, when it had a rich mythology of its own.

Tiru was now up and joined the Minister on the Sofa, rubbing his eyes in disbelief.

"Our Kamala and Lata, whatever could have become of them," said the Minister in despair.

"If, it weren't for the highway accident, just think we could be with them at the bottom of the sea," said Tiru.

"Jeevan, I wish you were more forceful with me. It's my mistake for not taking you seriously. But for my stubbornness Lata, Kamala, and hundreds of others would be alive today. I should have stopped that flight altogether."

"Sir, my mission is to protect you and your staff. I failed to persuade Kamala and Lata to join us on the Niagara trip. I sabotaged the limousine so that we would never make it back in time."

"What? You did that!" shouted the Minister looking for someone to vent his frustrations on.

Tiru was too overcome by emotion to say anything. He hugged his Sikh friend and wept uncontrollably.

The trip to London, England on the Global Express was put on hold. The Minister got orders from New Delhi to stay in London. He was expected to participate in the Canadian enquiry into the disaster.

In the following days and weeks, more information emerged. It became obvious that the Kashmir Princess was downed by a terrorist bomb. The Deccan Dhaku alliance was labelled as a global terrorist organization. The Minister, Jeevan, and Tiru appeared at a press conference. They were grilled for what they knew prior to the disaster.

However, all attention turned to Passarelli and his CISIA contacts when it became known that CISIA was warned well in advance that a terrorist attacked was being planned. All hell broke loose when it was further revealed that a junior CISIA officer had deleted voice, video recordings, and surveillance notes regarding the two major suspects, Godsé and Phadké. The surveillance of two foreigners, at the request of their third world Government was not on the top of CISIA's priorities. It was legally impossible to detain either of the two. CISIA's claim that their mandate was to collect intelligence and the RCMP's duty was to act on its own cognition with the available evidence, did not sit well with the press or the public. In reality 329 of the 529 killed by the explosion were Canadian citizens. This made it the worst act of terrorism against Canada.

Passarelli decided to take an early retirement package that was offered to him. His continued presence was an embarrassment to the force. Mavis was so disillusioned with the combined ineptitude of the CISIA and the RCMP, that she resigned and started a security business. She phoned to apologise to Tiru and told him of her new plans. He consulted with the Minister and Jeevan and they promptly invited her back to the team. They gave her company a contract to protect Indian Government Staff whenever they were in North America or elsewhere.

The duel between the AGA Government, and the Deccan Dhaku moved to a new arena. CISIA advised Scotland Yard in the UK that Godsé was now in England. But apart from a sparse description of his physical appearance, and the fact that he had light blue eyes, they were unable to provide any more details. The Deccan Dhaku had not stopped the peace initiative but merely delayed it. The world saw the Deccan Dhaku as a less than perfect terrorist hit team. They missed their target and needlessly slaughtered hundreds of innocent victims.

The Transportation Safety Board of Canada chaired a series of public meetings. These meetings were held in order to answer many questions surrounding the tragedy. The RCMP's report, distributed at one of the meetings, exonerated their staff. It hinted that the problem stemmed from the Indian Government's inability to contain its home-grown terrorism within its own territorial confines. Many victims' families left the meeting in disgust. They were convinced that the report was a face saving gesture.

The Minister, Tiru, and Jeevan met for the last time before they departed in-different directions. Tiru and Jeevan observed that the Minister appeared to have aged considerably since the disaster. The Minister was annoyed with is own complacency. This was brought about by a sense of optimism about India's future prospects. His government underestimated the evil alliance's ability to attack Indian interests outside India.

"Jeevan," he said, "You and Tiru will travel to U.K. while I return to India. I have spoken to your boss, Lieutenant General Anwar Khan and arranged that you be seconded to the Ministry of Defence. You are appointed as Military Attaché to the Indian High Commission in London, England. Your sole mission is to apprehend Anil Godsé before he gets up to any more mischief and destroys Tiru's efforts with NATO and CANDO. The future of hundreds of millions of people that live below the poverty line depend on it. If those lunatics have their way, our Government will collapse and our hawkish opposition will take control. Our meagre funds will once again be diverted to an arms race."

"By apprehend you presumably mean that I co-operate with the local law enforcement," inquired Jeevan seeking clarity on his new job description.

"Yes of course you need to do that but I would advise you to apprehend Godsé before the local authorities get to him," said the Minister uneasily.

"Apprehend Sir?" persisted Jeevan.

At this point Tiru leapt to his feet and yelled, "Kill him, yar! Kill him, kill him! Do it before the Brits get to him or else we'll have another pointless self-serving investigation on our hands. They could release Godsé because of his human rights, since nobody will believe the "third world" evidence we have against him. We have ample evidence to tie him to the Lonavala bomb. I am sure he used the same type of calibrated pressure transducer triggered bomb, hidden in unaccompanied baggage, to bring down the Kashmir Princess. The bomb exploded soon after the aircraft reached its highest, sustained, cruising altitude over the Atlantic. If he is caught and then released, it will then give him official sanction to destroy all that we have worked for. Kill him before they get to him!"

The Minister was shocked at Tiru's outburst but said nothing to contradict him. His silence on the matter indirectly gave Jeevan his marching orders, but without compromising the morals of his Government for unofficially sanctioning murder. However, the wise and experienced politician was saddened by the thought that a once soft-spoken, fun loving and intelligent professional like Tiru, had let the turn of events compromise his values. He had changed from an unbiased, truth-seeking intellectual into a revengeful person. Perhaps, reflected the Minister, the first casualty of war or an act of terrorism is not just the truth, but also the loss of innocence. It converts good people into those that seek revenge, at any cost, and at the expense of any principle.

While Tiru and Jeevan prepared to depart for England, the Minister stayed a little longer in Toronto to co-ordinate the salvage operations. The recovery operations concentrated on retrieving the bodies of the passengers and also the flight data recorder and cockpit voice recorder. The latter were required to establish beyond any doubt that Air Kanishka, Flight 281, was sabotaged.

The flight and cockpit data recorders continued to ping acoustic signals, which helped to locate them. This greatly aided the search. A towed underwater acoustic ping detector determined the best region to investigate. This was followed by extensive sonar scanning by an autonomous underwater vehicle. This device flew over a predetermined grid and soon dispatched images of the debris field. A French company continued the search using remotely piloted submarines. They were equipped with powerful searchlights and robotic arms that could be manipulated from a mother ship above it. Fortuitously the debris field came to rest on the shallow continental shelf. The flight recorders were found and were dispatched to Air Kanishka's flight training centre in Mumbai for analysis. Only 131 bodies were recovered; some still strapped to their seats.

Chapter 7: Canadian Visitor

A month after the Air Kanishka salvage operations, were completed, Jeevan found himself at the office of Chief Inspector Paul Lestrade of the Anti-Terrorist Branch of New Scotland Yard, London, England.
"Welcome, please take a seat Commander Gill," directed Lestrade turning around from a computer monitor.
"Thanks," said Jeevan as he took a seat and looked around at the many photographs mounted on the walls. All seemed to be in locales other than the UK. Lestrade appeared to have had a lot of field experience.
"I understand you have flown in from Canada. Settling down okay?"
"Yes thanks, I arrived a few weeks ago with Mr. Krishnaswamy, also from the Indian Ministry of Defence. We have set up office at India House."
"How are my friends at the Indian High Commission?" asked Lestrade in a jovial tone.
"Do you know some of the staff there, Sir?" asked Jeevan.
"Oh yes, yes I do. We go back a long way. During the war, that established Bangladesh as an independent country, a pair of zealots entered the Indian High Commission. They were armed with knives, and would you believe, imitation handguns. They were planning to take the High Commission's staff hostage. My unit responded, as in those days we were assigned to protect the diplomatic enclave. The two intruders were shot dead. The staff had a terrifying experience. I remember the High Commissioner praising the Yard for its prompt action. Ever since then, we have had good relations and full co-operation from their staff. This was the seventies, somewhat before your time but the story is kept alive, I suspect from one generation to another. This is why I would like to keep the good working relationship going. I hope I can count on your full co-operation with this nasty terrorist bombing, which killed so many Indians."
"Well, this is academic in view of the human tragedy," said Jeevan, "but as a matter of fact there were only a handful of Indian citizens on the Kashmir Princess. This included two of the Defence Ministry's senior civil servants and of course the Indian flight crew. The passengers' list breaks down into North American, European business people, many of them British, and other nationalities. The bulk of the passengers, about 329, consisted of mostly Canadian parents and children traveling to India to spend a summer vacation with family. It was essentially a nursery ship. Some of the husbands or wives would have joined them later when their vacation started."
"If that's the case, then I am surprised as to why the Canadian Government hasn't taken a bigger interest in this investigation," said

Lestrade. "All that's happen to date is that the Canadian Inter-Services Intelligence Agency, CISIA, contacted MIQ, the intelligence branch of the British Secret Service, set up after 9/11 to deal with global terrorism, with a claim that the alleged terrorist, named Anil Godsé, is now in the U.K. They haven't been able to substantiate this yet. All they could provide us with is a vague description of the suspect."

Jeevan reached into his briefcase and placed a file folder and a DVD disk on Lestrade's desk. "This file," said Jeevan pointing to a buff coloured folder marked "Top secret" in English and Hindi, with a the characteristic Indian Government four lion "Ashoka" crest on it, "contains a briefing on the Deccan Dhaku terrorist organization, which Mr. Godsé belongs to. We can trace his involvement right from the time they exploded a test bomb in Lonavala killing 37 students and teachers on a school picnic, to his entry into Canada. From that point on, CISIA tracked Mr. Godsé's movements in the Toronto area, bugged his hotel room and tapped cell phone conversations. In addition, based on our intelligence reports, we warned them that an attack on the Kashmir Princess was eminent. They never took us seriously. They perceived the issue as a petty dispute between a third world government and a political rival. CISIA only issued a low-key advisory to the RCMP who is responsible for Airport security. They did little or nothing to prevent the bombing."

"Wait a minute," said the alarmed Lestrade, "didn't CISIA track the suspect?"

"Yes, they had video and voice records to support his arrest and detention. They let him go because a clerical error by a junior officer destroyed all the evidence."

"What?" exclaimed the amazed Lestrade.

"The folder contains an updated version of the same content that we gave CISIA. Believe me, Godsé is in the UK and is up to no good. His mission to assassinate the Indian Defence Minister failed; instead, he murdered hundreds of innocent people. We need to stop him before he completes his new mission."

"And what would that be?" asked Lestrade.

"We believe he will try to disrupt the CANDO conference. It has been rescheduled for about 18 months from now," replied Jeevan.

"Oh, you mean the Mano Foundation's Conference. Last I heard was that, following the London tube bombings, they will be moving it out of London. I don't know the new venue."

"Chief Inspector, we need to find, arrest Godsé without further delay, and extradite him to India where there is ample evidence to link him with a bombing."

"Steady on with the use of the royal "we" old chap. While in the UK, you are not to do anything but observe and report to me about any more information you have about this gentleman. The Yard will then bring him in for questioning. Do I make myself clear?" admonished Lestrade.
"Yes, Yes of course. My apologies Chief Inspector," said Jeevan in a contrite tone. "My department wants to get to the bottom of this and will cooperate in any way." And then added tongue in cheek, "If you don't mind me asking, what have you done so far to trace Mr. Godsé?"

Lestrade seemed to be somewhat taken aback and searched for a convincing answer.
"Well, well er ... you see Commander Gill, after being briefed by CISIA over the phone, I put out a bulletin to all ports of entry but no person with that name, gender, and description has entered the UK. I have opened a file on him and the Yard now only refers to him by a code name."

Jeevan stifled a yawn while there was a lull in conversation. Lestrade pored over the contents of the file. He glossed over the lengthy notes on Deccan Dhaku and picked up a grainy video camera based black and white picture of Anil Godsé and glared at it for a minute.
"It might have helped if CISIA sent me this picture earlier. Rather good looking but effeminate little bugger isn't he?" said Lestrade with a sly smile on his face.
"Don't be deceived by his looks. The man belongs to a society of professional assassins. They won't stop at anything until their mission is accomplished. With one fell swoop they tried to wipe out the entire peace mission, me included. Deccan Dhaku failed in their first attempt. They will try again," asserted Jeevan.
"What evidence do you have that a bomb brought down Air Kanishka?" asked Lestrade.
"The salvage crew off the coast of Ireland found the cockpit voice recorder and the flight recorder. The flight recorder showed nothing unusual until a sudden decompression is recorded. It starts in the cargo hold and spreads from lower to upper decks. Other recorded parameters show that the out-gassing of pressurized cabin air from the rear lower fuselage area caused the aircraft to first yaw and consequently roll, due to the uneven lift forces on the wing," said Jeevan illustrating these manoeuvres with the palm of his hand.
"The Airbus 380," continued Jeevan, "has fly-by-wire electronic controls. This means that there are no hydraulic pipes going through the length of the aircraft as in the case of older aircraft. Moreover, its systems have multiple redundancies. If one system were damaged, another spare system would kick in immediately. Nevertheless, the autopilot could not cope with the lack of coherent information due to the catastrophic damage and promptly disengaged leaving the flight crew to fly the

airplane manually. The Captain did attempt to correct the roll and instinctively throttled back to lose speed and altitude. Theoretically, this was the right thing to do, in order to counteract the loss of cabin pressure, get more oxygen into the cabin, and improve manoeuvrability. However, his actions may have inadvertently accentuated the roll. Since the aircraft flew at 82% of the speed of sound, this generated tremendous g-forces that acted on the Airbus fuselage and wings. This caused it to break up in mid-air."

"Well, you seemed to have done a thorough analysis of the incident. What's on the DVD?" asked Lestrade.

"I saved the best for last," said Jeevan with a gleam in his eye.

"What I have on DVD," continued Jeevan, "is the last three minutes of the cockpit voice recording, which is much more interesting and relevant. My narration will help you understand the sequence of events on the voice recording. The Captain, Rohan Kapadia was one of the finest pilots in the Government's Executive flight crew. He was a much-decorated veteran of two regional wars. I had met him on his last flight for the Government. He was all excited about his new assignment with Air Kanishka International and the opportunity to fly the Airbus A380. The recording starts when a stewardess brings in a young boy to the flight deck for a visit."

Lestrade slipped the DVD disk into his computer and turned up the volume on the speakers.

"Hello Marcia, is this the young man you were telling me about?" asked Captain Kapadia.

"Yes Sir, this is my precocious cousin Murli who made me promise, in a moment of weakness, to arrange a visit to the fight deck if we were ever to fly together."

"Hi Murli," said the Captain and co-pilot almost in unison.

"So what grade are you in Murli," asked the Captain.

"I've just finished grade 8 and will start high school in September."

"Do you have an interest in aviation?"

"Yes I do, my father says civil aviation is expanding in Asia and they will need a lot of pilots out there. I would like to be an airline pilot."

"Your father is right we'll need many good people in the years ahead."

"Rubbish," said Marcia. "Don't believe this little rascal. All he wants to do is ogle at the good looking stewardesses."

"That too!" said Murli.

There is laughter all around.

"Come a little closer son," said the Captain, "see (presumably pointing to the instrument panel) we are flying at 35,000 ft at Mach .82. Do you know what that means?"

"Did you guys hear that?" asks Marcia interrupting with a sense of concern in her voice.
Almost immediately, a number of cockpit alarms are heard.
"We're losing cabin pressure in the hold and lower deck Captain. The auto-pilot has disengaged," reports the co-pilot.
"Opps …we've got some side slip." remarks the Captain, "Quick 70% thrust and lets get down to 10,000ft. PAN, PAN, PAN …Irish Control this is Flight 281 heavy, request emergency decent to 10,000 feet."
"Copy 281; Clear to decent to 10,000 ft. Advise about emergency," says the Irish air traffic control.
"Marcia take Murli, back we'll talk later," orders the captain.
"Yes sir."
Sound of door opening.
"Wait! Don't open the…" yells the co-pilot.
A loud whooshing sound heard followed by screams from Marcia and Murli as they are sucked out of the door into the passenger area. Screams of other passengers heard in the background.
"Captain, fire in the hold! I can see a large area of the lower fuselage blown out on the internal video camera …"
"Quick, pull hard right we're beginning to roll. Come on, pull hard right! Holy shit, Mayday, Mayday, Mayday…"
There is a crackling static sound followed by deadly silence.
Jeevan looked at Lestrade's ashen face. The Englishman had a stiff upper lip but his lower lip trembled a bit.
"Sorry to put you through this. You've just heard the death throes of 529 people. There have been all kinds of speculation in the press ranging from a meteorite strike, navy test range missile strike, to aircraft structural failure, due to the use of large amounts of new technology, composite material. I want to leave no doubt in your mind that this crash was caused by a terrorist bombing."
"I don't need convincing," said Lestrade in agreement.
"I take it then you'll marshal your troops and arrest Godsé as soon as possible?" asked Jeevan standing up and preparing to leave.
"Absolutely old boy, now that I got all this to work on," replied Lestrade pointing to the folder that Jeevan had given him.
Jeevan shook Lestrade's hand and turned to leave but as he got to the door and opened it, Lestrade said, "Oh, by the way, the code name for Mr. Godsé is ...Canadian Visitor. You see, we didn't know his nationality only that he arrived from Canada. Anyway, that's how we will refer to him, in all our communications from now on."
"Canadian Visitor, Ehh!" said Jeevan as he shook his head with amusement and walked through the door.

Jeevan met with Tiru and briefed him on his meeting with Lestrade. Tiru was sceptical about the Yard's commitment to locating and arresting Godsé. He urged Jeevan to be independently vigilant. Tiru brought Jeevan up to date with the week long meetings with NATO and CANDO. It turned out that the downing of Kashmir Princess and the near miss that Mr. Pinto and his team had experienced drew world wide attention to AGA's policies. Their attempts to curb the arms race in South Asia was better understood. Their support for a Carbon Abatement policy that would be linked to the Nuclear Escrow Agreement won universal approval. At the talks, the delegates were now eager to work with the Indians. They now saw them as comrades in the fight against global terror. Tiru's proposal was debated at length and approved. Much work needed to be done to develop the Escrow monitoring technology. The European Union appointed Norway to head a Nuclear Escrow monitoring committee made of members from the EU.

With CANDO funding assured and the prospect of billions being allocated to rural projects in India, the impoverished majority finally saw something in it for themselves. At the general elections, they turned up at the polling stations using anything from bullock-carts to bicycles to vote Alfred Pinto's AGA party into power!

Chapter 8: Cynthia Amis

It was early September, over two months after the Air Kanishka disaster. CANDO appreciated AGA's majority election victory. This would result in quick decisions that would have been nearly impossible if they had to deal with a coalition. CANDO set about inviting UK towns and cities to submit competitive tenders for the honour of hosting the CANDO conference. The committee was oblivious to the existence of Canadian Visitor as MIQ and Scotland Yard regarded this as a national secret. Many towns and cities bid to host the conference. This included the beautiful English Cathedral city of Lincoln in Lincolnshire, in the English Midlands. They knew nothing of the security threat this brought with it.

Cynthia Amis, a special education consultant for the Lincolnshire County School Board, was looking forward to lying in on this Saturday morning. Instead, she reluctantly got up early to make her way to an unusual assignment. It had been a tough previous week at meetings with few positive results. She was constantly losing the battle for getting more resources assigned to her department. The annual review of the school budget was in. It did not look good for Special Education. The Finance Department had increased her budget by about 10% and then increased the workload by 30%. She stormed into the board headquarters and demanded a meeting with the Director of Finance and a board Trustee. This Trustee was the head of the board's budget committee. They were about to present the budget to the board for a final vote the next week. Cynthia had one last chance to change their minds.

Cynthia had established herself as a strong advocate for the special education (special ed.) needs of children. She negotiated with the school board on budgetary matters, curriculum development, new technology, early detection, and teaching techniques. Her responsibilities covered a variety of intellectual disabilities. These included Autism, Asperser's Syndrome, Dyslexia, Pervasive Development Disorders, and Mild Intellectual Disorders. Her specialty included working with gifted children.

She enrolled in an online Master's course with the University of Edinburgh's special ed. department. Two consecutive summers were spent attending on-campus courses in Edinburgh. She earned her Masters in special ed. with distinction. Her Master's Thesis focused on gifted children with a learning disability.

Cynthia established herself as a leader in special ed. She published papers in many peer-reviewed journals, made presentations and gave keynote addresses at conferences in the EU. Moreover, due to her advocacy, the teachers' union, to the dismay of the school board, appointed her as their chief spokesperson for all matters related to special ed.

At the previous week's meeting, the Trustee and the Financial Director, teamed up against her, and stonewalled her suggestions. She prepared alternative strategies, which would in some cases have saved money and used these savings for much needed programs. The meeting had not ended well. Cynthia accused the school board of being insensitive to the needs of special ed. students. Name calling earned her yet another reprimand from her principal who added a 'letter in her file'. This implied that she was a step closer to being fired for cause and ruined her promotion prospects.

On the way out, she picked up her mail from under the door. She was delighted to recognize the familiar handwriting of her childhood friend, Veronica Sears. Veronica persisted with personal snail mail but used email for business. She got into her car, opened the letter, and read it. Veronica had applied for a job in the human resources department of Lincoln University. She hoped to resign from her job at a staffing and recruitment company in the West End of London and move back to Lincoln. Her family lived on an estate on the outskirts of Lincoln. They owned a chain of convenience stores in Lincolnshire and Northumberland. Veronica, being the only child, was under pressure to join, and manage the family business but she chose to go her own way. She graduated in business studies and got her present job in London. When she had left Lincoln for London, she was excited and full of adventure. Cynthia was pleasantly surprised to hear that she would leave all the bright lights and excitement of London, to come back to Lincoln.

She folded the letter, put it into her handbag and focused on her drive to her assignment. She found herself driving a familiar but lengthy stretch of a dual carriageway. To break the monotony she allowed her mind to wander back to Veronica and all the great times they had together. They were the best of friends, and she missed her company. Unlike Cynthia, Veronica could be quite the party girl once she got going. She recalled how they met the first time. It was Veronica's first day in the lower sixth form of St. Cuthbert's Comprehensive School. Cynthia was the head girl for the house. Veronica looked prim and proper in her shining new blazer and plaid skirt, but looked out of place as the girls rarely if ever wore their blazers in the sixth form. She was looking for the homeroom when Cynthia saw that Veronica was anxious and lost. Cynthia walked over to introduce herself. Their friendship grew from that point, and soon they became inseparable friends. She persuaded her to bike to school or take the bus so as to avoid being perceived as upper class and aloof when she arrived in her family's chauffer driven Bentley. Much to the consternation of Veronica's mother, Cynthia talked Veronica into lightening up her wardrobe. The girls would go shopping for accessories, shoes and jeans. Veronica tried hard to fit in with the rest of the of Cynthia's nerdy clique; the University bound sixth formers. She did well and was soon popular particularly after the whole group was invited to spend a weekend at the estate to celebrate her 18th birthday.

Veronica did not get to know Cynthia's friend, Michael Caruthers, very well. Michael's father worked as a machinist at Ruston Corporation, a local engineering company. He resented people of privilege and dismissed the tall skinny blonde haired Veronica as not being his type. He was, in those days at least, devoted to Cynthia who tutored and encouraged him to get enough O-levels to justify his presence in the lower sixth form. Michael and Cynthia's other friend was Murphy O'Neal, or Murph as they called him. Murph was a slight, sickly kid with a runny nose who hung on to Michael's coattails. He was often picked on and bullied in the schoolyard. Michael had come to his rescue on several occasions. Murph's parents, who were from Ireland, first settled in Liverpool but then moved to Lincoln where Murph's father got a job in Ruston's scrap metal yard.

Cynthia drove on and reflected on how quickly the years had gone by. Everyone had moved on to bigger and better things. She had persuaded Michael to leave after lower sixth form and take some courses in real estate management at Lincoln Polytechnic. She noticed that Michael, from an early age, had shown entrepreneurial skills. He was always wheeling and dealing with things that appeared to have "fallen off the back of a truck." Such as expensive car radios, MP3 players and tablet devices. He was never short of money and the first in their circle of friends to buy a car. He did well at the real estate courses and soon got a job with a local real estate firm.

Cynthia's mother was diagnosed with breast cancer. Nevertheless, she performed brilliantly in school and took her A-levels in the first year of sixth form. Based on these results she already secured a place at Royal Holloway College, London University. She delayed her departure for another year so that she could stay back and help her mother. Her parents divorced when she was only 4 years old. She persuaded her maternal uncle, Norbert (Noby) Clark to move in with them. Her mother had a mastectomy but the cancer had metastasized and spread to her lungs. Sessions of chemotherapy were interspersed with radiation treatment. It was clear that she was fighting a loosing battle. The end finally came in the third year of her study at Royal Holloway, in the midst of her finals. With her brilliant record, the college made every effort to allow her to write her finals after her mother's funeral. Uncle Noby was a retired Royal Air Force pilot and the last family member that Cynthia had left. He was a pillar of strength for her. She could not imagine what she could have done without him. Michael used to visit the family at the hospital but he was constantly on his cell phone. He was pre-occupied with wheeling and dealing in real estate.

She returned to Lincoln after a further year of teacher's training. She got a job to teach at her old school, St. Cuthbert's Comprehensive. She hoped to further her relationship with Michael whom she had developed a fondness during their earlier years together. Michael had changed in many ways in the years she was away. He became quite an accomplished real estate agent and consistently led his sales team in annual sales. He had the personality and powers of persuasion to turn prospects into a committed sale. He no longer needed her, as in their school days. He had matured considerably as their separation had taught him to stand on his own feet. He stood tall with a mop top Beatles styled hair and had a way with women clients. He knew for them location alone was not enough to make the sale.

Murph certified in the skilled trades and often undertook odd jobs for Michael. Murph later worked exclusively for him to upgrade properties that Michael had bought for a song. He became a kitchen cabinet maker and also excelled at refurbishing bathrooms with exquisite tiling and customized shower and bathroom fixtures. When a couple called on Michael's services, he would show them the spacious kitchen and gleaming fixture rich bathrooms. Then, if the price and the location were right, there would be a quick sale. Alternatively, there could be a bidding war between two and sometimes three couples who coveted Murph's handiwork. The pair became better with each project and soon the duo's reputation spread across Lincoln. Eventually, Michael opened his own business, Cathedral Realties Inc., located in an office tower in downtown Lincoln.

Due to the seasonal nature of the renovation business, Murph found part-time employment in a printing and graphics company, Patel Printers, owned by an Indian couple. They immigrated to the UK from Gujarat, India, decades ago. Mr. Patel was a successful chartered accountant. He bought the printing business to supplement his income. He lived with his wife in a spacious flat above the print shop. They had no children of their own but soon after some religious riots in their home town of Ahmadabad, in Gujarat State, Mrs. Patel visited Ahmadabad, leaving her husband to look after the shop. She returned with Mr. Patel's 12 year old orphaned nephew, Susheel, whose parents were killed by a terrorist car bomb during the riots. The Patels enrolled him in St Cuthbert's and as the boy settled down, for some reason, not quite clear to them, his English friends all called him what sounded like Patelji. They interpreted this ending as the respectful Indian addendum "ji", and hence chose not to correct his friends. He soon developed a Northern English accent flavoured with local colloquialism that they found difficult to follow. They chose to speak to him in Gujarati. He was Susheel to the Patels at home but Patelji to everyone else, including his teachers.

Cynthia drove on, but her mind wondered back to Michael. It occurred to her that he could help to find accommodation for Veronica, when she moved back to Lincoln. Although Cynthia and Michael had been intimate in the past, the years of separation had taken its toll on their relationship. She knew monogamy wasn't his strong suit. It all ended between them, when she stopped by at his flat on a Sunday morning. She hoped to entice him to go to a local hotel for brunch and see a movie. A young good-looking girl, dressed in nothing else but Michael's shirt, greeted her. Cynthia was told politely, by the young nymph, that Michael was asleep, and was not accepting any commercial visitors that day!

Michael's politics and views on race relations had bothered her more than his occasional sexual indiscretions. He was a card-carrying member of the British National Party, which over the years, had adopted a rather myopic view of Britain and its place in the global economy. Its strategy of "Britain First" advocated removing the U.K. from the European Union and among other things, encouraging the repatriation of non-European immigrants to their countries of origin.

After the breakup, Cynthia immersed herself in her career. The school board promoted her to the position of special ed. consultant. St. Cuthbert's was now one of the schools she was assigned to service.

Michael was distraught when Cynthia broke up with him, and secretly hoped she would take him back one day. When they were together, he treated her differently than the other women he would date. He had a deep-seated respect for her intellect and her work but never revealed it. Eventually he got over their breakup by devoting himself to his successful real estate work, driving out into the countryside, and having wild weekends with Murph and female companions. There was no shortage of loose women in his life. Some found his rustic looks, preference for fast cars, and his lavish life style attractive.

Michael's pet project, which was helped along by Murph, was the Saracen's Head. There were rumours that he acquired this pub under shady circumstances when the previous owner defaulted on mortgage payments. Michael had privileged information through his real estate contacts. He settled with the owner, before the property could be listed. He bought it for a song even though it was located in a prime area in the downtown section of Lincoln. The Saracen's Head, was renovated with new bar fixtures, Video Lottery Machines, and a Karaoke stand. There was a beautiful hard wood floor and a bandstand, which was partition off from the pub area from Mondays to Thursdays. It was party time with dancing to a live band during the weekend evenings. The pub's reputation spread and very soon people had to be turned away on Friday nights.

Cynthia drove further east and passed Michael's current project at the Evergreen Estates. If the Saracen's Head made Michael wealthy, the Evergreen Estates made him a millionaire.

It all started with Michael's business dealings with a prominent City Councillor, Clair MacMillan. He had sold her a farm that belonged to a retired farmer. The old farmhouse was demolished. The councillor commissioned Cathedral Realties to construct a modern country manor in its place. The spacious grounds contained a swimming pool, a tennis court, and a mansion full of all the amenities anyone could imagine. Questions were raised on an ongoing BLOG, as to how the councillor could afford such an extravagant residence on her salary. These were countered by an anonymous submission claiming that she had inherited wealth and hence this was nobody's business.

Soon after Michael completed the construction of the councillor's mansion, he solicited funding from a group of merchant bankers. They financed the purchase of a large piece of land that had been owned by Lincoln City. The UK Government originally appropriated this land during World War II for use as a Bomber Command Centre. In the sixties, the Royal Air Force (RAF) leased this to the US Air Force. They used it as a staging post for American bombers en route to Vietnam. The airbase also contained a storage area for the infamous Agent Orange defoliant. After the end of the Vietnam War, the RAF returned the airfield property to the City.

The airbase remained unused after the hasty withdrawal of the Americans from Vietnam in the seventies. In the eighties after a superficial cleanup, the City leased the land to farmers to graze their cattle. This turned out to be disastrous. The cattle aborted their calves. The City realized that there were serious soil contamination problems. The environmental regulations in those days were not as strict as in more recent times. All the City did was to build a chain linked fence around the property they named Evergreen Estates. 'No Trespassing' notices were posted at high traffic areas. The fields remained fallow and barren for over two decades. Very little vegetation survived within its confines.

When The City submitted its bid to host the Mano Foundation's CANDO conference, it found itself in an expensive competition and publicity drive to promote their bid. Funds were urgently required to spruce up and market Lincoln City, wining, and dining the visiting selection committee, and buying expensive gifts. The City also needed the money to renovate and extend the existing convention centre. The construction of a five star hotel, adjacent to the convention centre, had already begun. This could be used to house the convention attendees. It was decided to raise this money by selling Evergreen Estates.

The new generation of councillors were unaware of the previous problems, with the exception of Councillor MacMillan. She had served on the council the longest. Soon after the City's bid for the CANDO conference, Councillor MacMillan reported that an environmental assessment had been completed. The land was cleared for residential development. She also reported that Cathedral Realties came up with the best offer. No one dared to challenge the experienced councillor. The council rejoiced that the funds would be available for their pet project: the CANDO conference.

Cynthia hadn't driven past the old airbase area in years. She remembered fondly the time she would visit Uncle Noby with her mother. Uncle Noby returned from a training assignment in India to act as RAF liaison officer with the United States Air Force (USAF). Now nothing remained of the long runways, control towers, hangers, storage areas, and miscellaneous offices. Demolition, earth-moving equipment, and an army of building contractors had transformed the airbase into a residential suburb of Lincoln City. It offered a variety of housing options from town houses to detached residences. A school and a shopping mall catered to the needs of a community of 20,000 residents. The vast property allowed for the creation of an artificial lake, a convenient jogging, rollerblading, and cycling track. The paved track circled the perimeter of the lake and snaked its way through other areas on the community that conveniently backed on to it. A football field and children's playground were located close to the school. Evergreen Estates used of tube wells to supply fresh water. This avoided the cost of piping municipal water from Lincoln City to the estate. Cathedral Realties claimed to pass on these savings in the sale of each unit. This was a strong benefits statement in their sales pitch. Needless to say, Michael, the estate's sole landlord, made a tidy profit.

The required exit off the dual carriageway was in sight, and Cynthia shook herself out of her past recollections and started to focus on the task at hand. She had been directed to visit the Lincolnshire Youth Detention Centre on the outskirts of Lincoln, to interview a troubled teenaged girl who had been through chronic bouts of runaway incidents. She had gone absent without leave from several foster homes.

"Good morning, Ms. Amis," said the educational psychologist consultant, "I'm Dr. Tom Hodicroft, educational psychologist for the Lincoln County School Board."

"Yes, I have heard of you Dr. Hodicroft," said Cynthia, and bowed her head reverently.

"And, I've heard of you Ms. Amis and have read many reports and recommendations you have made about your special ed. students," said Hodicroft, struggling with his display of modesty.
"I don't of course work here, as you may know," continued Hodicroft. "I am a consultant for this centre as well as the school board. The director of the detention centre and the superintendent of special education have both asked me to deal with this file as soon as possible. This situation needs to be resolved quickly. I have had to ask you to attend this weekend meeting. The school board has collaborated in the past with Youth Social Services in order to place this student in a number of foster homes and on each occasion, she ran away. The police have been called in to find her. Now we have run out options since her former residences refuse to take her back. I recommend that she be detained and attend school at the in-house training facilities offered here."
"What?" exclaimed Cynthia, in a more surprised than angry voice, which nevertheless startled Hodicroft. His days were filled with quiet decorum when communicating with other school board staff. They were intimidated by him and rarely questioned his judgment.
"You can't be serious," asserted Cynthia, "the child has no criminal record and yet you chose to put her in this dump where she could be influenced by common criminals and raped by lesbian inmates!"
"Come now Ms. Amis, don't be melodramatic!" countered Hodicroft, "Other youth have survived here and have been integrated back into their communities."
"Over the years, I can count those on the fingers of one hand," countered Cynthia, "Once they get into the criminal system, they end up in a cycle of crime and detention, which increases in severity. They become professional criminals by the time they are adults. If your department were to do a psychological assessment of these inmates, they would find that about 60% of them have learning challenges and shouldn't be here in the first place."

Hodicroft's face reddened as he struggled to maintain his composure. He had heard of Cynthia's reputation for being outspoken and had prepared himself for this. But the woman not only dared to question his "better" judgment but had gone on to lay the blame for the incarceration of learning challenged youth on his department's shoulders!
"Our task is not to find a solution for society's problems. We offer a workable option within the special ed. budget. My decision is final!" he said in a calm and collected even toned voice.
"You mean your recommendations are final. You are now a consultant at the detention centre and are wearing that hat. I'll speak for the school board and will deal with its fiscal shortcomings."

An uncomfortable silence followed while the two adversaries stared at each other. A knock on the door interrupted this impasse. The head of a female staff member peered around the door and announced, "Intern 182, is here to see you Sir."
"Send her in!" barked Hodicroft.

Chapter 9: Long Hair, Skinny Legs and Shinny Teeth

The door opened and a teenaged girl walked sheepishly in. She wore a white sweatshirt and a pair of jeans that was obviously a size too short for her. Cynthia was struck by her appearance. She had a slim athletic look and stood at about 5ft 7"; tall for her age. She had a dark chocolate brown complexion and facial features, which spoke to her Trinidadian heritage. Her long black hair was held in a ponytail. Cynthia asked herself, "What would make such a beautiful child runaway from her foster home and do so repeatedly?"

The girl stood nervously in the centre of the room until Hodicroft motioned towards a chair. "This is Lisa Whittaker," he said.

"Hello Lisa, I'm Cynthia Amis from the school board. I have come to see how you are doing".

Lisa cracked the tiniest of a smile but said nothing. She avoided eye contact and looked at the big desk in front of her. Cynthia watched her intently. She had the poise of an elegant gazelle, trapped, and nervously looking from one predator to the other, but not knowing whom to fear the most.

"Lisa," said Cynthia in a slightly raised voice, hoping to draw her attention and encouraging her to look straight at her, "You don't belong here. I will try to find you new digs as soon as I can. Please be patient. Help is on its way."

She rewarded Cynthia with a wide and beautiful smile but this seem to be extinguished like a dowsed flame as Hodicroft shook his head and rolled his eyes to the ceiling.

"Lisa, why do you keep running away from your digs? You have been placed in the best foster homes but you don't seem to stay put anywhere," said Cynthia sensing that she needed to get to the bottom of this problem soon.

Lisa half open her mouth to speak but clamed up again glancing anxiously at Hodicroft. Cynthia turned to Hodicroft and said, "Dr. Hodicroft, could you excuse us for a while."

Hodicroft pushed his chair back and strode out saying, "Okay, but lets be quick about it. I have other appointments to keep and don't have any time to waste."

Cynthia stood up abruptly and followed him to the door. She had an angry and resolute expression on her face and as she approached Hodicroft with her fist clenched. He feared she was about to strike him and backed out quickly. He stopped short of bracing himself.

Cynthia stopped a foot away from him and whispered intently, "You better make time for this. You are condoning a gross violation of the Charter of Fundamental Rights of the EU, as far as this child is concerned. I am in damage control mode here. We need to find a solution before the press gets wind of this and it blows up in our faces." With that, Hodicroft just nodded and made a hasty retreat.

Cynthia returned to her chair. She looked across at Lisa. She had the air of a regal swan tangled in a web of institutional indifference. Cynthia moved her chair closer to Lisa, reached out, and held her hand. A gentle smile appeared on Lisa's face, but it was a sad smile; a smile that conveyed a sense of quite resignation to her fate.

"Lisa," said Cynthia "We don't have much time. I understand that we have just met and it is difficult for you to trust me. Nevertheless, believe me, I am here to help. I need to know what is happening with you. I need to understand why you keep running away. Have those people you live with been mean to you?"

Lisa gazed desolately at the floor and shook her head.

"Well then what is it? Has the food not been good or were your digs noisy and crowded? Did anyone hurt you?" persisted Cynthia.

The last question appeared to jolt Lisa. She stiffened and looked up at Cynthia. Her expression deepened and a tear rolled down the side of her face.

Cynthia consoled her and said, "Now, now love, I'll take care of you. You're going to be okay."

"Did any children or your foster parents hurt you?"

Lisa just shook her head. Cynthia's mind went through a quick process of elimination but could not resolve who could have hurt her.

She stood to leave and walked to the door saying, "I'm going to look into this further and contact you."

Lisa jumped off the chair and used her long legs to leap after her in two magnificent strides, taking Cynthia completely by surprise.

"Please Miss! Please, don't let them send me to another foster home! Please, Please I beg of you!" she screamed at the top of her voice grabbing and pulling at Cynthia's arm.

The door open abruptly and a uniformed staff guard entered and was about to wrestle her away from Cynthia, when Cynthia held up her free arm and nodded to the guard implying that the situation was under control. Lisa's behaviour shocked Cynthia. In all her years, she never encountered anything like this. The child was not just afraid, she was terrified of something or someone she found difficult to even talk about.

Cynthia drew her closer and hugged her. "It's okay love, you're not going anywhere for the time being. A dump, this may be, but you are safe here. If you can't tell me then I've got to find out for myself what

has spooked you. Give me a few days and try to keep out of trouble. I will come back to visit soon."
"You promise?" implored Lisa.
"I do," replied Cynthia. With that, Lisa let go of Cynthia. Cynthia walked briskly towards the exit, to find Hodicroft smoking his pipe, and stroking his little beard, on the steps of the detention centre. At first, she chose to ignore him and walked straight past him but then she turned around and asked, "Could I request a ban on visitors for Lisa Whittaker please?"
"Easily done." replied Hodicroft, and continued saying, "Who would want to visit that troublesome little black bitch anyway?"
Cynthia realized how lost, alone, vulnerable and uncared for Lisa was in the system.

Cynthia got back to her office and logged on to the special education database. She had access to all special ed. students within the jurisdiction of the Lincoln School Board. The recent introduction of a Web based document management system allowed her to access the entire dossier of any student. This included miscellaneous documents such as birth certificates that were scanned and converted to electronic files. All available information on Lisa's last 2 years with the school board was only a mouse click away.

It told a forlorn tale of a child whose single mother struggled to make ends meet as a bar and club entertainer. Lisa's firsts 6 months with the school board showed she was barely achieving a pass mark in most of her subjects. A report by her form teacher stated that her reading skills were at first form level, two form levels below her current third form expectations. A request for transfer to special ed. was on record with a strong recommendation for her to have a psychological assessment.

Cynthia could find no record of a psychologist's report under the professional records area of the document management system. However, the records showed a sudden change in venue; a new school. Cynthia scrolled to the Personal data section to see if this had anything to do with a change in address when she read a special note that said that Lisa's mother, the only relative in U.K., had died of a drug overdose leaving her a ward of the state. Lisa was then put into foster care and transferred to a school that was closest to the foster home. From this point, everything seemed to take a nosedive. She was failing in every subject. An Individual Education Plan, which is legally mandated for special ed. children, could not be found. It was as though the request for special ed. had fallen through the cracks, when transferred to the other school. There was a lack of advocacy on her behalf. The only bright spot was her high marks in music and physical education and sport. She seemed to excel at trumpet playing and in sports. She was the captain of the football team and had the fastest 100 metre sprint time for her age group, in the school board.

Detailed notes on her truancy incidents were available. After her third and last runaway attempt, she ended up at the Lincolnshire Youth Detention Centre. Cynthia noted that the same Case Worker and liaison for the school board had been maintained for all her placements. At least, thought Cynthia, there was some consistency. Cynthia made a mental note to contact the Case Worker to see if he could shed any light into why Lisa kept running away.

Cynthia went through the motions of transferring some files to her flash memory stick. She got up to leave, and the phone rang.

"Hello, hello,..." said a hesitant voice, "is that haa, is that ahhh mmm, ... Miss Amis?"

"Yes, Cynthia Amis here. What can I do for you?"

"My name is Jasu Patel. I am Susheel's uncle. Susheel Patel-Gan…" said the voice and stopped before he could complete the full double-barrelled surname. "My nephew is better known as Patelji," he continued.

"Oh yes! I've heard of the wonder kid. He's the little guy who amuses his friends, in the cafeteria, by remembering long numbers like the decimal equivalent of pi and answering questions from the Encyclopaedia Britannica on astronomy and mathematics."

"Yes, yes, he is the one," responded Mr. Patel.

"What's up? Did they run out of volumes of Encyclopaedia?" said Cynthia trying to lighten things at the end of a difficult day.

"This is no joking matter madam," said Mr. Patel sternly. "The boy has refused to go back to school."

"Did you ask the school to send a social worker to visit and speak to him?"

"Yes, yes, a young lady came to talk to him."

"Has anything unusual happened recently?" asked Cynthia.

"A few days ago, he returned from school with his shirt covered in blood. His nose was bleeding, and he had a swollen eye that later turned black. His glasses were broken. His teacher took him to emergency to have stitches. He insisted that he fell down the stairs at school. But when the young lady questioned him closely he admitted that some bigger boys beat him at school."

"Looks like a case of schoolyard bullying to me. Have you talked to the school councillor?"

"She promised to look into it but so far we have heard nothing from her. We discussed this at the Parent-Teacher Association (PTA). The quality of our nephew's education concerns us."

"Well, Mr. Patel, your nephew's unusual behaviour interests me. But, it's late and I need some time to find the underlying cause of this. Could I interview your nephew?"
"Yes, please do. Please help us if you can madam," pleaded Mr. Patel. After she got off the phone, she let her curiosity get the better of her and searched Patelji's file on the system.

Cynthia had already heard of his intellectual exploits in the staff common room. She suspected that he might be gifted. She was unprepared for what confronted her. The professional reports section had reports from both the board psychologist and a privately hired psychologist. Both indicated high scores excepting reading and comprehension where English as a second language was an issue. In most other areas, such as abstract reasoning and numeric skills they were exceptionally high and the family's psychologist went on to say, in a hand written comment, that he was borderline genius and recommended a gifted school.

The health report section showed the school nurse's comments. He was underweight. The nurse started to monitor his weight. Her last note stated that it continued to fall but was not yet at a critical level for his age and height. Cynthia thought to herself that he could be a young eccentric prodigy with an eating disorder. Bulimia was not confined to runway models after all perhaps savants were afflicted with the same problem; but why Patelji?

Uncle Noby sensed that his niece had a tough day at work when she walked in and snapped at their border collie, Bandit, when it pranced around her, vying for her attention. She flopped down on the settee and used the remote to switch on the late evening news. Uncle Noby handed her a glass of stout. He watched her take a refreshing sip and licked the foam of her upper lip. The colour seemed to come back to her pale complexion and brighten her cheeks. Cynthia was an attractive woman, approaching thirty, not tall, and bit on the plump side. She had a large oval shape face with a few freckles that persisted from her youth. Noby always thought that Cynthia had so much of her mother, his older sister, in her. Not just in looks but in character. She had a Yorkshire firm jawed determined characteristic that ran in the family. She was tenacious and dogged in pursuit issues until their resolution. However, all this hard work took its toll on her personal life. He was concerned that she had wasted her time on Michael Caruthers. He was glad she had finished with him. It was time for her to move on, he thought to himself.
"Your dinner is on the kitchen counter, love. You're rather late today. What's up?" enquired Noby.

Cynthia took another sip, turned to him, and said, “I’ve had the strangest day one could imagine.”
“Is the school board administration being difficult again, love?” asked Uncle Noby sympathetically.
“No but I think my case load has gone up by a count of two as of an hour ago. Looks like they’ll take up a fair bit of my time in the future,” said Cynthia. Little did she know they were to become her future.
“You need to ease up dear and make more time for yourself,” said Uncle Noby.
“How can I do that? These kids have been abandoned. One of them went to jail for running away from her foster home and the other, a genius kid, who should be the pride of our education system, has been so badly beaten up that he is terrified to go to school and yet in neither case nobody seems to care. What has happened to this country? We used to be the leaders in Europe as a welfare state. Now we would barely register on the social conscience radar! I guess we can’t blame it on Governments that we voted into power. They decided to spend all our education funds in Iraq and Afghanistan!”

Those were fighting words to an ex-RAF officer. However, his time with his niece had tempered his views on Britain’s foreign policy.
“I agree with you on Iraq but if we don’t help out in Afghanistan, we’d have to fight them on our streets here in UK. You can see what happened in the case of the London tube bombings. Anyway, tell me more about these kids,” said Noby. He really wanted to help to calm his niece’s nerves.

Cynthia went on to tell Noby about Lisa’s situation. She started to tell him about Patelji when a news flash caught her attention.
“ … following a lengthy investigation, the Lincolnshire Constabulary headed by Inspector Jim Paradis, a Youth Service Case Worker has been arrested and charged with the sexual abuse of female children in foster care, that were assign to his supervision ...”

She knew Jim Paradis. They volunteered their time on a committee called, 'Youth in Trouble'. Jim showed interest in the welfare of adolescents who through circumstances often beyond their control found themselves on the wrong side of the law. This was the constabulary’s community outreach program. Over the last year, they learned much from one another. She shared with Jim her concern for the high incidence of offenders with learning disabilities. She maintained that their lack social skills and poor parental support, and weak academic record, contributed to truancy and involvement in petty crime. This included anything from shop lifting to drugs. They usually ended up in the Youth Detention Centre.

The TV newscast switched to a conference with Jim answering the reporters' questions from the podium. He identified the alleged offender as Jake Turnbull.

The rapid sequence of events filled Cynthia with an instinctive sense of panic. The speed at which events were unfolding did not give her time to process the information in a rational way. To Noby's surprise, she jumped off the settee and rushed to her study to set up her workstation. She agonized during minutes it took to open Lisa's file.

"God Almighty, Uncle Noby it's the same guy that Jim has arrested. He is also Lisa's Case Worker!" exclaimed Cynthia, pointing to a line on the screen.

"Lisa? You mean the girl you just told me about and whom you visited at the Detention Centre?" asked Noby.

"Yes, the poor thing. No wonder she clung to me for dear life. That monster probably abused her and the other kids before he was finally caught."

It all started to make sense. Lisa's truancy stemmed from her efforts to avoid the Case Worker. Her futile runaway attempts were acts of desperation to get away from the child abuser. However, no matter which foster home she would be sent to, he would always catch up with her, as her board appointed Case Worker. The sanctuary of the Youth Detention Centre ironically spared her from his abuse.

The next morning Cynthia called Jim Paradis and made an appointment to interview Lisa. They drove to the Detention Centre. This gave Jim a chance to appraise Cynthia on most of what he knew about Jake Turnbull. It turned out that a school janitor disturbed Mr. Turnbull, while in the back seat of his car, undressed, at night, at a remote corner of the high school parking lot, with a female student. It would have been a matter of time before Jim's team would link him to Lisa when they examined his full caseload.

Lisa smiled widely at Cynthia but looked curiously across to detective inspector Jim Paradis as Cynthia introduced him.

"Lisa", said Jim, "Listen to what I have to say and answer my questions very carefully."

"Yes Sir...," Lisa started to say when Cynthia interrupted and said, "Just call him Jim. Remember we are trying to help you."

Jim nodded appreciatively in Cynthia's direction. He held up a collage of mug shots for Lisa to look at and asked if she recognized any person.

"That's Jake my Case Worker," replied Lisa, pointing to Jake Turnbull's mug shot, without any hesitation.

"Lisa, I will be direct and to the point. Was Jake's behaviour with to you inappropriate?" asked Jim. She greeted him with a blank stare.

"Did he do or say anything to you that would be considered inappropriate?" repeated Jim.

Lisa appeared confused and glanced at Cynthia with an increasing expression of alarm and anxiety on her face.

"In what?" she asked.

"Does she have trouble understanding English?" Jim blurted out impatiently to Cynthia and immediately regretted saying it.

Cynthia frowned at Jim, shook her head as if in disbelief, and then said, "Lisa dear, did Jake touch you up. Like put his hands on your breast," motioning inwardly to herself

As this point Lisa broke down and cried, "Please, Please Miss, don't let them send me to Trinidad! I want to stay here! I want to stay here!! I'll be good. I won't run away. I'll do anything Jake asks me to do."

"Come now my dear," said Cynthia, as she knelt beside her chair and offered her a handkerchief, "Nobody is going to send you away. You were born in England."

"But … but," sobbed Lisa, "Jake said that if I told anybody they would send me back to Trinidad, where my mother came from."

Jim paced the floor behind her said as he brandished his badge, "I'm a police officer, and I won't let that happen."

Lisa looked at the badge and seemed to be reassured at the sight of it. She gradually regained her confidence and nodded her head.

Cynthia asked her, "Did Jake touch you anywhere else?"

"Yes ... down there," said Lisa hesitantly.

"Where did all this happen?" asked Jim.

"He would tell my foster parents that he needed to speak to me in private to make his weekly report. At first he would take me to my room and then he started to drive me to a hotel room and do bad things to me there."

"Did he force you to have sexual intercourse with him?" asked Jim firmly.

Lisa looked a bit bewildered so Cynthia translated lowering her voice to almost a whisper, "Did he try to fuck you?"

Lisa looked at the floor embarrassed and ashamed. She nodded at first then to their surprise, she stood up and yelled, "He always used to undress me and made me spread my legs and forced me to have intercause! It hurt but there was nobody there to help me!"

"Intercourse you mean. Keep your voice down," admonished Jim.

"Well, we are here to help you," reassured Cynthia who had witnessed many children throw temper tantrums much worse than this. She would have preferred if Lisa to rant and rave for a while so that she could get it out into the open and out of her system. There would be time for all this later she thought to herself.

Jim glanced at his watch and said, "I've heard enough."

They said their good byes to Lisa who sought reassurance from Cynthia that she would visit again soon.

Once they were in the car, Jim turned to Cynthia and said, "You realize that I would have to bring her in for further questioning and arrange for a medical examination. Let's hope she isn't pregnant."
He then paused and asked, "She seamed very immature for her age, at 14, don't you think Cynthia?"
"Her dossier points to the fact that she may be intellectually challenged. I plan to schedule her for a psychological assessment and may have to get it done privately as we just don't have the budget. If I were to insist, she could end up with Hodicroft's people. A fat lot of good that would do!" countered Cynthia.
"Wouldn't that cost a fair penny?" asked Jim.
"Well, I know a private clinic where they need to return a favour for the amount of referrals I have sent their way. I need to ask you a favour, Jim," said Cynthia.
"Shoot … but I can't promise," replied Jim.
"Can you just leave Lisa out of this entire investigation? You already got enough to convict that bastard and put him away. Lisa has gone through such a lot. Why put her through all this and have her confront her abuser?"
"Come now Cynthia, you know I can't do that! A rape conviction of an under-aged female would remove him from civilized society for a very long time. We owe the public this. He is only charged with indecent exposure in a public place. The girl was over 16."
"Well then Jim, why don't you look up Jake Turnbull's file? I am sure in there you will find several other kids with similar abuse. I recommend you focus on a child that has well-healed parents. They will have the resources to pay for an expensive lawyer who would keep their child away from unnecessary interrogation. Lisa has nobody in her corner. The prosecution will drag her into the courts to make their case. The school board has neglected her and now the legal system will take advantage of her!"
"My, my," chuckled Jim not having seen Cynthia so worked up before, "Aren't we are cynical this morning?"

Cynthia remained silent for a while. A wry smile covered her face, which worried Jim. What scheme was she dreaming up now he wondered? In the days that followed, Lisa travelled in and out of the detention centre to face a barrage of tests and evaluations. The medical tests confirmed that the child had lost her innocence but apart from that, there were no other signs of physical abuse or complications. The psychological assessment confirmed Cynthia's concerns. Lisa faced many intellectual challenges. She was diagnosed with both Dyslexia and

Autism. She had a Pervasive Development Disorder (POD), which caused deficits in her abstract reasoning, numeric skills, and fine motor skills. Her dyslexia affected her reading and comprehension. The diagnosis was disturbing but there was hope and much work ahead thought Cynthia.

Cynthia's research made her aware of a hypothesis that suggested that females are able to cope with learning disabilities better than males since they are wired to make better use of both sides of the cortex and hence develop compensating strategies. Males favour the left brain and hence have a greater difficulty in coping with learning disabilities. However, after puberty, depression and anxiety are diagnosed at almost twice the frequency in females than in males.

She persuaded the clinic to write a strong letter, which referred only to the highlights of their findings. This nevertheless made it clear that Lisa's comprehension skills were diminished to the extent that she would not make a reliable witness for the prosecution. She could be manipulated by the defence and become a hostile witness.

Jim received a copy of the letter. It contents disappointed him. He would need to dig deeper into Jake Turnbull's caseload to find a reliable witness. This gave him some relief him since he did not wish to displease Cynthia. He should have just listened to her in the first place.

Chapter 10: The Bully Boys of St Cuthbert's

The next day Cynthia remembered her promise to follow up on the conversation she had with Mr. Patel. She arranged to have a meeting with the school counsellor, the Board's social worker, and the school nurse. Principal Gail Mortimer got wind of the meeting and invited herself to it. She sat at the head of the table in the teachers' common room and proceeded to take over the meeting.

"Now, ladies I don't want to waste too much time on this incident. However, I want to make sure all issues regarding young er … Sh … Shushi in future be referred to me."

"His name is Susheel but the lads call him Patelji," prompted Cynthia, "and since he is special ed., I'll deal with him if you don't mind Gail."

Gail grimaced as she always did whenever Cynthia spoke up at meetings.

"I called this meeting," continued Cynthia "with all the support staff because his guardians have lodged a complaint directly to me as head of the special ed. department. Apparently they spoke to you first (looking at Principal Mortimer), and you told them to contact the counsellor."

Cynthia turned to the counsellor and remarked, "They haven't heard from you yet. The lad has missed three days of school and no one has done anything about it!"

The counsellor looked helplessly at the principal for support. Gail said, "We are not going to do anything. That Indian kid got into trouble off school property. It has got nothing to do with us."

Cynthia turned to the nurse and said, "I read your report. Could you elaborate on the extent of Patelji's injuries?"

The young nurse looked hesitantly at her boss, Gail, who fixed her with a blank stare. The nurse then said, "One of the girls brought him to the infirmary. I understand that Patelji tutors her in math and science and he was attacked when they were walking home together."

"He has tutoring assignments? That's interesting," interrupted Cynthia, "Sorry, carry on."

"His nose was bleeding profusely, and they punched him while he had his glasses on. The broken lens narrowly missed his eye but left a nasty gash on his eyebrow. I drove him to the emergency at Lincoln General and they decided that he needed a few stitches. The attending surgeon performed a thorough examination and found he had a broken rib and badly bruised shin where he had been kicked."

"Good Grief!" exclaimed Cynthia "This kid's been beaten to within an inch of his life and nobody had the courtesy of contacting his aunt and uncle? Did you think that all this would just go away! With the nurse's report in place, I am surprised that the Patels have not lodged a police complaint."

"Exactly my thoughts Cynthia," said Gail Mortimer in a manner as if she had the clinching argument. "When they do we will be ready for them. We need to protect the School Board's position if there were to be a lawsuit and hence I had urged my staff not to say anything that would jeopardize our position."

Cynthia shook her head as if in disbelief and thought to herself; who are we here to serve and protect; the school board or the children? In her mind, there was no doubt.

She turned to the nurse and asked, "Did you get anything out of the girl who was with Patelji?"

The nurse replied, "She claimed that there are two or three fifth form lads who regularly torment Patelji. They steal his lunch and demand 'protection money'. On the day of the attack, Patelji did not have any money. They did not believe him, which is why they beat him up."

"What was Patelji's weight when he first joined St Cuthbert's?"

"110 pounds. He has lost 10 pounds," replied the nurse.

"That does it for me," said Cynthia "The kid was bullied and starved because his lunch money was stolen and yet contributed by helping others. I am recommending that this brilliant child be transferred to our school for gifted children at Surrey Place where the environment and level of instruction would be more in keeping with his talents and abilities."

"Nothing of the sort," retorted the principal. "That's my jurisdiction. No student is transferred out of my school without my permission. Besides, who do these people think they are? Mr. Patel has been using the Parent Council to make similar demands. Surrey Place is unique and serves schools for miles around. There are only a few spots available for St. Cuthbert's and these should be reserved for our English kids and not for some foreigners from our former colonies who waltz in here and take what they want."

"Well, the process is competitive, and Patelji is the best this school has in the gifted department," replied Cynthia.

"Lets leave that for the Annual Review and Individual Educational Plan review shall we? Dr. Hodicroft and I will be happy to discuss this issue with you at that time Cynthia," responded Gail Mortimer.

"When could we schedule an Annual Review for both my special ed. students, Patelji and Lisa Whitaker?" asked Cynthia anxiously.

"None of these students have been in our school board long enough to justify an Annual Review . The earliest we could even discuss this is next autumn. You will have to support them with the existing resources that are at your disposal or get some volunteer help from the corporate sector."

With that, the meeting ended and Cynthia left empty handed as she had with so many other meetings for children with special education needs.

Chapter 11: A Strange Encounter

A year had past since the Air Kanishka disaster. Lieutenant General Anwar Khan grew impatient by the day. Commander Jeevan Gill offered no positive news. At the weekly video conferencing calls, Jeevan expressed his frustration about the lack of perseverance from his British counterpart, Chief Inspector Paul Lestrade. MIQ were not anymore helpful. In an email directed to Anwar Khan, Jeevan gave the U.K. perspective. It allowed Khan to change his strategy and call for action. This was to get Jeevan out of London and reduce his dependence on Scotland Yard and MIQ and to be more proactive in his search for Canadian Visitor.

Jeevan stated that the UK authorities were taking the same stance as the Canadians and were destined to learn from their mistakes, when it was too late. The prevailing thinking in the UK was that this is an "Indian" problem. It represented a petty dispute between the Indian Government and one of the many terrorist groups that were operating in India. The UK directed its anti-terrorist activity to deal with the fallout from the London tube bombings. Moreover, there was increasing public unrest about the rising casualty figures from the wars in Iraq and Afghanistan. The Kashmir Princess bombing was front-page news for a week, and now one year later those responsible for this crime were still not caught. The media turned its attention to other things. The search for Canadian Visitor was still a state secret. The British public were still unaware of the threat the Deccan Dhaku posed to the CANDO conference.

Anwar Khan brought Jeevan up to date on actions taken against the Deccan Dhaku in Puné. After several months of bureaucratic wrangling, RAG got permission to send Dr. Karmarkar's team to Puné. However, even with Prof. Paranjpé's help they only found some junior Deccan Dhaku members. Karmarkar's infamous Pain Protocols only extracted rudimentary information from them. This included that Anil Godsé was in UK, and that the disruption of the CANDO Conference was still their goal. They did not know his exact whereabouts. The other significant intelligence was that he was a transvestite and known to frequent gay bars. His electronic medical records showed that he was diabetic. Jeevan had no idea where to begin his search for Godsé, but this information would help to narrow down the search.

The conference committee announced a short list of six cities that they were considering. These included Torquay, Brighton, Liverpool, Blackpool, Lincoln, and Newcastle upon Tyne. Torquay, Brighton, and Blackpool were tourist seaside resorts with good conference facilities. They were rumoured to be in the lead. Since Torquay and Brighton were closest to Jeevan's London base, he focused on these locations. He started to make secret scouting expeditions with the hope of running into someone who knew of Godsé.

Cynthia's only indulgence was golf. In spring and summer, she would drive for about 50 kilometres away from Lincoln, to a golf club, relax in different surroundings, meet with, and play a round of golf with people that had nothing to do with work. Jim Paradis, also a member, recommended the club to her.

In late June, when school was out, she had still not made any head way towards getting any support for either Lisa or Patelji. With no business experience, it was difficult to get corporate sponsorship for her special ed. department. She spent months networking with businesspersons at events sponsored by various chambers of commerce. She followed many leads that showed promise but none led to anything substantial. Most businesses supported well-established charities and took the stance that public education was already funded by their corporate and personal taxes. She realised that she needed to focus on in kind contributions. She required a more creative approach. Since there were no positive results to show, she decided to take a break to rejuvenate herself and come up with innovative solutions for the next academic year. She wanted to get away and to take her mind off her special ed. problems. She looked forward to golf all week long and was up and about on the links for an early tee off. Cynthia was rewarded with excellent weather and had an enjoyable and rigorous 18 hole round. She played as well as she ever did. To top this off she sat at the clubhouse bar and chatted with some club acquaintances, she had not seen for a while, over a pint of beer.

At mid afternoon she decided to drive back home. It would normally be a half hour drive, along the A57. She selected a Nora Jones track from an album that she downloaded using a gift card that Uncle Noby gave her for her birthday. She enjoyed the silky voice of the jazz singer and wondered about her interesting pedigree. Other than golf, a piece of news that cheered her was that Veronica had been interviewed for a job at Lincoln University and got the job right away. She relished the thought that Veronica would be back in Lincoln. It would be like old times. With these happy thoughts in her mind, Cynthia drove on and pondered on how she could help her to settle down again.

It would have been a perfect day but for Cynthia this was not to be. As she approached her exit, she had slowed down as the traffic built up. This was just as well since she heard a strange clunking sound. She pulled over, parked on the hard shoulder, and discovered she had a flat tire. Not being mechanically inclined, she made no attempt to replace it with the spare. Instead, she reached into her handbag for her cell phone and realized that she had left it at home. She put her hazard lights on to warn the swarm of other drivers that whisked by. She was not too concerned, as she believed eventually a police car or a tow truck would stop by. Fifteen minutes passed by and she had no luck. She continued to look wearily at the traffic. She noticed a forest green station wagon. It slowed as it approached. The driver wore glare glasses. He glanced at her as he drove past and then stopped a few car lengths ahead of her vehicle.

A slim looking man of average height opened the driver's side door and walked towards her. Cynthia smiled gratefully at him, but he remained expressionless, and in a businesslike tone asked, "Can I be of assistance?"

She couldn't place his accent. He had a light olive/brown complexion and Cynthia guessed he must be South-Asian. He wore a purple cashmere sweater worn over a black pair of slacks. He sported a full head of glossy black shoulder length hair parted almost down the middle. He had the bearing of a young college professor.

"I appear to have a flat tire," said Cynthia motioning toward her car. She looked at his clean well-manicured hands and surmised that he may not be the man for the job.

"Do you have a cell phone?" she asked

"No," he replied.

"Do you have a spare wheel in the trunk?" he asked.

"Trunk?" asked Cynthia a bit confused, "Oh, you mean the boot? Yes but this model of Volkswagen Beetle has the spare under the bonnet," she said as she pointed to the front of the car.

"Bonnet?" asked the stranger and suggested, "It's under the hood, I presume."

Trunk? Hood? Where is this chap from? Cynthia asked herself. It turned out the wheel jack was missing.

"Sorry to take up your time. I will need a tow after all," said Cynthia.

The stranger nodded and started to walk back to his station wagon. Cynthia's gaze followed him. She noticed that his vehicle had Irish registration plates. He then glanced back at her just before he opened the door and asked half heartedly, "Do you need a ride into Lincoln City?"

By this time, Cynthia's curiosity got the better of her. She thought for a moment and convinced herself that it would be too much of a coincidence that a serial rapist of South-Asian origin would drive from Ireland to plan this rendezvous at this time and place, just to have his way with her.

"Yes please! I live in Lincoln. Where do you need to go to?" she blurted out.

"I am looking for Northampton Hall on the Lincoln University campus."

“Great,” said Cynthia, “We are a five minute drive from the Brayford Campus. If you drop me off I will give you the directions.”
“Oh, I’m Cynthia Amis,” she said after they settled into his Volvo station wagon.
“I’m Paresh … Paresh Naik,” said the stranger barely glancing at her. They drove off in silence. In an effort to break the ice she asked, “Did you take the ferry to Liverpool from Belfast and drive the rest of the way?”
“Yes,” said Paresh as he looked anxiously at the unfamiliar terrain.
“Will your family be joining you from Ireland, Mr. Naik?” she asked.
“From Ireland? Of course not! What family? I have no family!” he yelled. The words were almost spat at her through barred teeth with such viciousness and hatred that Cynthia cringed back in her seat and mumbled, “I’m sorry, it’s just that I am a school teacher and if you had kids...” She didn’t complete the sentence as she realized the futility of pursuing that topic.

Cynthia thought to herself, maybe he is not a serial rapist but more likely a murderous psychopath with a fetish about Irish Leprechauns. Cynthia avoided antagonizing Paresh any further by giving him curt and precise directions to her home. As they approached the City, Lincoln’s famed cathedral loomed majestically ahead, bathed in the late evening sunlight. Its twin towers appeared radiant against a blue cloudless sky.
Cynthia couldn’t resist commenting, “That’s our famous cathedral; a major tourist attraction.”

Paresh glanced wearily at it but said nothing. He dropped Cynthia off at of her home and drove off without so much as a wave. As he left, Cynthia realized that she had forgotten to give him directions to the Lincoln University campus. She mused to herself that he may just get lost in the myriad of those old Roman streets and she would never see him again.

Chapter 12: Lady's Man

A few weeks passed by since Cynthia received the good news of Veronica's relocation to Lincoln. Cynthia persuaded Michael to rent her a house on Evergreen Estates. Michael not only selected the best-placed unit in the complex, but to impress Cynthia with his generosity, he threw in a months free rent. He also wrote into the contract an option to purchase the property. Veronica's family wanted to send their chauffer driven Bentley to pick her up at the Lincoln Station. She had informed them that she had made other arrangements and would visit the family estate when she had settled in. This being further evidence of the strained relationship she had with her overbearing and affluent family. This conflict started when since she decided to make her own way rather than settle for the convenience of working in the family business.

Cynthia had asked Michael for the use of his Land Rover to pick Veronica up at the station. The bulk of Veronica's London apartment contents were to arrive later that weekend through a moving company.

Veronica's train from Euston station, London arrived on time. Cynthia scanned the platform while Michael appeared to be engrossed in a business discussion on his cell phone. Cynthia noticed a gleaming set of designer suitcases emerge from the First Class compartment followed by Veronica. She looked elegant in a pleated skirt, a pink blouse, and a vibrant red scarf. She wore calf length leather boots, which made her look even taller. Cynthia rushed forward to give her a hug. The ladies turned towards Michael. Michael's jaw dropped at the sight of Veronica. He had not seen her in over five years. When she traveled from London to her visit family, he had missed or avoided her. She seemed nothing like the awkward skinny blonde he knew in school. She had grown into a beautiful woman, and Michael could scarcely take his eyes off her. He switched off his cell phone in mid conversation and stepped forward with his hand out stretched and said, "It's great to see you again Veronica. My, you changed lass! I'd have never recognized you on the street!"
"Changed for the better I hope," said Veronica cheerfully, clearly happy to see Cynthia and to be back to a city that was once home. Michael took one look at the huge suitcases of assorted sizes and beckoned a porter. The group walked to the short term parking area. The luggage was loaded into the Land Rover and they drove up Main Street. Michael caught Veronica's eye in the rear view mirror and asked, "What convinced you to return to Lincoln, Veronica? Cynthia told me that you made quite a name for yourself in Human Resources in London."
"Living in London isn't much fun anymore. Driving around the City is very restricted. It could take an hour to commute each way if you live in the suburbs. The tube bombings were the last straw. Closed Circuit

Cameras (CCCs) are everywhere and armed cops roam the streets. So I thought I needed to get away from London and go back to my roots where it is safe and free."

"You made the right move Veronica," remarked Cynthia, "Things are booming with the University of Lincoln expanding and if the City wins the competition to host the Mano Foundation Conference, your University colleagues will have their hands full with organizing and convening the conference sessions. Besides, which terrorist organization would want to waste its time on us in Lincoln? Thankfully, they have not heard of us. We are not on their radar. So you're safe and sound here, love".

"You can thank me later if they win their bid," said Michael with a proud smirk on his face, clearly trying to impress Veronica with his good citizenship, "The money from the sale of Evergreen Estates helped finance the Conference Bid and will more than pay for the cost of hosting it. The City will also benefit from all the tax money it rakes in from local businesses, if and when it takes place."

"You are into everything around here aren't you Mr. Lincoln?" remarked Veronica patting Michael on the shoulder. Michael turned and smiled at her.

They soon reached Veronica's new home in Evergreen Estates. Michael ensured that she got one of the best locations. As they drove in, they noticed Murphy O'Neil on the driveway, in blue overalls and ready to leave.

"What's up Murph?" demanded Michael "I hope for Veronica's sake everything works."

"I've checked everything guv. I have aired the unit as you asked and vacuumed the carpets. The heating and lighting function and the new appliances work."

"Good work Murph but hang on a bit because we need your help with getting these cases in," said Michael motioning to the back of the Land Rover.

"Heelloo Murph!" said Veronica cheerily "I haven't seen you in ages."

"Oh, it's good to have you back Veronica," said Murphy.

After Veronica settled in, Michael and Cynthia prepared to leave. Veronica came on to the driveway to say goodbye.

"Thanks for all your help you two. By the way Michael, you've got a nice set of wheels," remarked Veronica.

"I was hoping to upgrade to the latest model but some wog company in India has taken over Land Rover," responded Michael rather despondently.

Cynthia shook her head apologetically and feigned a loud whisper to Veronica with her hand shielding her mouth and said, "He

hasn't changed much has he? I think that reference to Mr. Lincoln earlier was somewhat misplaced. Abraham must have turned in his grave!"
"No, it doesn't look like he has changed much – at least not in that department!" agreed Veronica and turning to Michael she asked, "Do you still belong to that, 'send immigrants back to where they came from party'? What's it called, British Front..?"
"British National Party," asserted Michael and continued saying, "Yes, I'm a proud card carrying member and one of their major campaign contributors in all of Lincolnshire," retorted Michael.
"Mike, you'll have to get rid of your Jag too. That's also been taken over by the so called wog Company," teased Cynthia. Both Cynthia and Veronica giggled at the frustrated expression on Michael's face.
"You women may laugh but I'll have you know there was nothing out here eighteen months ago. Murph and I built up this development as entrepreneurs from scratch with no help from any government. These religious zealots and coloured immigrants from our former colonies, come here, demand handouts, take our jobs, overload our health services, and if we don't conform to their religious beliefs, they try to kill us! Why Veronica, in your case, those people have chased you out of London!"
Veronica always up for debate replied, "It's not as simple as that. Some misguided people in this country have been caught up with this fundamentalist malaise that is sweeping the world since 9/11 and -"
"Okay, okay you guys! Let us save the heavy debate for a drink at the pub. It's Veronica's first day back and let's not get embroiled in all this crap," interrupted Cynthia hoping to diffuse the argument.

Michael drove Cynthia towards her home and stopped at a traffic light. A shiny red vintage convertible Mercedes 300 SL pulled up alongside, which immediately caught Michael's eye. However, its occupant was even more interesting. She wore a saffron scarf and had delicate and a beautifully sculptured Indian face much like the ones in Bollywood movie posters. Michael hated Bollywood movies and the entire genre but this face caught his attention. Moreover, she turned, smiled, and waved. Michael was somewhat flattered before he realized that she appeared to have recognized Cynthia. Cynthia waved back just as the lights changed. The sports car pulled away with gentle rasping gear change sounds, which spoke volumes about the driver's skill in handling a high performance vehicle. Before Michael's bulky vehicle could lumber across the junction, the saffron and red apparition was out of sight.
"Oh blimey ... who, who … wha …, what was that!" stammered the rarely speechless Michael.
"Quite a day for the good looking birds Michael!" laughed Cynthia, "Sure you can handle all of them?"
"Sure I can! Present company included," replied Michael.

"Don't even go there," rebuked Cynthia, "that's Bina Apté. She has a contract with the school board to teach meditation, yoga, music and high-spirited Bollywood styled dance exercise routines as part of the art and craft classes. She has a nice little studio on Church Lane and is very popular with the kids. They call her Miss Bolly."

Both Cynthia and Veronica kept in touch by phone but were too busy to meet. Veronica went through a learning curve for the new job. With the new school term approaching, Cynthia's office got calls from several local schools. Many parents needed her intervention and advice for the special ed. needs of their gifted and learning challenged children. The next term would be busy but she decided that Lisa and Patelji would to be her special research projects. The procurement of a solution for these two children, using a new approach, may help the other kids.

Despite her workload, her mind would wonder back to that beautiful day in late June when she encountered that strange man whose abrupt mannerism distracted her from finding more about him. She often wondered what had happened to him. She could only remember that he had something to do with Lincoln University. Most eligible men that she would run into would at some time get around to asking her if she would like to meet for a coffee or at least turn the conversation to topics that would ensure that their paths would cross. She did not have of whimper of interest from this one. Maybe Veronica could track him down. Hardly did that thought cross her mind when the phone rang. It was Veronica.

"Hi Cynthia! What's going on? We haven't spoken in weeks," said Veronica.

"I was just going to call you sweetie. Enough of email and phone calls lets do lunch!" said Cynthia. Veronica suggested they meet at the Renaissance Restaurant. The restaurant was a co-op training centre for the Hospitality Department, which gave a diploma in Catering and prepared students for careers in the Hotel and Hospitality industry anywhere in Europe. The cuisine was known to be exquisite, but the setting was formal. This suited the ladies, as they wanted to get away from the madding crowd. Veronica preferred to avoid the Lincoln University cafeteria where she could run into freshman or staff who would need to consult with her. They met at the Renaissance a week later.

"How are your folks?" asked Cynthia, "I haven't seen them for ages. The Lincoln Chronicle had a picture of your mom speaking at a local Rotary club. I must say your folks are great philanthropists."

"Talking of philanthropy, you should know my parents are supporting the new chair in Virtual Reality Animation," said Veronica with a regretful tone in her voice.

"Wow! That's fabulous," said Cynthia, "but you don't seem happy with that."
"Well, when I first applied for a job here, I had no idea this was going on. Now I am wondering whether I got this job because of them or was it on my own merit," said Veronica.
A young student waitress appeared and said, "Good Afternoon ladies..."
Veronica detected a French accent and said, "La carte des vins, s'il vous plait."
"Bien sûr, madame!" obliged the young French student.
Cynthia recalled the time when she visited Veronica one summer many years ago when Veronica's parents had packed her off to a Swiss finishing school in Geneva for a year before she started at Royal Holloway College. Veronica only spoke to her in English but she spoke to everyone else in French.
"Vin Blanche peut-être? Est-que vous recommandez quelque chose, mademoiselle?" asked Veronica.
"Aujourd'hui, le Chardonnay est très bien, Madame," recommended the waitress.
"Chardonnay will go nicely with the Atlantic Salmon," said Cynthia.
"It's my treat," said Veronica, "I feel rich today."
"How come? Did you get paid already?" enquired Cynthia.
"No but that meddling mother of mine called Cathedral Realties, changed my rental contract to a purchase plan and paid off my mortgage!" said the reluctant heiress.
"Is that so?" asked Cynthia trying to hide her envy.
"How are your two special projects coming along?" asked Veronica tongue in cheek half expecting the usual litany of complaints and disillusionment.
Cynthia seemed unusually subdued and said, "If it's to be, it will be up to me. I think these kids are on their own, and no one in our public education system cares enough to go the extra mile for them. I am looking for fresh ideas and pro bono resources outside the school board."
"As a matter of fact there is someone you should meet," said Veronica, "He is the new Prof. they hired to run the new Virtual Reality program that my family is funding."
"Why would he be of interest to me? That seems so way out of the ordinary and nothing to do with special ed."
"Well, it's just a hutch I have that there may be something he can do for your kids."
"Such As?" asked the curious Cynthia.
"Well, from the discussions I have sat in on, and everybody is really excited about this, his research team will be taking the conventional eLearning stuff to new heights with Virtual Reality."

"But that's old hat with all these 3-D computer games and online virtual villages where you can take on the role of an avatar."
"Yes but if you have ever tried any of the really high definition stuff, where the characters appear as life like as humans and the avatars are realistic and not the usual cartoon like characters? The present technology gives a rather poor response rate and it's too slow for instructional programs. Dr. Naik, that's his name, has a novel way of using the mother boards of several computers that are then run in parallel."
"Parallel? What does that imply?" asked Cynthia.
"Oh, I don't know much about this myself. I learned that parallel processing allows one big problem to be tackled by several computers simultaneously thus speeding up the solution. It's how a working woman's brain works when she solves the complex problem of balancing her career and looking after her family by multi-tasking. However, the beauty of it is that PC motherboards are inexpensive and yet the grid of motherboards increases the overall problem solving speed hundreds of times. The Computer Science Department is amazed at the results that Dr. Naik is getting with initial test cases."
"Veronica," said Cynthia with a mischievous glint in her eye, "if you ever date this brilliant Dr. Naik of yours, please don't ask him about his family or else he will bite your head off."
This left Veronica open mouthed in amazement. She was taken aback at the thought that Paresh and Cynthia had already met.
"You know this chap? Where did you..."
"Don't ask!" interrupted Cynthia anticipating the question, "I'd much rather forget the whole incident. The man is intense and scary if you ask me."
"I don't know much about him, since he was hired before I got here. I know he has quite an international reputation. At a recent wine and cheese party, senior staff including the Vice-Chancellor who was listening intently to what he was saying surrounded him. I would not let his eccentric mannerism get to you. I've spoken to him briefly in my office to discuss his benefits package. One thing that did surprise me is that he has a mysterious past with no known next of kin."
"I don't think he's got any kin. The man is probably a woman hating mad scientist," said Cynthia feigning her lack of interest in Paresh Naik.
"Oh come on, give him a chance. The Virtual Reality Teaching Theatre could be extended to develop modules specific to special ed."
"I would broker a deal with the devil if it would help my kids," said Cynthia and she conceded by saying, "You may have a point particularly when it comes to social skills and the broad area of soft skills. Virtual reality could be used as a teaching aid."
"There you go," said Veronica.

The young French waitress carried in the pièce de résistance. The two ladies sat in silence enjoying their meal for a while. Cynthia broke silence and asked if Veronica could set up an appointment with Paresh. Veronica smiled to herself as she keyed in a memo into her smart phone. "Since I am setting you up with young Einstein, this reminds me of something else that I needed to talk to you about, girl to girl," said Veronica.

Cynthia used a napkin to wipe her mouth, took a refreshing sip of the Chardonnay, and looked across to her long time friend. Veronica fidgeted nervously with her cell phone and avoided eye contact with Cynthia.

"What's up love?" asked Cynthia leaning forward.

"Well, it's Michael," said Veronica and paused to take a deep breath. "He's been sweet and has been calling the house a couple of times a week to ask how things are. Whenever there is a problem, he'll send Murph around to fix it. Last week I had mentioned to Murph, in passing, that the water tasted flat, as you know all the homes on the Evergreen Estate have their own well water. So yesterday evening the pair of them turned up with a water softener device that makes the water palatable."

"Charming," said Cynthia at her cynical best, "Remember love he's just earned a bundle on the sale of your house. He's hardly being generous."

"Well, that's not all. Michael presents me with a bunch of long stem pink roses and asks me out to dinner saying that it would be my welcome back to Lincoln treat. I know he's your ex so I told him I would think it over and let him know," said Veronica.

"I wish you had turned him down flat, love. He's a snake in the grass and is only looking to put another notch on his belt. You can do much better than that."

Veronica had a pouting expression on her face, while she contemplated the bottom of her wine glass. A look that Cynthia recognized and knew so well. Veronica always liked to test the limits and eat the forbidden fruit. The classic pout came on when someone stopped her from being adventurous. Cynthia was aware of the typical conundrum faced by women on either side of 30 as they try to balance their love lives and relationships with their careers. The childbearing biological clock ticks on relentlessly. She was a beautiful heiress, well educated and had everything going for her but was unlucky in love. Were the nice guys just too intimidated to ask her out? She was obviously lonely and missed her circle of friends in London.

"It's okay by me, love," said Cynthia trying not to sound sympathetic, "Just stick to dinner. But, you know what? You're a big girl now and you can take care of yourself. I have done my bit and warned you."

"Cynthia dear, I've not been on a date in ages. I'd be flattered if a dog humped my leg. My parents have been trying to fix me up with the sons of their business associates for ages. Every time I go home for Sunday lunch, there's some doctor, stockbroker, or lawyer being entertained for my benefit. I despise them for humiliating me like that," said Veronica almost tearful.

"Well, sweetie they are only thinking of your interest," consoled Cynthia.

"Oh, they just want grandchildren to carry-on the business," said Veronica firmly. She never understood why Cynthia sided with her parents particularly since they always thought of her as a liberal rebel and a bad influence on their conservatively raised daughter.

Veronica caught the young French waitress's eye and said, "L'addition, s'il vous plait."

The waitress responded with a cheerful, "Bien sûr, madame!"

Cynthia and Veronica parted company, and Cynthia went back to her home office. She couldn't focus on work. It wasn't the glass of Chardonnay. The discussion on relationships had her thinking again. She was as bereft of male companionship as Veronica. She hadn't been on a date in ages. She realised that she was not just lonely and longed for male companionship but was also unhappy. A UN sponsored survey showed that the Danes were one of the world's happiest people because they were more accepting of their achievements in life even if these were lower than their expectations. Their neighbours, the Norwegians were richer but no happier and the Swedes were no better off in this department either. Perhaps she could try to be happy following the Danish example and settle for less and accept that love and marriage, were currently out of her reach. She decided that the special project she had undertaken to help Patelji and Lisa would become a personal goal. She would care for these two special needs orphaned children like her own.

In order to adopt this new live style, she applied to be a foster parent. She discussed this with Noby and looked for his support to apply to the Social Services to allow Lisa to move in with them. The old bachelor was set in his ways and took some persuading. He rose to the occasion and relished the opportunity to refurbish the spare room and convert it into a bedroom. Lisa was overjoyed when she heard the news. Once the authorities did their round of house checks and background checks, Cynthia's application was soon approved.

After Noby met Lisa, he regretted his earlier reticence in accepting her. He soon developed a routine to help Cynthia to care for her. He cooked snacks and meals. He ensured that she was ready in time to have breakfast and catch the school bus. Besides, he now had a willing audience for his yarns about his days as a RAF test pilot and later for British Aerospace on the Hawk Trainer aircraft support missions in India, Australia, and Malaysia. Best of all, he discovered they shared a common passion for football!

Bandit considered Lisa as a member of his flock that he needed to care for. Lisa on her part accepted her share of chores. She enjoyed the company of Bandit and would take him for walks. Bandit made himself at home in Lisa's bedroom. He slept at the bottom of Lisa's bed at night.

The security and love showered on Lisa began to have a positive impact on her test scores at school, which Cynthia monitored. Lisa still had a long way to go. The years of neglect and abuse took its toll on the child. It showed itself in the time it took for Lisa to trust her guardians. There were those days of total silence. On some weekends, she would only venture out of her room for her meals and to walk Bandit. She would occasionally wake up crying in the middle of the night. Bandit who sensed her grief would whimper and alert the household. Cynthia or Noby would rush to her side and to assure her that everything would be all right and no one would harm her.

Chapter 13: Cynthia's Special Projects

Cynthia procrastinated about visiting the Patels for some time. With Lisa, settling in well she finally got around to calling them. They promptly invited her to drop in for some chai and samosas, on a Friday afternoon.

The Patel's print shop, Patel Printing, was located close to the Lincoln City centre in a row of houses that were zoned as residential businesses. The Patel's did well with University business and work orders from local businesses in the City Centre that came in at a regular pace. Cynthia followed instructions and drove through the narrow side laneway past the storefront that faced the street, to the rear of the two-story building. She saw a notice saying, "Private Residence –Suppliers please report to the front desk at Patel Printers." Cynthia tried to ring the bell just when Mr. Patel opened the door. He must have heard or seen her drive in and park.

"Come in, Come in, welcome, welcome Miss Amis!" greeted Mr. Patel cheerfully as he led the way up to the Patel residence above their Print shop. As Cynthia climbed the stairs, she encountered a blast of pungent spicy cooking smell that makes some people nauseous and others mouths to water.

"Something smells good here," remarked Cynthia.

Mrs. Patel entered the room and bowed her head with a fervent Namaste. Not to be out done Cynthia replied with hands folded in front of her. The sitting room was lavishly furnished with a beautiful Kashmir carpet, which bedecked a polished pinewood floor. Cynthia walked around a hand carved teak coffee table and sat down on a black leather sofa.

An awkward silence followed that Cynthia decided to break and asked about a large multi-armed deity whose three hands appear to hold something of symbolic significance and the forth pointed to an ugly creature or monster trampled underfoot.

"That's Lord Shiva," explained Mrs. Patel. "He dances and balances good and evil in the universe."

"He must be a busy lad," mused Cynthia.

"Yes, yes , veery veery beejee," chuckled Mr. Patel, "These bad, bad things are happening all over the world."

"But there are good things happening too," reassured Mrs. Patel.

There was another pause in the conversation. Cynthia came to the rescue again. She remarked how well Patelji was doing academically. "Ever since we took steps to ensure that bullying was not going to be tolerated at school and a volunteer group of observers was set up by the parent council, there have not been any reported incidences of bullying and Patelji is settling down. He functions at four or five years ahead of

everyone else in the science and Math subjects. His teachers have remarked that he has lost interest and appears to be bored with the course content. He needs an environment that challenges him," said Cynthia to open the discussion.
"These are our thoughts too Ms. Amis, and hence I have asked for the support of the parent council to send Susheel to that gifted school place where the clever children go to study," said Mrs Patel.
"Oh, you mean Surrey Place. Yes, that definitely is within his reach, but the parent council is not the best venue to make your case. I brought you the application form, which is the first step in the process," said Cynthia handing Mrs. Patel an information booklet that also contained the application form.
"The next thing you need to do is present Patelji's - I mean Susheel's requirements at the Annual Review, which will be scheduled in a few months. It turns out that I will be going to the same meeting, for the first time as a guardian and foster parent of the child that has been placed in my care. The principal will chair the meeting. The board psychologist and other staff from the school board office will also attend. They decide on a case-by-case basis the type of resources to be allocated to each special ed. student. You need to convince them that Susheel is a good candidate for Surrey Place."
"What must we do to prepare?" asked Mr. Patel. Before Cynthia could answer, Mrs. Patel rose to go into the kitchen. "Please keep talking. I can hear you from here," she urged Cynthia.
"I think you have done the smartest thing already. That is to get Susheel tested by a private educational psychologist. Her report is vital to support your case. His school reports are excellent apart from English and the expressive language based subjects such as history and geography, but even in these subjects he has improved, and his scores are now above average."
"What are his chances of being accepted?" asked Mrs. Patel from the kitchen.
"To be frank with you his chances are slim. I suspect the Principal has already made up her mind as to who would represent the school at Surrey Place," said Cynthia. Mr. Patel wore a forlorn expression.
"His good marks should get him in on merit," he remarked, his voice choking with emotion. "He is my niece's child. My niece and her husband were killed in a terrorist attack in Gujarat, India, soon after the communal riots. Later there were threats against young Susheel's life, his father's family contacted us and asked us to take him to England where he would be safe. However, Shanti and I have no children of our own. We have no child rearing experience. We didn't expect these problems. We knew the child was bright but that is an understatement. Aside from

the traumatic loss of his parents, he has moved thousands of miles away from his family and friends to a foreign country. Now he has to deal with kids stealing his lunch money and beating him up. If he went to another school, where he could be among other students of his calibre, he will be happier and safe."

"Now Jasu don't bother Miss with our problems," said Mrs. Patel carrying in a steaming tray of samosas.

"It's okay Mrs. Patel, it helps to get some background information on my special ed. students," assured Cynthia.

Mrs. Patel motioned towards the samosas and Cynthia didn't need a second invitation. She dipped a samosa in red tamarind sauce and took a big bite.

"Mmmm … delicious," proclaimed Cynthia, "I've never eaten home made samosas... incredible!"

Mrs. Patel's bespectacled small round face beamed appreciatively.

"I didn't come here to only give you bad news. I wanted to let you know that I have taken on your grandnephew and my foster child's Lisa's case as special projects. I am researching into other ways in which special needs kids can be helped and use fewer resources from the school. In my experience, parents and guardians have unrealistic expectations. They think that allocating more resources to the special ed. department is all that is required. In practice, there can never be enough funds for special needs children. This is an issue that affects 12% of the student population and doesn't have the same political clout as other general issues such as bussing, computers and infrastructure maintenance and improvements. Under the special ed. Special Projects banner, I propose to look outside the school board for support."

Both Mr. and Mrs. Patel looked on with polite interest but Mr. Patel frowned and asked, "It sounds like a good idea but are you going to go around to businesses asking for donations?"

"Not at all, not at all," assured Cynthia, "I will be looking for in-kind contributions. For example, I plan to visit the Education Research Department at Lincoln University to see if they can develop some visualization applications using virtual reality. It would cost us nothing and yet it could form the basis of a research topic for a masters or doctoral candidate. We could provide the students that would participate in the project."

"What kind of tools could they develop?" asked Mrs. Patel.

"I am thinking along the lines of social interaction modules that would engage students with fictitious virtual reality characters from schoolyard bullies to bank tellers, which would help to improve the communication skills and the social skills of our special ed. population. In practical terms it would serve to draw Susheel out of his isolation and encourage him to communicate in a non-judgmental environment."

"Good idea, Good idea," said Mr. Patel, "but this will take a long, long time to accomplish. The boy needs help now."

Mrs. Patel entered the room with a tray of piping hot chai.

She started to explain to Cynthia how Indian chai was made when Cynthia interrupted and said her Uncle Noby who lived in India had taught her how to make the boiling hot brew with plenty of sugar, milk, and cinnamon. Uncle Noby also claimed they used condensed milk that made it taste better.

"Oh, you have an uncle who has been to India? Which part of India did he visit?" inquired Mrs. Patel.

"He was stationed in Poona in the early sixties and returned years later to support the Hawk jet trainer program. He has now retired from the RAF," said Cynthia.

"We would love to meet him," said Mr. Patel.

"We have a very good customer, also from Puné. A beautiful young lady called Bina, Bina Apté. Jasu is always happy to see her," said Mrs. Patel with a coy look on her face.

"No, no ... she's like daughter," said the embarrassed Mr. Patel.

"It's okay Mr. Patel. She's quite a looker and I've seen the effect she has on men. Bina is a colleague. She works under contract to the school board, but we call her Miss Bolly because she is so pretty, poised, and glamorous," said Cynthia.

"She always enquires about Susheel, how he is, what his hobbies are etc. etc. She has even offered to enrol him in her Indian Classical Dance class and give him free lessons because there is a shortage of male dancers. But our Susheel is shy and doesn't want to dance with those girls he says," said Mrs. Patel giggling to herself.

"Classical Indian dancing would be excellent for Susheel," said Cynthia, "It would focus his mind on non-technical things and develop team spirit. Moreover, the expressive and interpretative nature of the dance form will serve to bring out the extrovert in him."

"But he is stubborn and he won't go," said Mr. Patel.

"Let me think about this. A batch of students is scheduled to go there every week. Perhaps I can get Susheel to go with someone he knows," said Cynthia.

Cynthia took a last sip of the cinnamon tea and stood up to leave.

"It was really nice of you folks to see me at such short notice." she said and walked towards the door when Mrs. Patel hurried towards her with a plastic samosa filled container.

"This is for Uncle," said Mrs. Patel. As Cynthia thanked her, she heard someone singing at the top of his voice from the print shop below. She strained her ears and recognized the refrain.
'When Irish Eyes are smiling, sure it steals your heart away...' She then recognized the voice. It was Murphy O'Neil! On Friday afternoons, he would return from the Saracen's Head, under the influence and turn the rest of the afternoon at Patel Printing into a sing as you work event!

The Patels hid their embarrassed well and said nothing.

Cynthia's mind was full with the new ideas that were discussed at the Patels. She always learned a lot from involved parents and guardians. The next step was to plan a meeting, with Paresh Naik. She was dreading meeting with him again but with the children in mind, she needed to ask for his help. She spent the best part of all the spare time she had to write up a proposal on the "Use of Virtual Reality Teaching Aides to Enhance the Social Skills of Special Education Students". She emailed it to the Dean of the Educational Research Dept. and blind copied Veronica.

The Dean called her within a week and sounded very enthusiastic about the proposal. She remarked that there was potential for much research in that area and they had the best person for the job. She wasn't surprised when she mention Paresh's name and offered to schedule a meeting as soon as possible.

Cynthia arrived early for her appointment and visited Veronica's office. She had brought both Patelji and Lisa with her hoping to introduce them to Paresh Naik. Veronica had not expected that Cynthia would bring her students with her. She suggested to Cynthia that she should have an initial discussion with Paresh before introducing him to the children.
"Prof. Naik is expecting you. I'll show you to his office but I'll take the kids to the computer lab where they can play with some computer games. You can call me on my cell when you're ready," recommended Veronica.
"Thanks, Veronica, I shouldn't think they'll have too wait long," said Cynthia confidently.

Cynthia knocked and entered Paresh's lab/office. He had is back to her. Cynthia noticed that that Paresh's office was behind a glass-framed door adjacent to a spacious computer laboratory.
Paresh said, "Will be with you in a moment," as he hurriedly attached leads to an array of similar devices stacked together in a special purpose shelf.
"Parallel grid computing..." said Paresh dismissively as he waved at the shelf.

He walked around a table, which had a myriad of computer parts spread all over it, folded his arms, half sat on the edge, and looked at her. Cynthia hadn't seen him since their previous encounter. She now had an unhurried opportunity to take a closer look. He wore a black polo neck sweater and navy blue slacks. She remembered his long black hair parted down the middle. There was something that grabbed her attention that she hadn't noticed. It took a few moments for her to realize she was rudely gazing at him before it jumped out at her. His eyes - they were a marble like, light blue in colour so unlike the shades of blue or blue/grey prevalent in Europe.

"Nice to see you and thanks again for rescuing me," she said. His face was tranquil and expressionless. She looked for a chair to sit on. Some were located at other parts of the lab, but none was offered.

"I am afraid I need to ask for your help again," continued Cynthia smiling persuasively.

"I've read the proposal that the Dean forwarded on to me. It's interesting but it is a matter of priorities," said Paresh.

"What are your priorities?" asked Cynthia boldly, "Can you not fit my proposal in with the rest of your plans for this year?"

"Our present research concerns virtual simulation of business based models input into stochastic algorithms. We hope this will provide business models that will make better use of market research and surveys in order to determine merchandising outcomes," said Paresh.

"Sounds like a load of bullshit to me," challenged Cynthia raising her voice, "I'm giving you an opportunity to affect the lives of real people and you are going on about business models."

If Paresh was offended by her outspokenness, that on many occasions had not endeared her to school board officials either, he did not show it. He remained collected and expressionless and said, "Our sponsors in the business community control what we do."

"Oh really? How can social conscience ever challenge big business interests, hey?" said Cynthia.

"You aren't the only one in this room with a social -" Paresh started to say when there was a gentle knock and a young Chinese lady poked her head around the corner and said, "Professor Naik,... can we meet now please?"

"See you in five minutes Vivienne," said Paresh and when she left Paresh said, "That's one of our Doctoral candidates, an international student from China, who will be working on the Business Virtual Simulation project."

Cynthia who felt that she was fighting yet another losing battle for special ed. whipped out her cell phone and selected Veronica's name to call.

"Hi, sweetie I'm ready to leave. Come rescue me from big international business," she said as she glared at Paresh who now looked around sheepishly as though he wanted to hide his conscience behind the bank of computers. Soon the door opened and Veronica ushered in Patelji and Lisa and left saying she would catch up with Cynthia later. Lisa was sporting a new spring jacket and sneakers that Cynthia had bought her on their last shopping trip. She beamed at Paresh.

"This is Lisa and Patelji," said Cynthia.

"Good morning Uncle" said Patelji.

"Hello ... how are you guys?" asked Paresh.

"Patelji, won all the chess games on the computer downstairs Miss!" said Lisa with admiration.

"You play chess? What level did you go up to?" enquired Paresh.

"Level 7 Uncle," said Patelji as if he had broken something.

"What! But that's almost at Grand master level!" said Paresh looking at Cynthia.

"What can I say Dr. Naik, the kid's smarter than he looks!" said Cynthia.

"Did you help Patelji?" asked Paresh looking at Lisa.

"I don't play chess Sir. Patelji showed me how to use the fashion program," said Lisa.

Patelji hid is mouth with his hand and tried in vain to stifle a giggle.

"Hee, Hee, Hee …It's that program where you dress naked bald women…" he blurted out, while bursting into an uncontrolled infectious laughter with Lisa and then Paresh joining in.

"They are not bald silly," said Lisa, "We had to select hair dos for them."

"I presume they were computer models of manikins," corrected Cynthia struggling to keep out of the hysterical din around her.

"How old are you kids?" asked Paresh.

"I'm 14 and he's 12," said Lisa patting Patelji affectionately on the head.

"But that's the same age as my ..." said Paresh but quickly checked himself.

"How are you kids doing in school?" he blurted out to change the subject. Cynthia smiled to herself as the slip didn't pass her unnoticed. She noticed a different side of him emerge as soon as the children arrived.

"I am doing okay now but those bully boys still threaten me in the boys' wash room and call me Paki," replied Patelji and continued saying, "Uncle Paresh, could you please help my friend Lisa to read better and get better grades? Bullying is a bad thing for me but bulling is nothing as bad as that wicked person who raped Lisa..."

"Patelji!" yelled Lisa, "that was our secret! Only Miss and you are supposed to know about that."

"Raped? But she is a baby, just an innocent child!" said the astonished Paresh looking to Cynthia for an explanation.

"And abused and neglected for years by the system," confirmed Cynthia and nodded solemnly. Just then, there was another feeble knock.

"Okay kids lets go. Dr. Naik is busy," instructed Cynthia.

To her surprise, Paresh raised his hand to indicate that he was not finished. He was sorry to see them leave.
"I hope you will bring them back for another visit soon," he said as he walked them to the door.
"Well, that would depend on your business priorities, won't it Dr. Naik?" said Cynthia curtly as she ushered the children through the door and closed it behind her.
She then reopened the door enough to stick her head through it and whispered, "If you want to see them again, you'll have to reconsider my proposal."
The door closed and Paresh stared at it for a while. He had a premonition that after this visit his life would never be the same again.
"Come in Vivienne," he said.
"Vivienne," said Paresh as she entered, "I am going to forward you a proposal. Please read it and search the databases to see what's been done on the application of Virtual Reality Simulation for learning challenged and gifted children."

Veronica and Cynthia met in the University cafeteria and decided to treat the kids to ice cream while they caught up over a cup of coffee.
"Well how did it go?" asked Veronica.
"It's hard to say. I think the children made a bigger impression on him than I did," answered Cynthia dolefully.
"I'm sure he will like you once he gets to know you better," reassured Veronica.
"He was very genuine with them and wants to help. That's what I like about him. To be fair he has established research interests and I now regret launching this on him from out of the blue. But he almost let on he has children of his own about the same age as Patelji and Lisa," remarked Cynthia.
"Really! Oh so he's married," said Veronica with a sense of resignation in her voice.
"I'm not sure what is going on," said Cynthia, "but I suspect he's had a messy divorce and his ex has him over the barrel with alimony payments and denied access to his children or something. There is much bitterness there, which explains why he is so reticent to talk about his family. How did your date go with Michael?"
"Nothing sleazy to report I'm afraid. The conversation would occasionally wind back to you. The hunk still has feelings for you," answered Veronica looking guiltily into her coffee cup.
Cynthia motioned to the kids and stood up saying, "Now, sweetie, for the umpteenth time, I've dumped Michael and moved on. I advise you to do

likewise. Let some other unsuspecting woman deal with him. I've got to get these truants back to school. I'll talk to you soon."

Chapter 14: Inglish with an "I"

The next day, Cynthia juggled her department's budget in order to find money to support special needs children. Her wide screen monitor had multiple worksheets opened side by side, filled with budgeting data. She tried to reconcile differences, when she heard a firm knock. She expected it would be the Finance Director coming to bug her about her report and once again admonish her for trying to sneak in unbudgeted items.
"Come in," said Cynthia reconciled to facing the music.
Cynthia looked up to see the outline of a tall, sculpted figure in her doorway. The smiling face of Miss Bolly beamed at her.
"Bina! It's great to see you! Take a seat," greeted Cynthia.
Miss Bolly as always immaculately dressed wore an olive business suit but with a light silk saffron scarf around her neck and two inch pumps that made her look about 5' 10''.
"Happy to be of service," said Miss Bolly. Miss Bolly reminded Cynthia of the way Paresh looked with many similar features and complexion but not the way they spoke. Paresh's accent appeared to be a blend between a British and North American accent with gentle Indian overtones. However, when Miss Bolly spoke, you were left with no doubt that she was Indian. Her diction had the typical singsong mannerism, not unlike Southern Welsh folk.
"How are things at Bollywood Song and Dance?" asked Cynthia.
"Very busy, thanks to our contract with the school board. I am also trying to catch up with my journalism career, which has been neglected ever since I set up the dance school," announced Miss Bolly and noticing a smile on Cynthia's face, she asked "What's up?"
"When do you get the time for all this stuff? I didn't know you wrote for a living! Which magazines will you be submitting to?" asked Cynthia.
"Various Indian eMagazines, the Indian online content industry is on the rise, with a voracious appetite for news of relevance to India from Europe. I came to England to cover the Mano Foundation's CANDO conference but with that stalled for the time being, I had to find something else to do so I started up Bollywood Song and Dance. But now I hear rumours that Lincoln City might well get to host it."
"Wouldn't that be great if Lincoln were selected? I know so many people who would benefit. Will you be writing in English?" asked Cynthia.
"Of course! There is no other market with about 500 million English readers. However, it's Inglish with an 'I', I mean Indian English. Somewhere along the way, in the last 300 years, we have developed our own brand of English. The vocabulary and syntax that we prefer to use is different from what is prevalent in UK, North America South Africa, and Australia. Indians throw in many Indian words into their diction but its

still understandable to non-Indians. This is what I mean by 'Inglish'. Eventually there will be more Inglish speakers in India than at least in Europe and North America combined. Most people will be speaking and writing Inglish," predicted Miss Bolly.
"Shakespeare will turn in his grave before that happens," countered the school teacher, "I called this meeting to ask a favour."
"Anything I can do to help?" offered Miss Bolly. "You helped me to get the school board contract after we met by chance at the 'Business After Hours' networking event organized by the Lincoln Board of Trade. An Indian always returns a favour."
"I would like to send two special ed. students to your classical dance class but this would have to be pro bono since there are no funds to support this project. One of them is someone you know ... Patelji."
"Oh, you mean Susheel! I would love to have that little rascal in my class. Money is no problem. I have talked with the Patels for some time but Susheel has resisted my charms," said Miss Bolly enthusiastically.
"Well, here's the solution," said Cynthia, "I have paired him up with another student, Lisa Whitaker. They both get on very well. Susheel tutors Lisa with her Maths and Science work and Lisa keeps an eye on him because we have had issues with bullying at St. Cuthbert's. She also got him to play football. If Lisa enrols, we might be able to persuade Susheel to tag along. What do you think?"
"It might just work. This is good timing as I am developing a dance sequence based on ancient mythology, which will depict Lord Krishna and his consorts. Guess who could play Krishna?" said Miss Bolly with a twinkle in her eye.
"Oh no! Poor Patelji," giggled Cynthia.

Lisa started to attend classes at Bollywood Song and Dance. It took a lot of persuasion to get Patelji to go to the dance studio. When he first got there, he sat with his head in his hands. He refused to practise the warm up sessions for stretching and balancing. Miss Bolly made some inroads with him by getting him to play the tabla instead.

She first started by showing him the basics of the tabla ritual. Patelji learned that the smaller of the two, the right drum is called the tabla and the wider drum, is called the baya or left. The baya's wider surface allowed the pitch to be varied by pressing down on it with the palm of the hand while the fingers struck the surface creating the characteristic beautiful hollow resonating tone.

As weeks went by Miss Bolly gained his confidence. The lessons became longer. Miss Bolly decided to move Patelji to a separate spare room adjacent to the dance studio. Patelji concentrated on his tabla lessons and avoided the distracting name-calling, winks, and smiles of the girls. This embarrassed him since he had not yet overcome his shyness. Patelji progressed at a steady pace that surprised Miss Bolly. Cynthia's parting advice to her started to make sense, 'Careful with Patelji, he doesn't show it but he is gifted beyond measure.'

His giftedness surfaced when she lent Patelji a on the theory of classical tabla music. Patelji devoured the entire contents of the book over a weekend. He soon had a deep understanding of this ancient art form, which amazed Miss Bolly. He could answer any question on the beat structure such as, 'Teen Taal' or 'Ek Taal'. He understood how the tabla was played solo or played in accompaniment with a sitar. In a short time, he even grasped the intricate beat sequence for the classical Indian Bharata Natyam dance.

The mathematical sequence in the beats appealed to Patelji. These ranged from 3 beat cycles to 108 beat cycles. The popular Teen Taal, for instance, consists of a cycle of 16 beats. Typically Teel Taal could play out as: 1,2 1,2,3 1,2 1,2,1.

Patelji's coordination improved, and Miss Bolly took him to the next level of complexity. It turns out that each sound produced with the hand has an equivalent sound syllable that can be vocalized. These are called 'bols'. A tabla artist typically announces to the audience the particular improvisation for the selected taal (Teen Taal, Jhaptal etc.) by vocalizing the basic elements of the improvisation. For the 16 beat, Teel Taal the bols could sound like:

Dha Di Dhin Dha, Dha Di Dhin Dha, Dha Di Dhin Dha, Dha Di Dhin Dha ….

A professional artist could take could be up to minute or more to complete the sounding out of the bols. The artist would then play out the sequence on the tabla.

At first Patelji was timid with the utterances of the bols but with Miss Bolly's guidance, he gradually began to vocalize them. As the months went by, well past his 13th birthday, his voice changed, and took on a more manly tone. Patelji's bols sounded almost professional. To everyone's surprise, he soon improvised well within several taals.

Patelji started his perilous journey into manhood under the tutelage of Miss Bolly. He followed her instructions and longed for her approval. She captivated him with her charm and beauty. One day she persuaded him to leave the privacy of the Tabla room and join the dancers in the main hall. There were about 15 girls about Lisa's age. They represented a mixed group of English, Caribbean, European, and South Asian girls who had abandoned ballet classes in favour of Bollywood Song and Dance.

The girls dressed in their casual school clothes for the practice sessions. They wore payals around their ankles. Payals are circular necklace like ornaments made up of a number of small brass bells or silver bells. The Bharata Natyam dance involves communication through intricate hand, eye, head, and feet movements. These could depict the behaviour of an animal or a human being or portray events. The feet movements involved delicate stomping or tapping motions. These cause the payals to ring in unison with feet movements. The ringing of the payals follow the same taal beat sequence. The dancers would replicate the tabla sequence for a particular taal by ringing their payals during an improvised dance movement but respecting the same beat sequence.

After months of practice, Patelji found a new dimension to his skill. The young tabla maestro now had the best-looking and talented girls totally under his control. They danced to whatever mathematical combination of rhythmic beats he could conjure up. His self-esteem improved and his confidence grew to the point that the girls could not keep up with the bols he mischievously devised. They protested, and Miss Bolly had to intervene.

Cynthia's strategy appeared to show dividends as Patelji's shyness disappeared. His reputation with the Tabla spread. To Lisa's chagrin, he began to have a large female fan base. His tutorials now consisted mostly of females with chronic maths and science problems. However, his newfound popularity only spiked the ire of the bullying nemesis that continued to taunt him with racial slurs and occasionally punched him when no one was looking. This problem had not been solved but much progress had been made elsewhere.

Chapter 15: Bandit at 12 O' Clock

Cynthia never got used to Uncle Noby's habit of inviting acquaintances to tea at short notice. His years overseas in the RAF had made him impulsive and very 'un-English' thought Cynthia.

"Oh, Cynthia love, I've invited Mr. Naik from the College over for tea. You know the bloke you went to see a few weeks ago. He needs to collect some application forms for my archery club," said Uncle Noby.

"And when may we be honoured by Mr. Naik's visit Uncle?" enquired Cynthia whimsically.

"Oh... I had asked him to come tomorrow, Saturday at 4 pm. That's okay with you pet isn't it? You're not off playing Golf are you?"

"Well I planned to go but I also need to get an answer from Mr. Naik," said Cynthia, "He still hasn't got back to me on whether he can help Lisa and Patelji. I'll have to cancel Golf."

Bandit had been on his best behaviour for weeks. Both his mistress Cynthia and Noby were pleased with the new Bandit. His incarceration in the backyard kennel had cured him of his 'bad habit'. Life, as a domesticated Border collie, thought Bandit, was so different from that on a Yorkshire farm where there were sheep to keep in check. Humans were easier to coral, much easier to predict, and were not really much of a challenge. It was September and Cynthia was busy with her schoolwork again but this Saturday she was in the kitchen making high tea. Uncle Noby was in the backyard tending to the never-ending problems with the sliding framed glass roof of his prized greenhouse. Bandit caught a whiff of Cynthia's lemon meringue pie, wandered into the kitchen, and lay down with his chin on the tiled floor. He kept one eye on the pie, that he saw browning through the glass window of the oven, and the other on Cynthia.

"Behave yourself at tea. We are expecting a visitor," warned Cynthia. Visitor! That was music to his ears. That meant another gullible soul that could be charmed out of a few crumbs at teatime.

Bandit's peaceful sojourn on the kitchen floor came to an abrupt end. His sensitive ears picked up footsteps on the sidewalk. They were a man's footsteps moreover, he sensed the visitor wore trousers with turn-ups. Bandit cocked his head and tracked the footsteps to the front gate. They turned and moved along the pathway towards the door. Bandit couldn't resist the urge to investigate. So, with a short yelp, he bounded towards the door. He went through a small movable flap at the bottom and barked widely as he saw the turn-ups on the visitor's trousers. Bandit's momentum and enthusiasm carried him well past his target. Like a combat aircraft, he prepared for a second sortie and ran in a wide semicircular path across the lawn. He decided tactically to attack from the rear, while he barked furiously.

To Bandit's surprise, the stranger turned and confronted him. Bandit stopped short of his target by a few feet, eyed the nearest turn-up, and then looked up to see a pair of cold blue penetrating eyes glaring at him. Bandit sensed something was terribly wrong. Why doesn't this person panic or shoo him away or even do what usually amounts to a highland jig? Bandit's bark reduced to a growl but he could only get himself to take a timid nibble at the nearest turn-up, a far cry from previous attacks where he had ripped the turn-ups off his victims trouser legs and then shook the piece of cloth vigorously, as if it were a piece of torn flesh. However, today he felt intimidated, bewildered and actually relieved when Noby rushed out of the backyard to admonish him.

"Bandy, you naughty boy! How many times must I tell you not to do that?"

He then turned to the visitor and said, "So sorry Mr. Naik, I'll be with you in a minute. Let's put this rascal into the backyard."

Bandit whimpered as Noby led him away by the collar, and even cast a doleful glance towards Paresh, but there was no reprieve for him. Uncle Noby returned to usher Paresh Naik into the sitting room where Paresh almost bumped into his niece in the lobby. The commotion had brought her out of the kitchen with an anxious look on her face.

"You've met my niece Cynthia, I believe?" asked Noby.

"Yes," replied Paresh, ignoring Cynthia's partially extended hand and walked to the chair offered to him.

Noby Clark sat in his favourite chair and pushed a sheaf of papers towards Paresh Naik. "Here's the application form for the Archery and Bowling Club, the club's brochure, and regulations."

Paresh studied the first page of the form with a furrowed brow and turned the page over at which point he sharpen his gaze at the requirements at the top of the document. He straightened himself and said, "This will not work for me."

"Oh," said Noby sounding disappointed, "What's up? Anything I can help you with? If it's the deposit, I can arrange to have you pay it in instalments ..."

"No..." said Paresh, as he seemed to be inventing an excuse, "Well, it's just that I don't know how long I will be around here so I don't want to make any long term commitments."

"I recommend the option to pay as you use the range. There are hourly range fees." suggested Noby, "Non-members use the ranges at off-peak times. The best time slots are reserved for members, league matches, and tournaments."

"That would work for me. But I am not filling any forms," said Paresh firmly.
"Well sir, you would have to go through an initial safety orientation session with our ranger and sign an insurance waiver since our club insurance only covers members. This means that you will need to show evidence of your own insurance arrangements."
Paresh had a harassed expression and said, "Okay, fine then. I won't be bothering you anymore about this. I'll take you're leave now Mr. Clark." He then stood up to leave.

Just then, Cynthia walked in from the kitchen, pushing a tea trolley. The top shelf had her prized lemon meringue pie and her best china tea set with a steaming pot of tea. The bottom shelf had a number of goodies she had been toiling over all morning. These included cucumber sandwiches, scones, shortcake biscuits and jelly in various shapes and colours. Bandit followed on her heels but kept away from Noby. He slumped down closer to Paresh. He obstructed Paresh's passage to the door and still eyed the forbidden turn-ups. Cynthia, though busy in the kitchen, kept tuned into the conversation, sensed the tension in the room. She decided to diffuse the situation by doing a burlesque like removal of her apron and draping it playfully over Bandit. Bandit leapt up and ran around in a circle, to dislodge it, almost knocking against the trolley. Uncle Noby threw his head back, laughed heartily, and said, "Serves him right for bothering you, eh ... Mr. Naik."

Paresh maintained an expressionless composure but conceded a little by just frowning less and nodding his head.
"We're going to have a spot of tea. Would you care to join us Mr. Naik?" asked Noby. Paresh responded with a half-hearted nod.

Paresh felt trapped by the dog and his increasing curiosity about a woman who he met once just by chance and then again two weeks ago. Cynthia occasionally wondered into his thoughts. She stood there with a smile on her face half expecting a polite compliment, a remark of some sort from their guest for the fine fare just presented, or at least a cheerful comment about her antics with the dog. However, she was confronted instead by a cold gaze of a person who seemed to be preoccupied with something else more important to him. All these distractions appeared to obstruct a noble cause.

Uncle Noby noticed that his niece had put on her favourite tight fitting, black party dress with a white hand-embroidered silk blouse. She had also made an unusual effort with her makeup. He came to her rescue and said, "Looking particularly dapper this afternoon my dear." And added, "You weren't expecting anyone special were you?"
"Thanks, Uncle," said Cynthia and to ensure that Paresh would not take offence she added, "One esteemed guest is more than I can handle." Then

turning to their reluctant guest she asked, "Would you like a cup of tea Mr., I mean Dr. Naik?"
"No, thanks," said Paresh, "But may I have a piece of that pie?"
"Well, of course Dr. Naik," said Cynthia, thinking they were finally breaking the ice with him. She placed a generous serving in front of him.

Paresh didn't wait for the others to be served but instead grabbed the thick end of the wedge and took a big bite. He then indulged in a series of nibbles and while doing so began what seemed to Cynthia, to be a curious movement of his head. It was a hybrid of a conventional nodding affirmative and a negative side-to-side shake. Aviation buffs would call it a "Dutch Roll". Cynthia had seen a similar Dutch roll like head movement communicated between two Indian musicians on TV, at a point when they both appeared to reach some sort of unison in timbre and taal. Paresh reached his own unison at least between himself, and his rapidly diminishing piece of pie.

While Cynthia observed all this with polite curiosity, she noticed with the corner of her eye that Uncle Noby was getting redder by the minute with a valiant effort to stop himself from laughing. This being contagious, she found herself struggling to stifle a giggle. To add to their collective discomfort, Paresh's enthusiastic demolition of the pie left him with an unnoticed blob of cream on the side of his mouth.
"Excellent, excellent," he pronounced to Cynthia and turned to Noby and said, "Many years ago, as a graduate student at Imperial College in London, I would often miss tea at the department's cafeteria. There was a very kind tea lady who worked there. She would always save me a piece of her lemon meringue pie and bring it to my lab. I haven't had such a good pie since then."
"Perhaps, she fancied you," bemused Noby and asked mischievously, "Would you like to have some more cream?"
"Oh, Uncle!" rebuked Cynthia, coming to the rescue of the bewildered Paresh as he looked down at his empty plate, "Uncle meant pie," she said and served him a slice of pie before he could refuse.
"There's a serviette under the plate," she prompted. Paresh used a serviette to wipe his mouth with an involuntary action before he commenced with the pie. He then looked at Cynthia and hesitated as he summed up the courage to say something. He finally blurted out, "Miss Amis..."
"Please call me Cynthia," she offered.
"Yes..., er ... Miss Cynthia," continued Paresh, "With regards to the children that you brought to my lab, a few weeks ago. I have given it some thought. I think there may be something I can do to help. But I must warn you that I have no experience on how to devise a program of

instructions for children with special education needs, either gifted or those with learning challenges."

"Oh thanks so much for reconsidering!" said Cynthia, as she clasped her hands together, slanted her head to one side in gratitude, and continued to say, "Lisa is a lovely girl, and you'll enjoy working with her. She has had a troubled past and could do with any help you could give her. She has dyslexia and hence reading, spelling and comprehension are difficult for her. You just missed her. She lives here with us. I am her foster mother. She and Patelji go to the Bollywood Song and Dance Studio every Saturday afternoon. As for Patelji, he's just brilliant but lacks social skills. He needs to stand up for himself and needs a role model. In addition, the curriculum does not challenge him. He finds the course content too easy and gets bored. If you give me your email address, I could send you a ton of stuff I have found on the Web. This includes the use of information technology to support dyslexic students and computer based projects for gifted children. Beyond that, I just don't have the knowhow and computers to implement such intervention. All I have is a battered old school board supplied laptop that's on its last legs. It's good for not much more than email. I hope you can help."

Paresh reached into his jacket pocket for a pen. He scribbled his email address on a paper napkin from the tray and pushed it towards Cynthia.

Cynthia picked it up and read it out slowly, "k-a-n-i-s-h-k-a @ Lincoln dot ac dot uk. Kanishka? What does that stand for? Is it a name?"

"It's to remind me what I am here for," said Paresh mysteriously and got up to leave. Cynthia held Bandit back as Noby opened the door for him.

"So I'll look forward to your email," he said as he glanced at Cynthia and then with a brief nod to Uncle Noby, he walked briskly down the pathway.

"I'll work on it right away," said Cynthia enthusiastically after him.

Uncle Noby shut the front door and poured himself a stiff Scotch. He slumped on the sofa, looked up at his niece, and said, "That's your typical blue eyed Poona Brahmin for you my dear. They very rarely leave the country. I saw more than my share of them. A more arrogant, pompous lot you would never find anywhere. Indo-Aryan arrogance personified if you ask me. They had simmered down by the time I did my first stint for the RAF at the airbase in Poona, in the sixties. I met British Raj type Englishmen who retired there. They told me that in the good old days, the Brits never ventured into the Brahmin area of the city because they got treated like untouchables."

"But that was decades ago Uncle. Much has changed since then. The sub-continent's economy depends so much on foreign trade and investment now."

"That may be so, but some people haven't changed much. I first saw our friend at the Archery Club. He had walked in with the notion that he could just use the range as if it were his divine right. He was in a heated discussion with our membership director. I attempted to intervene and adopted a friendly approach. I found out he is originally from Poona. I told him of my work with the Indian Air Force in support of the Vampire to Hunter conversion program, and more recently on the Hawk Trainer program. He seemed the least bit interested however, I persuaded him to show me his crossbow."

"Crossbow? He has a crossbow?" asked Cynthia, surprised and curious.

"Well yes, I must say it's a thing of beauty," continued Noby, "I've never seen anything like it before. It's made of composite material, is as light as a feather and has sound damping. What's even more interesting is that it has a laser sight and a binocular sniper scope."

"Sound damping is used to reduce the bow's twang is it not, Uncle?"

"That's right. So, if you miss your quarry with the first arrow, you can at least get off a second shot without having spooked it with the sound of the first release."

"I've only seen conventional telescopic sniper scopes. What's with the binocular scope?" asked Cynthia.

"The twin lenses produce a high definition image on a digital camera sized LED screen," replied Noby and added, "I suspect they gather more light and give better depth perception. Crosshairs are superimposed on the electronic image. The laser sight produces a pinpoint of light on the target. This is used to adjust the binocular mount until the crosshairs intersect the laser dot illumination. This novel screen sight can be used like a smart phone camera; just line up the target with the crosshairs and shoot. He wouldn't be permitted to use that crossbow for league competitions, including the special purpose arrows. Would you believe it, Cynthia, they have razor sharp tungsten arrowheads with a Kevlar shaft and carbon fibre fins. They seem to be aerodynamically optimized and balanced for long range."

Cynthia, had seen her uncle adjust and repair longbows and crossbows, from the club, in his workshop.

She asked, "Did you ask him why he needed all these bells and whistles."

"I did and at first he ignored my question, just packed his gear and started to walk away. However, when I persisted, he just looked back and said, 'I don't like to miss.' "

Just then, Noby happened to glance at the application form that Paresh had read earlier.

"Ah-ha," proclaimed Noby as something caught his eye, "It's the references that got him bothered. That's what put him off. He either doesn't have any good ones or couldn't be bothered with bureaucracy.

Cynthia my dear, you were a bit hasty in putting our Lisa in his care. Who is this chap? We know nothing about him. Can he be trusted? If you ask me, I think he's a bid weird."

"He is dealing with culture shock and needs to adjust to English conditions. He'll soon settle down. Give him some time. Just think how you had to adapt when you went to India," said Cynthia in a conciliatory tone.

"Culture shock, my foot! He has lived in this country before and what's more he's Canadian. I don't know what you find in him besides I thought you didn't like that miserable sod."

"Well, I never said I disliked him," said Cynthia "I would like to keep an open mind besides, he offered to help me with Lisa and Patelji, and what's more he likes my lemon meringue pie. So you think he is a Canadian visitor. Just think, now my pie will be famous in North America!" she said cheerfully and then asked, "What makes you so sure he's from Canada?"

"That fancy crossbow bears a well known Canadian manufacturer's trademark. I know of them from their Website and online store. They are located in a place called Guelph, near Toronto. He probably worked closely with them in order to customize a unit like that. What bothers me is that it is designed more like a weapon, rather than a conventional sporting and recreational bow."

"Well, I admit that there does seem to be a dark, secretive side to his personality or perhaps we have made too much of a person who has awkward social skills and an unusual hobby," said Cynthia.

Chapter 16: Dr. Naik's Virtual World

Cynthia kept her promise and emailed Paresh a number of relevant attachments and links to sites on special ed. and technology. Paresh was surprised at the vast amount of work that had already been done in virtual reality that supported learning challenged children.

Paresh and Vivienne looked over the literature and realized that it would require a mountain of work just to catch up with the status quo. New funding for this project would be needed. Veronica Sears was the only member of the university's administrative staff that Paresh knew. He went to see her to ask for her advice.

"Come in," said Veronica cheerfully to Paresh as she glanced up from her laptop at him and added, "Just give me a second, while I read this news flash."

Paresh sat on a chair on the other side of the desk and watched her intently.

"Good grief! A bunch of terrorists have attacked the Taj hotel in Mumbai and set it on fire," exclaimed Veronica.

"They have murdered the staff at a Jewish NGO and laid siege to the main railway terminus," continued Veronica in a grim tone.

Paresh got up, walked to her side of the desk, and peered over her shoulder as she read the text in solemn silence. She scrolled through images of a railway station that showed bodies of passengers, men, women and children lying in pools of blood with luggage scattered in every direction.

Veronica hadn't noticed that Paresh had moved away from behind her and was now facing the glass pane of the large office window. The Venetian blinds were drawn up and Paresh had his palms against the windowpane and appeared to be muttering something in a language Veronica did not understand.

He then drummed his fists against the windowpane and said, "Why don't they just leave us alone?"

"Do you have any friends or family in Mumbai Dr. Naik?" she asked, hoping to coax him back to his seat, which he promptly did on his own. She saw he was very disturbed by the news. He appeared to be shaking his head in disbelief.

"No I don't, but I know that railway station well. In the old days, it used to be called VT or Victoria Terminus. Those poor innocent people..." he said in a heavy voice trailing off.

"Well, just you and I can't stop these lunatics or make the world a better place so lets return to the business at hand, shall we?" she asked in a firm business like tone.

"Yes of course," agreed Paresh recovering his composure.

Paresh informed Veronica that he was interested in helping Cynthia by developing simulation modules directed to assisting Lisa with her learning challenges. He could also engage young Patelji in some projects that would challenge his giftedness. The problem was that their anonymous sponsor had already signed off on a well-defined specification for a research into a virtual reality based simulation of a retail decision support system for marketing and promoting products and services.

Unbeknown to Paresh, was that the sponsors were Veronica's family business with their vast empire of chain stores. They had resources that they could use to spend on research and hoped to expand into the European Union but needed better market research tools before this could happen. In order to avoid allegations of a conflict of interest, Veronica was determined to keep this information confidential and in fact apart from Cynthia, no one knew who the sponsors were as the entire funding and communication with the university was through lawyers.

"I understand from your email you want to change the direction of your research or add new components," said Veronica.

"More like the latter; Miss Amis wants to run a pilot project in our lab. This would involve the development of VR modules focused on special education."

"Is this feasible? How difficult would it be to implement this change in research objectives?" asked Veronica.

"As far as general VR research is concerned there is already a lot of material available. The European aerospace industry has just designed an executive jet with VR tools. The work that Vivienne planned to do is also well covered but no one has taken a holistic approach to the development of a decision support tool that …."

"Okay, okay, Dr. Naik," said Veronica, as she looked at her wristwatch, as if she was expecting someone, "Spare me the technical details and give me the bottom line. How much more time would Cynthia's initiative take?"

Paresh was silent for about 10 seconds while he seemed to be thinking things over and said with some hesitancy, "Nine to twelve months."

"And Vivienne doesn't mind this digression?"

"No she doesn't and in fact she is quite excited with these new ideas. Special education is in its infancy in China compared to the EU. She sees many new opportunities to apply her research in China."

"Fine then, that would be all for now Dr. Naik. I'll talk to my contacts in the finance department and get back to you," said Veronica standing up to indicate the meeting was over.

Just then, the door flung opened and Michael Caruthers walked in unannounced.

"Big change of plans, love," he said, "I've been invited along with an assortment of City's business leaders and dignitaries to the City Hall. We'll first go to the City Hall to hear some announcement..." He stopped when he noticed Paresh.
"Michael, this is Paresh Naik," said Veronica motioning in Paresh's direction.
"Pleased to meet you," said Paresh.
Michael glared at Paresh and then blurted out, "What kind of Paki name is that? You don't sound like or look like your typical Paki. What sort of a wog are you?"
Paresh stiffened at uninhibited use of racial slurs.
"I'm a Brahmin from Puné," replied Paresh bluntly.
"Oh, one of those. I've a theory about you lot -" said Michael.
"Michael Please lets just leave," interrupted Veronica, embarrassed by Michael's crassness.
She turned to Paresh she said, "Don't pay attention to his silly politics."
"Wait a minute love...," said Michael now determined to make a point.
"When us British were out there civilizing you lot, establishing law and order, teaching you English, and building your railways and the like, we took over from you Brahmins and your caste system because we were whiter than Brahmins."

Paresh, who had heard the British civilizing influence argument before, was somewhat amused at the new racial superiority twist that Michael added.
"But that doesn't make sense," Paresh retaliated, "since Britain's earliest inhabitants were overrun by the darker Latin race of Romans who helped to civilize you in the first place and built a number of things right up to Hadrian's Wall, in the North."
The significance of Hadrian's Wall, built during the Roman Empire to stop northern invaders, from what is now Scotland, was lost on Michael. His limited knowledge of geography or history did not extend much beyond the confines of Lincoln's real estate market.
"That's it! We're leaving!" snapped Veronica and nudged Michael out of her office.
Michael tried to save face in front of Veronica, turned, half way through the door, and said in a conciliatory tone, "Come over to the Saracen's Head. My mate Murph and I would like to take you up on this over a beer."
"Thanks, but I am very particular about the company I keep!" said the Brahmin.

Veronica returned late from lunch and called Cynthia.

"Spectacular news sweetie! Lincoln City has been selected to host the Mano Foundation's CANDO conference!"

"Great news! Jobs, jobs, and more jobs all around. How did you find out about this?" responded Cynthia.

"Oh, it's on the City's Web site and besides the Vice Chancellor, who went to the press conference, has asked me to chair the Conference Liaison Committee. We will provide accommodation for the attendees in the halls of residence next summer when they are empty. There will be University tours to arrange and some of our staff from the Sociology Department plan on presenting papers at the conference," said Veronica, carefully concealing her presence at the press conference herself as part of a lunch date with Michael. She made no mention of the encounter between Michael and Paresh in her office.

"Hopefully by then, Paresh may be able to present the work he is planning to do," said Cynthia prompting her friend to divulge how her meeting with Paresh went.

"I met Paresh this morning. He really is a strange person," said Veronica.

"You're telling me! Why, what's he done now?" enquired Cynthia.

"He almost broke a window, when the news about the Mumbai terrorist attack came through. He was very upset," reported Veronica.

"Uncle thinks he is a shady character and doesn't trust him. It looks like anything to do with his family or terrorism strikes a nerve. Did you discuss funding for our proposed pilot project?"

"Yes we did. I have a simple solution to all this but this is just between you and me. Paresh never needs to know this. I'll just talk to my parents and ask them to inject more money into the project. Paresh could then broaden the business simulation project to include VR applications for special ed. as part of his doctoral candidate's research. Oh shit! This will mean more Sunday lunches with boring suitors."

"Why don't you ask Michael to go with you? That will avoid dealing with your parents' choice of life partners," blurted Cynthia and immediately regretted she had made this suggestion.

"I can't believe you said that. You mean you want me to date Michael?" asked Veronica, hoping that her developing relationship with Michael would get Cynthia's approval.

"No I didn't imply that you should date him. Just take advantage of that jerk whenever you can!" said Cynthia.

The university's finance department accepted Paresh and Vivienne's modified financial proposal and hence the project went ahead within weeks of Paresh's visit to Veronica's office.

The VR lab gradually took shape. LED elements covered the walls and ceiling of the simulation room. If anyone entered the lab with a head set, microphone, 3-D visor, and a wireless joystick, strapped to their arm, they would be surrounded by a seamless world that would depict any scenario that they wanted to simulate and interact with. Vivienne discovered that powerful VR tools could be purchased online with an extensive cast of library characters. Even Paresh was taken aback at the degree of realism in look, speech and movement most of the library characters represented. VR had come a long way from being limited to cartoon like characters. The robots or avatars resembled and behaved like humans being filmed in a studio or a film set. The background scenes were actual offices, homes and streets.

After the initial excitement of the new VR lab and accompanying software died down, Vivienne worked on the development of the pilot VR modules. After two weeks, major snags began to appear. Vivienne found the sluggishness of the VR presentation frustrating. The movement of the characters she created appeared jerky. The images of the avatars were too grainy. Moreover, the avatars' lip movements and gestures did not synchronize with their dialog. What's more, the simulation and the server rooms were unbearably hot. Very often, a server would freeze and bring the whole system down. On top of all this, the maintenance staff complained about the large power usage.

Vivienne and Paresh met to discuss these problems. To Vivienne's surprise, Paresh seemed calm and collected. He merely pointed to Phase II in the specifications that dealt with implementation following the initial installation and shakedown of the VR hardware and software testing.

Cynthia and Paresh exchanged email on a regular basis on the progress of the VR lab. Cynthia sent Paresh an enormous amount of information on the latest research on Dyslexia. Most schools took longer to absorb the new material and implement new intervention strategies. Early detection was still a problem.

The speed at which Paresh assimilated the material sent to him impressed Cynthia. However, his understanding of dyslexia, giftedness, and the best teaching strategies for these challenges left much to be desired. On her part, Cynthia knew nothing of the world of virtual reality.

Cynthia and Paresh agreed to meet in person in order to sort out these concerns. They decided to meet in the cafeteria after 2 pm. At this time, most students would have finished lunch and would be in classes. Cynthia had looked forward to the meeting all week for a reason she couldn't explain. After all, it was just a business meeting with urgent priorities and not a high school date. What's wrong with that? Isn't he a colleague? She reasoned.

They met at the cafeteria entrance, ordered tea, and chose a secluded section of the cafeteria.

Paresh remarked, “I am still in the dark about dyslexia. The material you sent me clarified one misconception I had, that dyslexia is a visual perceptual problem and the popular myth that dyslexics laterally invert some letters such as ‘b’ to interpret it as a ‘d’. My question then is that if her problems don’t stem from visual processing, what is the origin of Lisa’s disability?”

“Let’s, just step back for a minute. I am surprise that you haven’t challenged me on my assertion that she is dyslexic in the first place,” said Cynthia.

“I wouldn’t dare. Your reputation precedes you!” said Paresh with a slight smile.

“Thanks, but diagnosing dyslexia is no trivial problem. Fortunately for Lisa, some years ago, I attended a dyslexia conference in New York. I signed up for a workshop, which featured a treatment based on the well-known Orton-Gillingham approach. Although this treatment works and is well recognized in the US, our school does not give it any credence. They bundle dyslexia into the diagnosis of learning disabilities. Dyslexics have difficulty in associating sounds of a single letter or even easy combinations of consonants and vowels that represent a syllable. They don’t have phonemics awareness. This is the ability to associate a sound with a consonant or a vowel. They lack the ability to breakdown syllables into separate sound components or phonemes.”

“What causes this auditory problem?” asked Paresh.

“Research has shown that the brains of dyslexics are structured differently from the norm. The connectivity between the left and right hemispheres is significantly different due to the lack of ‘normal’ neural connectivity between the left and right hemispheres. This leads to fogginess in auditory processing. In fact, in the case of dyslexics, the right hemisphere is of the same size as the left, which makes it bigger than the norm because in non-dyslexics the right hemisphere is approximately 10% smaller. Because of this, dyslexics have a larger that average brain mass. It may surprise many that some dyslexics are smarter than the average person and this increase in brain power allows them to compensate for the poor language processing by memorizing the sounds associated with the images of words. They can get away with this with lower demands on vocabulary up to the age of 7 or 8, and go almost undetected in the early years. But after this, when the vocabulary that is taught has multiple syllable words, their reading and comprehension skills don’t advance and could remain at this level, unless diagnosed and exposed to remedial teaching methods. That's Lisa’s predicament. She’s in form 4 with Patelji but her reading and hence comprehension levels are well below form 2.”

“Does Lisa show these dyslexia symptoms?” enquired Paresh.

"I am afraid she does. I have not rushed to this conclusion. Lisa has been living with my uncle and me. This has allowed me to observe her. An educational psychologist could make her pronouncement after a day or two of testing. A battery of standardized tests is used. I had a private psychologist examine Lisa and she came to the same conclusion. She is also challenged in her fine motor skills and displays an impairment in written expression. You will notice that her handwriting is almost illegible. Her gross motor coordination seems to be normal as witnessed by her success in sports. She may be the school's fastest sprinter and a star football player but her spelling is atrocious. This goes back to her poor auditory memory, which again is another characteristic of dyslexia. Of course a useful pointer would have been some a close relative who was also dyslexic since dyslexia could be inherited. Her only relative, her mother, passed away due to a drug overdose."

Cynthia paused, leaned forward across the table and whispered, "I hope I am not boring you with all these details?"

"No, no you're not; please carry on. I have never been exposed to this interesting topic," responded Paresh.

"The other issue is co-morbidity," continued Cynthia, "My psychologist friend has confirmed that Lisa has a Pervasive Developmental Disorder or PDD. This implies that apart from Dyslexia, she also has another disorder to deal with. All this and I haven't told you about Patelji's issues with social skills, bullying, and truancy."

"Getting back to Lisa, what are the symptoms of PDD?" asked Paresh.

"The understanding of abstract concepts is the key problem area for most youth on the Autism spectrum. This varies for individual to individual. No two children with autism present exactly the same symptoms. Communication skills and developing relationship are a challenge. Children with PDD like continuity and don't cope well with changes in their environment. This is why moving from one foster home to another, was troubling for Lisa."

Cynthia noticed a troubled expression on Paresh's face. He asked with a furrowed brow, "Can nothing be done to help Lisa and Patelji? Lisa is such a beautiful and friendly girl and Patelji is so bright. They are both talented in different ways."

The genuineness in his voice and his deep concern struck a chord with Cynthia. This was no scientist preparing lab specimens for an experiment. He cared deeply about the children. Why did he agree to change the course of his research? She had no idea why he was drawn to the children after knowing then for such a short time. The mystery of Paresh Naik continued.

"Much could be done Paresh, but it will take time. Thankfully, the brain is not hard wired but rather that it is plastic; more like muscle that could be trained or rewired and changed through mental effort, " she assured him. “For Lisa, I have already started instructing her with a remedial reading techniques based on the Orton-Gillingham method. The school board should assign a professional who is certified to deliver this treatment. Both the kids go to Miss Bolly’s Song and Dance Studio. This has helped their self-confidence and self-esteem; they both need social rewiring. Patelji is quite the technical genius but let us hope he does not grow up to be a lonely wizard who has a hard time getting a date. He needs to improve his soft skills in particular interpersonal skills. Lisa needs help in this area too. She should be able to distinguish between good and bad authority figures and learn to trust professionals who could help her. Because of the systemic neglect and abuse she has been subjected to, she often stops caring about herself and other people. She needs to develop more empathy and take an interest in the concerns of other people.”

Paresh displayed a defeated expression on his face. “This is a tall order. I am nonplussed and wouldn’t know where to begin. In the short term, could we do something for these kids?” he asked.

Cynthia stared at her tea in silence while she churned a few ideas in her head. After almost a minute of contemplation she spoke up, “I think I've got it! We could develop a module that has both Lisa and Patelji interacting with one another and with other students to deal with Patelji’s bullying problem.”

“That’s a great idea! It would be possible to simulate social scenarios. In fact, we planned to do this in our original business simulation model. Why don’t we go upstairs to see what we have right now? Vivienne has a VR demo that she wants to show you. This way you will have an idea what is practical,” offered Paresh.

Paresh led the way and walked right past the lift towards the stairs. Cynthia motioned towards the lift but Paresh walked on saying, “I am supporting project Small Foot.”

Cynthia followed him up the stairs and asked, “Project what?”

“Small Carbon Foot Print or Small Foot for short,” said Paresh, “It is an inter-departmental competition, which will determine the department with the smallest carbon footprint per person. Everyone keeps a weekly tally of all alternative activities that result in green house gas reduction. Some people are walking or bicycling to work or using public transportation and have signed on to a campus wide campaign to switch unused electrical devices off.”

“Wow, what a good idea! I think we should do this for the schools in our school board,” said Cynthia.

Vivienne waited for Cynthia and Paresh to arrive for the planned VR demo. It featured a library module about a customer at a bank who required a mortgage. She ushered Cynthia to the imaging station with a blue screen background. Vivienne had Cynthia stand on a pedestal that rotated while digital cameras photographed every square inch. Cynthia was amused to see Vivienne bring up a 3-D image that kept rotating at the same speed as the pedestal. This process captured almost all her features and clothing in detail. Next, Cynthia donned a firm fitting mesh outer garment that looked like chain armour and was covered with countless motion sensors. Once activated, every minute movement including the briefest smile was duplicated on her avatar.

"Please Miss Amis, please I would like now to calibrate your avatar," requested Vivienne.

"Calibrate? That's not going to hurt is it?" asked Cynthia.

"No, no, no ..." giggled Vivienne "Just read what on screen and pretend, you in bank, yes?" said Vivienne with a grin on her face. Cynthia obliged and thought to herself what a charming contrast to her unsmiling pre-occupied boss. She read out terms, which included compound interest amortizing period, term of loan, true net worth etc. and further obliged the system by moving about and sitting on a chair, then getting up and shaking hands with an imaginary person.

"Enough, enough, enough … thank you, thank you. Please wait a few more minutes yes?" pleaded Vivienne.

Vivienne typed at a key board for a few more minutes. She used a screen stylus to make final adjustments to Cynthia's avatar, on a large touch screen monitor.

Cynthia slumped down on a chair, gradually losing her patience. This better be good she thought to herself or Paresh will have hell to pay! Vivienne then placed a large wireless headset and visor over Cynthia's head, and pointed to the door of the VR theatre. Cynthia hesitated but Vivienne bowed gracefully and pointed again, with her open palm, to the door.

"Remember, press green button for third person view, yes? The red button is for scary first person view," she said as she issued her final instructions and enjoyed Cynthia's nervous discomfort. Cynthia looked at Vivienne through the visor. She wondered if she was a robotic creation of Paresh. She wanted to reassure herself by reaching forward and pinching Vivienne's cheeks. This could after all be a conspiracy to create a robotic clone of her. She may return from the chamber of horrors and behave and talk just like Vivienne!

Cynthia's Yorkshire genes got the better of her as she grit her teeth and marched into the VR theatre. The door closed behind her. The third person view was activated by default. Cynthia surveyed the scene at the bank, including her own avatar, from an external vantage point. She used the well-labelled library function buttons, on her hand held console, to control her avatar. She could make the avatar shake hands, sit, and even sign a document. To her amazement, several bank employee avatars entered the scene. One leaned forward and asked her avatar if she had made an appointment with a mortgage specialist. She manoeuvred her avatar to greet the mortgage specialist and then followed him to his office.

This can't be too difficult she thought, so let's be more adventurous and press the red button. She soon realized why Vivienne called it the scary button. The visor now projected the electronic image of the world as seen through the eyes of her avatar. Moreover, each 'eye' saw its own true image. The depth perception took her by surprise. She staggered backwards and almost lost her balance and grabbed a chair to steady herself. She immersed herself in the virtual bank and had a surprisingly realistic discussion with the mortgage specialist. She even signed a fictitious mortgage agreement.

When finished, she pressed abort, and the door slid open. Vivienne helped Cynthia to remove the equipment. Cynthia glanced at her watch and was surprised how quickly the time had flown by. She must have been in the VR theatre for about half an hour but was so engrossed that she didn't notice the passage of time. She planned to attend other meetings before the day ended and hurried to Paresh's office to say goodbye.

She found him watching his monitor with a bemused expression on his face. He was looking at her avatar barking out financial terms as it spun around on the pedestal.

"So, I'm under your control Dr. Naik. What are you going to do with me?" she asked as she sneaked up on him from behind. Paresh reacted like an employee caught watching porn at work and instinctively hit the delete button. He looked back at her with a sheepish grin and asked, "So, what do you think? Does VR have the potential to help your students?"

"Oh certainly; I am amazed. It went beyond anything I could imagine. Apart from our discussion in the cafeteria, I could think of several applications that could support my students. But I can't stay and discuss this with you right now as I need to attend some parent/teacher meetings."

"I'll walk down with you. We'll let Vivienne work away at this stuff," suggested Paresh. They reached the ground floor in silence. They walked out of the Engineering and Computer Science building, on to terraced steps that led to the car park at street level. Cynthia stopped to shake Paresh's hand. Paresh took her hand and shook it. She aroused feelings that had been dormant for more than two years. He held her hand somewhat longer than it would take to shake it. Cynthia made no attempt to release herself from his grip. She enjoyed the thought of developing a relationship with this enigmatic yet dedicated person. They held each other's hand for almost half a minute, and then mutually released each other, having made a point that their relationship wasn't going to be platonic.

Cynthia cleared her throat and asked, "I expect you'll call me when you want the children to visit?"

"Certainly," was all Paresh could get himself to say.

She walked towards the steps, then turned back to face him again, and said, "You could call me anyway, even if you just want to talk about anything."

"Yes," replied Paresh, "I would like to talk about ... er ..."

Cynthia nodded encouragingly.

"I would love to talk about anything," he finally blurted out with an awkward smile.

With that, Cynthia skipped down the stairs with girlish zeal until she reached street level. She looked back to wave a final goodbye, but the shy, mystery man was gone.

Chapter 17: The Annual Review

Cynthia was usually focused in what she did. The new school year was well on its way and her caseload kept her busy. However, things had changed meaningfully since her last meeting with Paresh. She found the VR lab and above all Paresh wondering into her thoughts. She did not have the time to daydream but she realized that she liked thinking of him. Perhaps he was a criminal. His past seemed blurred. Could it be because he was just released from prison? Perhaps, he was drinking and driving and his family was killed in an accident. No wonder he did not like to talk about his family. Worse still, he could be a convicted pedophile in Canada, and he came to England to make a fresh start. That could explain his reasons for going overboard to accommodate the children!

Ever since Paresh had visited her house, Uncle Noby had put a lot of pressure on her to have him investigated but she chose not to do anything. Eventually against her wishes, Uncle Noby contacted Jim Paradis and asked for his help. Jim found nothing in the U.K. Criminal and National Security database that matched his name. Some interest was generated when his description matched someone Scotland Yard were looking for. Although there was nothing on him, he was a person of interest to Scotland Yard. Nevertheless, a month had gone by, so if he were a criminal they would have picked him up by now thought Cynthia.

Not all this seemed to matter to her. She thought maliciously to herself, before they arrest him, for whatever he had done, she had better make good use of his talents. She even fantasized visiting him in prison. However, what really irked her most was that he hadn't called her. She was losing her resolve in holding back from calling him. She rationalized that it was normal and professional to find out how things were going and enquire when she could schedule an appointment for the kids. She resolved that if he didn't call by 4 pm, she would call him. It seemed to be the longest wait as she kept glancing at her watch every ten minutes. At 3 pm, she could wait no longer. She was not having a very productive day just waiting for his call. Just then, her phone rang, and her heart leaped. It was Paresh!

"Hello, Paresh how are you?" She asked in a flat business like tone hoping to conceal her pleasure at hearing from him.

"I, ... I, I'm fine." said Paresh "Vivienne sends her regards. I had meant to call you earlier, but we are in the midst of implementing Phase 2. I'm pleased to tell you that we have made good progress."

"What's Phase 2, again?" asked Cynthia.

"Oh, it's to do with increasing the processing power of the VR lab. When you last visited, we were nowhere near the computing strength required to

deal with the computational requirements of the VR lab. We also needed a new power source and a cooling unit."
"Did you buy a huge new computer?" asked Cynthia hoping that taking an interest in technology would act in her favour.
"Vivienne and I decided to build our own mini-supercomputer with several arrays of motherboards. We had no shortage of volunteers from the Computer Science Department offering to help and getting valuable experience in return."
"Are these motherboards similar to those in PCs?" asked Cynthia.
"Well, almost but with Vivienne's direction we've followed the direction taken by supercomputer designers and used a mixture of Central Processing Units (CPUs), commonly found on most computers and Graphical Processing Units (GPUs) hitherto confined to high end graphic boards used by video games enthusiasts. A correct mix of CPUs and GPUs can give optimum performance. "
"I've heard of the term CPU but GPU is new to me," said Cynthia.
"GPUs are better at rendering graphical images, which feature in our VR simulation work," commented Paresh and while Cynthia struggled to follow the techno speak, he continued saying, "Hundreds of PC motherboards were linked together to create a gigantic parallel processor that can do half a trillion calculations per second. We have named the beast, Ramanujan, after the famous ..."
"South Indian mathematician!" interrupted Cynthia gleefully, "See, even I know a few nerdy things! Wasn't he at Cambridge when he developed an algorithm to calculate pi accurately to many decimal places? One of my special ed. students did a project on him for the school's science fair."
"Yes that's right," confirmed Paresh, "A self taught mathematics genius with a natural gift for numbers. Vivienne has downloaded a number of supercomputer benchmarks and one of them is his famous algorithm to calculate pi. The trouble is that when Rama, that's the beast's nickname, is running flat out, it consumes a lot of electricity and generates heat. The room gets so hot that we had to install a new environmentally friendly power supply unit for Rama and its air-conditioner."
"Don't tell me, you got some windmill powering that computer!" joked Cynthia.
"Oh, no, no, we have a small natural gas powered gas turbine engine that turns the electricity generator, housed in a sound proofed shed on the grounds below."
A prolonged silence followed.
"Hello, Cynthia are you still there?" asked Paresh, who thought they were cut-off.
"Yes I am," said Cynthia, "A reminder just popped up on my laptop, which I had intended to talk to you about. It's about Lisa and Patelji's

Annual Review. This meeting is held every year for special ed. students in order to update their individual education plans. These plans determine the teaching strategies and the level of specialist intervention required to support the child. Specialists include speech pathologists, special ed. teachers, and even the hours allocated to a teaching assistant. Also up for consideration are resources such as gifted schools or classrooms settings, learning assisted devices, and software. I will represent Lisa, since I'm her foster mother. The Patel family has asked if you could be the spokesperson for Patelji. I'll send you the notes I have on their discussions with the school board and the justification made to transfer him to Surrey Place, the school for gifted students."

"Yes, I would be pleased to represent Patelji," said Paresh without hesitation.

"Good, that's it then. We'll meet next week at St. Cuthbert's," said Cynthia in a tone of resignation and not hoping to get more out of the stoic, mission-oriented scientist. However, he would surprise her.

"Thanks for involving me in this challenging project. I hope I am up to the task," said Paresh and continued saying, "I enjoyed our discussion in the cafeteria. You are welcome to come over again but perhaps it would be nice to meet away from work, for a change."

"You mean like a date? What did you have in mind?" asked Cynthia.

"Veronica's Birthday party is coming up and I've been invited. I could ask her if you could accompany me too?" suggested Paresh.

"Lisa and I are already on her guest list. I've known her since we were teenagers. I will ask her to seat us at the same table," said Cynthia before taking his leave.

The Annual Review was held in the staff room at St. Cuthbert's. The room smelled of fresh latex paint and expensive new curtains and carpets adorned the room. Cynthia heard that the chairperson of the Parent Council had persuaded her colleagues to spend the hard-earned money from the council's fund-raising activities on renovating the staff room. An alternative proposal to invest in eReaders and online software was disregarded. Needless to say, her child made the short list of students going to Surrey Place.

The Patels, Cynthia, and Paresh were ushered into the staff room and sat down at one end of a long oval shaped table. Cynthia had also brought Lisa and Patelji, but Dr. Hodicroft did not allow the children to attend the meeting. He insisted that they wait in the library. Cynthia, who was now in a reversed role of a parent instead of a teacher, was aware of the tactics parents had used in the past of bringing their challenged children to the meeting. This strategy could influence the Annual Review Committee to favour the parents' pleas for better support and resource allocation, due to the sympathy factor. Although she had encouraged parents to use this tactic in the past, ironically she was not allowed to use this in her favour.

The school principal, Gail Mortimer, was the self-appointed chairperson. She also took on the role of recording secretary. Other members of the Annual Review Committee were the School Board trustee, the head of special ed. for the school board, special ed. teachers, a language pathologist, and the homeroom teachers for both Lisa and Patelji. The meeting started with glowing reports from Lisa's homeroom teacher. She remarked that Lisa's reading skills had improved and that there were no further incidents of truancy. She concluded that no change to the current special ed. strategy or any more resources were required.

Cynthia remarked that Lisa suffered emotional damage due to her rape and abuse by a board appointed social worker and showed occasional displays of depression and withdrawal. She pleaded with the committee to provide Lisa with a child psychologist. Gail Mortimer intervened and being oblivious to the problems Cynthia experienced at home with Lisa, said that she did not favour changing a "winning strategy". Cynthia's requested for remedial help with Lisa's Dyslexia. She informed the committee that Lisa needed a language instructor well versed in the Orton - Gillingham approach. This too fell on deaf ears. Paresh protested saying, "It's clear to me or any non-partisan person that the young girl needs help. Most of her progress could be attributed to Ms. Amis's efforts. Isn't it time the school board contributed some resources and did its share?"

Dr. Hodicroft reddened at Paresh's remarks. He stirred uneasily and then said in as measured a tone he could manage, "Mr. Patelji, I understand you were admitted to this meeting as an observer. You have no right to speak. Criticism of the school board on a case that you are not familiar with is unacceptable. If you disturb the meeting again, I will ask you to leave."

"His name is Dr. Naik. He speaks for us. We sent letter to madam principal," asserted Mrs. Patel.

"That's fine, but he can't speak for Lisa Whittaker." said Hodicroft regaining his composure and added, "I won't tolerate any unfair criticism of the school board."

Paresh seemed dejected but caught a sly encouraging wink from Cynthia, which no one else noticed, and he rewarded her with a rare smile. This meant a lot to Cynthia. They were on the same page and now an inseparable team.

Dr. Hodicroft said that in the interest of time he would put forward a motion that the Annual Review recommends the existing teaching strategy for Lisa. Gail Mortimer seconded the motion, which passed by unanimous vote by other members of the committee, including the school board trustee. The parents and support groups didn't have voting rights.

Cynthia and Paresh looked at each other aghast and were dumb founded by the way the system steamrollered Lisa's needs. The meeting moved to the next item on the agenda. This involved a review of the request for Patelji to be transferred to Surrey Place.

Patelji's homeroom teacher stood up, gave a glowing report of Patelji's progress, and claimed that there were no more incidences of bullying and truancy due to checks that the school had put into place. Ms. Mortimer added, "Patelji is a bright boy but there are only a limited number of gifted school places allocated to St. Cuthberts. The selection process is competitive besides Patelji's truancy issues did work against him."

"In all fairness," protested Paresh, "surely, you can't hold that against him since he was being bullied ..."

"The altercation, I understand, occurred outside school property," interrupted Ms. Mortimer, "We are not responsible for incidents that happen out there."

"What criteria did you use in your selection process?" asked Paresh. The question took Ms. Mortimer by surprise. She hesitated for a while and then answered.

"I, I ... I'm afraid all that's confidential information that I cannot divulge."

"In that case, how can the process be judged to be fair and unbiased?" retorted Paresh.

"Mr. Nike! Mr. Nike!" shouted Hodicroft standing up, "Out! Out!" he yelled, pointing to the door.

The Brahmin didn't move an inch but stared Hodicroft down with his steely blue eyes. Hodicroft slumped to his seat and thumped the table with his fist, like a child angered by not getting his way. This startled Mr. and Mrs. Patel. Mrs. Patel covered her mouth with surprise. Ms. Mortimer rose to her feet and said, "The decision of the Annual Review Committee stands. Young Patelji will stay with us for the rest of the school year where things have worked well for him. As principal, I have the right to adjourn this meeting as to continue will not be productive."

The Patels, Paresh and Cynthia huddled together in a small group in the corridor. Mrs. Patel approached Paresh and in a ritual that Cynthia had never seen before, ran her palms down his cheeks and then clenched her fist and cracked her knuckles on the side of her head and said, "Thank you Bhetaa (son) for speaking for us. Everyone else has promised to do something for Susheel (Patelji); they all say he is very clever but nothing has been done to help. Where he is now, some boys call him names and others threaten him. We wanted him to go to better school with other children who are like him and would appreciate him. Just you and Miss are the only ones that are trying to help. We, ourselves are doing all we can to protect him."

Protect him? Perhaps she meant, "help him" thought Paresh to himself.

"Mataji (mother), it's been my pleasure. I am honoured to help," said Paresh folding his hands together.

"If you excuse us we must return to the store. We have left it in the hands of Murphy," said Mr. Patel.

"You know what he's like on a Friday afternoon," giggled Mrs. Patel.

"Oh, yes. Ohhhh yes," said Cynthia nodding her head, "That boy likes his TGIF booze!"

After the Patels had left, Cynthia noticed Paresh looking intently at Patelji and Lisa. Patelji looked well turned out in his jacket and tie. Mrs. Patel had coaxed him to dress formally for the occasion. She assumed that the Annual Review Committee would question him.

Both the children were oblivious to the downturn in the standard of education they could expect for the balance of the school year. They were engrossed in a chess game on Cynthia's cell phone. After having taught Lisa the rudiments of the game, Patelji was coaching her in strategies.

"Didn't I tell you to take the Queen at the first opportunity you had, even if you had to sacrifice a pawn?" he admonished Lisa.

"Now, now Patelji," said Paresh, "be patient with Lisa you know she has a learning disability."

"What? Lisa has a disability? I always thought that I had a disability and she is the successful one. Look how well she does in football and basketball. I could never be selected to play for the school team. Besides, she is the best dancer in Miss Bolly's dance class. She has so many friends and I have none," complained Patelji.

"Yeah right! What he's not telling you is that quite a few girls have a crush on him. He gets them all excited when he gets going on the tabla. I have a disability. I can't read and write and understand things as well as everyone else can," said Lisa.

"Perhaps, we should think of it as an inability rather than a disability. What you kids are unable to do now, socially or otherwise, you may be able to do in the future. You never know. We need a positive attitude in order to convert our inabilities into abilities. Remember what I told you about the brain being plastic. When there are no barriers to learning, there are ..." said Cynthia as she paused and prompted the kids to complete the

sentence. They didn't disappoint and shouted together, "No limits to growth!"
"You have taught them well," remarked Paresh and patted her on the shoulder. Cynthia reached over and placed her hand on his, while she turned to the children and said, "Why don't you kids run along and wait for me in the car," giving Lisa the keys.
"I'll race you to the car," challenged Lisa.
"No way, you're too fast," said Patelji as he handed Cynthia back her cell phone and then, without warning, he made a sly dash towards the exit saying, "Last to touch the driver side door is a donkey!"
Lisa chased after him but paused to do a graceful pirouette and shouted, "Bye Paresh!" while in mid-air.
"Aren't they just wonderful?" said Paresh straining to see who won the race.
"Well, I think they are very special. That's why they are in special education," said Cynthia with a whimsical smile on her face.
"I'm sorry if I made things worse for the kids by speaking up in there," said Paresh.
"On the contrary you asked the right questions and said the right things. I couldn't speak up since I'm an employee of the school board. That Hodicroft needed to be put in his place. He is an institutional bully." Then she leaned closer to him and whispered, "It's rumoured that he and Gail are having an affair. She'll do anything he tells her to do."
"Anything?" asked Paresh.
"Yes, including stuff that would shock your puritanical Brahmin mind. He gets off on her being a dominatrix. You hear a lot from students who play around with hidden wireless Web cameras."
Paresh looked at her in wide-eyed astonishment.
"But all this leaves us with nothing of real value to offer the kids," she continued.
"Well, as you know we may have a solution, but it would be much nicer to work with humans," said Paresh as he looked into the distance as if he had a plan in place.
"What do you mean?" said Cynthia, as she stepped back from him and looked alarmed.
"Rama passed all the supercomputer benchmark tests. The beast is as fast as we designed it to be. Vivienne has already created several educational avatars. She and her volunteers were on location at St. Cuthbert's video taping the required backdrop scenes that will be digitized. If things work out we could deliver at least some of the resources in virtual reality that the Annual Review Committee failed to offer in real life."
"You're kidding me! Well, I'm not sure about this Paresh. I know the bank demo was quite convincing but you'll have to be careful what you

do with children. Let's keep this to ourselves. If Hodicroft gets a wind of this, he'll create quite a stink and try to stop the project. Lisa is like an image processor. Due to her auditory processing challenge, she gobbles up images of words then assigns meanings to them rather than synthesizing their syllables into phonemes that get mapped into a neural network. The adage, "a picture is worth a thousand words," works well for her. If acquiring knowledge through reading is difficult, then realistic images that move and weave the same story or illustrate the same point might work better."

"I can see VR being used to acquire large amounts image based knowledge, which she currently avoids due to her reading issues," nodded Paresh in agreement and added, "It just occurred to me that if we could involve Patelji in the VR programming, that will not only challenge him, but also help him develop mature social skills as he works with Vivienne and other students in the VR Lab."

This brought a big smile to Cynthia's face as she reached up and gave him a high five saying, "Done deal!"

They held hands, as they walked to the exit. She leaned towards him and whispered, "Why are you doing all this for these kids?"

"Because I believe in incarnation," whispered back the mysterious academic.

"I was going to treat the kids to some decadent fast food. Would you care to join us?" she asked.

"Thanks, but I better head back. We will meet at Veronica's party soon," he reminded her.

"Will I be seeing you or will you be sending your avatar?" she asked.

"The world's a stage and we are avatars from another life. Don't underestimate the value of VR avatars. You can learn to love them even if they are imperfect. No terrorist can harm them or destroy their virtual world. They don't require commitments, but they will always be there to serve you as long as their software is updated, and their profile attributes are backed-up!" said Paresh with a smile and a wave as he hurried back to his lab.

Chapter 18: Mumbai Dreamin'

Cynthia got into the routine of dropping off and picking up Lisa at the entrance to the Computer Science building on Mondays and Thursdays after school. On the days she was not at the VR lab, she was driven to Miss Bolly's dance classes, to football practice, or to the athletics practice with the 100-metre relay team. Patelji would take a bus to the VR lab. He liked to work with Vivienne and rapidly picked up VR programming and made significant contributions.

One day, while driving Lisa to the University, she heard a report by a London based environmental group on the car radio. The organization had obtained a list of all sites in UK that stored Agent Orange during the sixties and early seventies. The lethal defoliant was flown to Vietnam from UK. This data was now available due to the freedom of information act, for each European country, that allowed the media access to this otherwise "classified" document. It had been hidden from public view for decades. Cynthia's heart skipped a beat when the airbase near Lincoln was mentioned as a major Agent Orange storage site in UK. Decades later this airbase was turned into Michael's real estate project now called Evergreen Estates.

The local press soon scheduled an interview with city Councillor MacMillan. The councillor reassured the press that the site had received a clean bill of health by an environmental lab before it was sold for conversion to residential properties.

Later that week, Lisa returned from the VR Lab with a big smile on her face.

"What's up love? You look more cheerful than usual. Have you been clowning around with those VR avatars again?" asked Cynthia.

"Paresh gave me a hug and kiss today," said the beaming Lisa.

"Wow!!" said Cynthia, "That is a major milestone! He's made of flesh and bones after all. What brought this on?"

"Vivienne asked Paresh about getting more sound bites (bytes) or something from me to improve my avatar's speech. Paresh asked me if I could sing a song that they could record. So I sung a song that I learned from my Indian friends in kindergarten. Paresh just loved it."

"Is it that simple? All a girl has to do is to get Dr. Naik's attention is to sing him a song?" asked Cynthia rhetorically, struggling to pay attention to the traffic.

"He always asks about you Miss," confided Lisa.

"Does he really?" asked Cynthia.

"May be you could learn the song and sing it to him," suggested Lisa with tongue in cheek.

"Come on then, sing us this famous song. Curiosity is killing me," pleaded Cynthia.
"I used to sing the words without knowing what they meant but today Paresh explained everything. I know you are going to laugh at me …" Lisa paused, took a deep breath and sung in a high pitched but melodious voice,
"Mera Joota hai Japani
(My shoes are Japanese)
Yeh Patloon Inglistani
(These trousers are English)
Sar pe lal topi Rusi
(The red hat on my head is Russian)
Phir bhi dil hai Hindustani
(But even so, my soul is Indian)"

They had stopped at the lights, with the car windows rolled down. The curious passengers in adjacent vehicles were treated to this impromptu recital by a Trinidadian girl, singing an Indian song to an English woman.
"That sounded great, but it would be difficult for me to learn," said Cynthia pulling away as the traffic lights changed.
"Paresh showed me a place where you can find an old black and white Bollywood video on the Internet, showing a famous Indian actor called Raj Kapoor singing this song. There are English words at the bottom of the screen," assured Lisa.
"Oh good, it has sub-titles you mean. I'll get to work right away!" said Cynthia enthusiastically.
"He said that some Indian parents teach their kids this song so that their souls will always be connected to their Motherland no matter where in the world they live. Their kids teach their friends to sing the same song so that way they are aaallll connected," explained Lisa, widening her arms as if to embrace the world.
"Ahh, that's a nice thought," said Cynthia.
"Miss, does Paresh have any kids? Do they live with him here in Lincoln?" asked Lisa.
"Well, all I know is that they don't live with him anymore," said Cynthia. After a brief thoughtful pause, Cynthia added, "And sweetie, never ever ask him about his family. Please remember that."
"Sure Miss,…but, it's sad that Paresh doesn't have any children. He would make a nice dad," said Lisa somewhat disappointed.

This was the moment when Cynthia changed the way she thought of Paresh. She didn't have to rely on her intuition. He had passed a more severe test; the test of a child's judgment. Very few adults survive that level of scrutiny to gain a child's trust. He may be a person of interest to Scotland Yard, thought Cynthia, but now he was of interest to her.

Veronica and Michael were seen together often enough at various venues all over Lincoln. Uncle Noby noticed them sitting together in the Saracen's Head in close proximity and obviously courting. Veronica made no guise of the fact that she was dating Michael. Cynthia resigned herself to the knowledge that her best friend was now courting her ex-boyfriend. The two women stopped calling and avoided each other on the Lincoln University campus. The invitation to attend her birthday party at the Saracen's Head still beckoned as an opportunity for them to reconcile their differences. Cynthia called late in the evening. She left a voice mail for Veronica that informed her that she and Lisa looked forward to the party.

Michael had gone overboard for Veronica's birthday party. There were balloons and streamers everywhere. A six-piece band with a lead singer had been hired. They were set up on a raised platform adjacent to the dance floor. Guests that numbered about eighty were seated at assigned tables. Veronica's parents were with Michael and Veronica. They joked and laughed with Michael and had clearly accepted him into their social circle.

When Cynthia and Lisa entered the party area, of the Saracen's Head, they were ushered to their table. They were surprised to find Murphy, Paresh and Miss Bolly seated at the same table. Paresh and Miss Bolly conversed in an Indian dialect.

Miss Bolly looked stunning, but somewhat out of place in a black evening dress highlighted with saffron embroidery down either side of each sleeve and down the front of her dress. The embroidery was hand finished and meticulous in detail. There were teardrop curves and crescents, which were filled with tiny mirror like fillings that flashed and shone like jewels every time she moved. Her outfit portrayed the hand of a modern Indian designer of international repute. The front of her dress had small saffron cloth buttons with symmetric patterns on either side of the button line. All buttons fastened modestly right up to her neck. She wore a white pearl chocker necklace with matching earrings. Her hair was gathered neatly round her shoulders. She had the regal poise of an Indian princess. Her attention was directed to Paresh. She seemed to lean forward and hang on his every word. Cynthia observed them for a while. She felt a surge of a strange emotion she had never experienced before even when she dated Michael, and other women flirted with him. This feeling was poignant, bitter sweet and unique. She realized for the first time, she was jealous.

Lisa gave Miss Bolly a hug and playfully sat on her lap and demanded to know what language they were speaking.

"It's Marathi," said Miss Bolly "I've just found out that this gentleman," nodding in Paresh's direction, "whom I have never met before, comes from the same part of the world that I do; Puné, India. We are both Maharashtrian."

"What does that mean?" inquired Lisa as she got off her lap and found a vacant chair.

"Maharashtrians live in Maharashtra State in India; Maharashtra means big country," explained Paresh.

"I didn't know you knew Veronica, Bina," remarked Cynthia.

"I'm Murphy's customer," explained Miss Bolly, "he did a super job with the pinewood dance floor at the studio and that's the connection..."

"Well, I checked with guv, he said it was alright to invite Miss Bolly," interrupted Murphy. "She's not just my customer, she's my prettiest customer," continued Murphy, who had helped himself to several drinks at the open bar earlier. He then threw his arm clumsily around Miss Bolly.

"Thanks," said Miss Bolly straightening herself with a slight embarrassed smile.

An awkward silence followed. Through the corner of her eye, Cynthia noticed Michael casting long curious glances at their table. She didn't think he was looking at her. The object of his attention was Miss Bolly!

The lead singer announced that the party was going to be treated to a historical mix of songs and tunes from the 40s to the present time. To please Veronica's Parents, they played several numbers from the Glen Miller era. The party cheered as Mr., Mrs. Sears took to the floor, and some of the other couples joined them.

Veronica and Michael made the rounds of all the tables greeting and chatting with guests. As they approached, Paresh tactfully rose, excused himself and walked towards the washrooms. When Veronica and Michael finally arrived at Cynthia's table, Murphy rose to his feet and said "Guv I think you folks have met everyone accept the glamorous Miss Bolly."

"Hello," said Miss Bolly, "Cynthia has mentioned you from time to time, but we have never met," she said looking at Michael.

"I have seen you around, but it's great to finally get to meet you," said Michael thrusting his hand forward enthusiastically. Miss Bolly shook his hand and Michael was somewhat surprised at the firmness of her grip.

"How is that you haven't taken to the floor? It's your birthday after all," Miss Bolly appeared to be asking Veronica.

"I'm not a good dancer but I'm sure that won't stop Michael from having a good time," said Veronica.

"Murph and I intend to get very drunk and dance every available woman of their feet," said Michael and added, feigning an old fashioned bow, "May, I have the next dance with you Miss Bolly?"

"Wait and minute guv, she's my date," protested Murphy jokingly.

"Now, now gentleman there is plenty of me to go around. I'll put both of you on my dance card," said Miss Bolly.

"See what I mean, a real lady. She's too good for you guv and that's why she is with me," said Murphy.

Michael smacked Murphy on the arm playfully, gave a broad wave to the table but couldn't resist giving Cynthia a parting peck on her cheek, while he whisked Veronica back to their table.

Veronica looked back at Cynthia and said, "Join us some time, my Mum and Dad would like to speak to you."

"Will do," nodded Cynthia.

As Paresh returned to his seat at the table, the band struck a lively disco beat and Murphy turned to Miss Bolly and said, "Let's go."

Miss Bolly stood up but turned to Paresh and said "Don't you dance, Paresh?"

"Yes, but right now I'm nursing this excellent stout," replied Paresh struggling to avoid the topic.

"Well, don't go away. I'll be back to speak to you some more," said Miss Bolly placing her hand on his shoulder and caressing his arm as she followed Murphy to the dance floor. Then she turned back, smiled, and waved playfully at Paresh.

"I think Miss Bolly fancies you Paresh," remarked Lisa.

"She's not my type," said Paresh firmly while looking Cynthia in the eye.

A few minutes later, Cynthia stood up, and with her best attempt at imitating an Indian accent said to Paresh, much to the delight of Lisa, "Don't go away. I'll be back to talk to you some more," and patted Paresh on the shoulder as she walked towards Veronica's table.

Bill and Melinda Sears returned to their table. By the time Cynthia reached the Sears table, she found Melinda Sears engaged in a heated discussion with Michael.

Malinda was a serious advocate of environmentally friendly business practices. She had established a corporate policy of energy saving and recycling at her retail branch plants. She consulted frequently with the Lincoln Environmental Protection Association (LEPA). Melinda was also their major benefactor. She had used her corporate network to raise funds for the non-profit association.

Evergreen Estates had caught the attention of LEPA. This happen soon after the report on the European locations of Agent Orange

storage sites had been released. LEPA had completed an extensive health survey of the area and had used a Geographic Information System (GIS) to produce a layered graphical display of population density with the incidence of skin rashes, ovarian, breast, colon and prostate cancer. A shocking correlation was demonstrated centred around the location of Evergreen Estates in terms of the incidence of Cancer and miscarriages. The executive director of LEPA and Melinda had a long meeting and most of this new environmental data was reviewed at length. They had also noticed that Evergreen Estates used its own tube wells for drinking water and were now demanding further investigation.
"Michael dear, why has your lawyer sent the executive director of LEPA a copy of a court order banning them from entering the Evergreen Estate's gated property? Wouldn't it be better to let them get on with the testing and put this sordid mess behind us?" asked Malinda.
"Melinda luv," reasoned Michael, "I have tried to make my peace with LEPA but they have been relentless ever since that damn report was made public. They won't accept the findings of the original environmental assessment that Councillor MacMillan commissioned years ago. She has also recommended to the City that this is sufficient and the City need not spend time or funds on further testing. LEPA is hell bent on making a name for itself in Europe but they could ruin us all if this baseless scandal were to hit the press. It could trigger a mass exodus from the Estates; put a stop to the Mano Conference, which would result in losses amounting to millions of pounds for businesses that are relying on the conference, including your grocery chain business. We need to put a lid on this nonsense before it gets out of hand. LEPA now wants the Evergreen Estates to foot the bill for the testing. They are not just asking for water sampling. They want blood samples taken from the residents of Evergreen Estates. The project would now include sample collecting, testing, analysis and reporting. This would amount to a sizable bill I dare say."

Michael paused to eat the hors d'oeuvres on the table.
"What's more, my lawyers' research department advised me that a control group would need to be tested for a demographically equivalent population that lived outside the Estates and used the municipal water supply. It would be near impossible to get such a sample since the Estates house a high income, older homogeneous and predominantly English cohort. Lincoln City has a multi-national heterogeneous population including that curried immigrant rabble who presumably get sick and die of other things, mal-nutrition I expect!" said Michael looking smug.
"Now, now Michael! Watch your language!" admonished Mrs. Sears.

She then continued with a worried expression, "Bill and I are also concerned about the ramifications on our business. We sell food through our grocery chain. The customers' health comes first, particularly those that shop at the store in Evergreen Estates. Granted your lawyers make a point but I am sure we could reach some sort of compromise here. Couldn't they start with testing the water?"

Much to Michael's relief, he didn't get to answer that question. "Mum, Cynthia is here," said Veronica pointing to Cynthia who waited and listened to the discussion.

Malinda turned to Cynthia and held out her cheek for Cynthia to plant a kiss.

"You people are talking shop," said Cynthia cheerfully, "Give it a rest. It's Veronica's birthday!"

No one could have been more relieved with the change in the topic of conversation than Michael. However, with Cynthia and Veronica sitting at the same table, he felt uncomfortable and looked for an excuse to get away. He glanced across the dance floor and saw Miss Bolly clearly dancing rings around Murphy. The tempo changed and the band played disco hits from the late 70s and 80s. The band embarked on a very good imitation of one of Bee Gee's numbers from 'Saturday Night Fever.' Michael saw his chance, stepped smartly up to the couple and asked to cut in.

Miss Bolly took the lead in replicating John Travolta's famous dance sequence almost to the last step with Michael following in close sequence. Michael who loved to dance was enthralled. He had finally found a partner that could not only keep up with him but also, to his chagrin, out dance him. The band switched back to the 50's and 60's rock 'n roll era. Many couples who vacated the dance floor just to sit and watch Michael and Miss Bolly dance, now got back into the swing of things with a brisk jive.

"How are things going on at the VR lab?" asked Veronica.

"They have made good progress. This stuff is exciting. The simulations are realistic and coming along well. There are two modules being developed now. One to deal with school yard bullying and other concerns dyslexia," said Cynthia. She turned to her parents who weren't paying attention. They were more interested in watching the couples on the dance floor. She continued for their benefit, "Your money is being well spent. Thanks to your generosity the university is going to break new ground in development of teaching tools for children with learning challenges."

Bill and Melinda nodded and smiled. Melinda spied an old friend on another table across the floor and excused herself to go and see her and likewise Bill walked over to a business associate at the bar.

With Veronica's parents gone, Cynthia leaned towards Veronica and whispered, “Looks like Michael is seeking greener pastures. I warned you didn’t I?”
“Well, you were right as usual. Things have cooled considerably between Michael and me. He got what he wanted and now he is ready to move on. I hope Miss Bolly is not his next victim. She is such a nice lady. I met her in the washroom earlier while she was checking her glucometer. She told me that she was diabetic…”
“I don't care what she's got! I rather she mess with Michael and leave Paresh alone,” snapped Cynthia.
“Oh, Miss Amis, what have we here? You really care about our mad scientist!” chirped Veronica pouncing on Cynthia’s unplanned revelation and continued, “Do tell, do tell, all the sordid details please!”
“Sorry to disappoint you. Dr. Ice hasn’t made his big move yet,” said Cynthia “but we are making progress. This is the first time we’ve gone anywhere together. This is hardly a date but it’s a start. He’s carrying a lot of baggage from a previous relationship. The mystery unravels one week at a time. For instance, I found out this evening he likes his dark stout.”
“Did you know he was not a bad dancer?” asked Veronica with a mischievous twinkle in her eyes.
Cynthia who had her back to the dance floor, furrowed her brow and asked, “Why, have you been dating him too?”
“No silly, just look!” exclaimed Veronica pointing to the dance floor. Cynthia turned to see Paresh jiving with Lisa and only slowing down to teach her a new move, which she picked up with ease.
“I’ve never known a guy from Mumbai or there about who doesn’t like to party!” said Veronica.
“Oh, they look so cute together,” said Cynthia as Lisa let out an embarrassed squeal as she spun around and held her twirling skirt down. Lisa seemed happier than Cynthia had ever seen her before; she smiled, waved and winked at Cynthia and Veronica.
Paresh caught Cynthia’s eye and beckoned to her.
“What are you waiting for?” asked Veronica, “Go get him girl!”

Cynthia ran over to Paresh and after a few hesitant steps, when they stepped on each other’s toes, Paresh and Cynthia soon got into rhythm. The lights dimmed as the lead singer slowed the tempo with a faithful rendition of, Frank Sinatra’s, “Strangers in the Night.”
“Thanks, for showing Lisa the ropes. You two were dancing up a storm. Lisa should go to more dances. It will help with her social skills,” said Cynthia.
“Dancing comes naturally to Lisa. It those Trinidad genes I suppose,” said Paresh.

"That's her gross motor co-ordination – she has no trouble with that. She has a problem with fine motor co-ordination. Cursive script and key boarding is where the challenge is."
"Yes, we've noticed that at the lab too," said Paresh. "Vivienne suggested that Lisa use the sound recording feature of a smart phone to record lectures. Voice recognition software could convert these sound files to written notes. She can also use the smart phone to photograph the contents of white boards when required." suggested Paresh.
"Getting her a cell phone is a good idea, but you've lost me on the voice recognition thing," said Cynthia smiling at him helplessly and hoping to change the topic.
"Your friend Michael appears to be staring at us," said Paresh as he manoeuvred his partner to the other end of the dance floor.
"Oh don't let him bother you. By the way he's my ex-boy friend," she said looking at him to judge his reaction.
"That could explain why he was rude and hostile to me when we met in Veronica's office," said Paresh dropping his guard just for a moment.
"Well now, Dr. Naik, I hope you don't think that I'm with you on the rebound!" teased Cynthia.
"Oh, I …I, I think we have a good professional relationship. Do we not?" mumbled Paresh.
"I am planning on taking the kids to the Lake District some weekend soon. Would you like to spend some un-professional time with me; I mean us?" asked Cynthia, enjoying his discomfort.
"Yes, it would be nice to get away from the lab," said Paresh.

Michael and Murphy sat on high stools at the bar.
"Just look at that wog messing around with our Cynthia," he said to Murphy as he glared at Paresh over a pint of beer.
"Oh come on guv, he's not a bad sort once you get to know him. Your big mistake was to let Cynthia get away," said Murphy. "Besides, you got Veronica to think about now."
"You're right about Cynthia. I should have never lost her love. Veronica is no match for her. Anyway, I fancy that Bolly bitch or whatever her name is. I might try my luck with her," said Michael as he raised his beer and smiled across the dance floor at Miss Bolly.
"That is not fair guv. You're going to dump poor Veronica just like that?"
"Well, I'm done with her. You can have her if you want!" said Michael.
"I have always fancied Veronica but she was with you so…"
"You sly little bastard! I would never have thought you had a thing for Veronica. Forget it! She's way out of your league mate!" said Michael who laughed and almost choked on his drink.

"She is not above me," snapped Murphy. "This is the 21st Century, and it's time to lay your class system to rest. No one is above me! That is why I like to work for Mr. Patel in his print shop. Mr. Patel treats me with respect, teaches me new computer skills and tells me that I could be anything I want to be. You are always putting me down! And another thing, I'll get further with Miss Bolly in a week than you will in a life time."
"You're on!" said Michael, "I bet you a hundred quid, I'll lay that bitch before you have a chance to put a hand on her."
"Done!" said Murphy like he had said to his friend for years and eventually lost to him almost every time. Michael always had the knack of cheating him out of a bet. Murphy walked across to where Lisa and Miss Bolly sat. As he approached their table, he noticed they were looking towards the dance floor, as were most of the guests at the party but with curious and embarrassed expressions on their faces.

A few minutes earlier, Cynthia who was dancing with Paresh, excused herself and told him she would be back in a few minutes. Paresh waited for her on the edge of the dance floor with his hands thrust in his pockets. Just then, the band started to play an old ballad from the Rodgers and Hammerstein musical South Pacific called, "Some Enchanted Evening." There was a collective groan from many on the dance floor who were looking for the tempo to pick up. Many decided to take a break and leave the dance floor to return to their tables or wander over to the bar. This left Paresh looking somewhat out of place, all by himself. Instead of following the rest, he stiffened as he heard the beautiful rendition of the original Rogers and Hammerstein song.

A strange transformation overcame him. He threw his head back and closed his eyes. It all came back to him now. He felt himself transferred back in time a decade and a half. He had just been engaged to Gita. A girl he met, just by chance few years earlier, while she was visiting his parents in Puné. She was the daughter of a close family friend and was on a group tour of southern India. The tour passed through Puné, and she had stopped over for the day at his parents' home. It was an opportunity to catch up with laundry, shower and have a home cooked meal after weeks on the road in and out dusty hot buses and trains. She was a tall North Indian beauty, wheat complexioned, with a perfect oval face and dove like fleeting eyes. His mother was helping her to dry her long luscious black hair when Paresh walked in. She had a warm dazzling smile that disarmed the technocrat. It was love at first sight for Paresh who didn't know what hit him! They corresponded while he was in graduate school in England, and then he returned to India to marry her. She was what he needed. He was a complete person with her at his side.

In time, she would encourage him to broaden his outlook on life and spend more time with family and friends.

Bandra is a jewel of a suburb on the north end of the island of Mumbai. It is picturesque with a beautiful promenade called Lands End, which looks west into the Arabian Sea. This gives its seaside residents a view of spectacular sunsets. Bandra always had a prominent Christian community. The suburb has a fair number of churches and a famous basilica on a hill. The December/January months comprise the wedding season. The brief Mumbai "winter" lasts only a few weeks. During this time, the temperature hovers between a comfortable 20 to 25 degrees Centigrade. Many local residents look with great anticipation to the New Year's Eve dance at the Bandra Gymkhana. It had to be held out doors in order to accommodate the hundreds of couples that had bought tickets months in advance.

Paresh and Gita made a beautiful couple in the midst of hundreds of others who enjoyed themselves on the vast outdoor dance floor, which were in fact six tennis court improvised for the occasion. There were several live bands, which took turns to entertain the revellers. It was truly an enchanted evening with a cloudless crisp night, and a full moon beamed down on the spectacle. Very appropriately, a lead singer started to sing, "Some Enchanted Evening". Paresh and Gita swayed to the music and danced cheek to cheek. They talked excitedly about their plans for their forthcoming wedding day, only a week away. Paresh also broke the good news that his immigration papers to Canada had been accepted. He would soon be traveling to Canada from his base in the UK to set up a satellite remote sensing business. Gita would follow and join him in Canada when her immigration papers came through. He mentioned the contract his company had just been awarded. It was to survey the natural resources of Canada's northern First Nations communities, track the environmental impact of the huge oil sands project, and monitor deforestation. Gita listened with polite interest, but the school system appeared to interest her more. Paresh realized that she was thinking ahead to their future family in Canada, so from that point on, all they talked about was kindergarten.

An uncomfortable murmur spread across the dining area at the Saracen's head. Cynthia returned to witness the spectacle of Paresh dancing all by himself in almost perfect unison to a foxtrot beat but with an invisible partner. He was totally engrossed, smiled and talked to somebody that nobody else could see and oblivious to the attention he had drawn to himself. He was in a trance locked in time years earlier, at a place six thousand miles away!

Murmurs turned to giggles from around the room, and some thought he was just clowning around.

Michael yelled, "Get that drunk out of here!"

Almost at once Cynthia and Lisa ran across and grabbed him by the arms.

Paresh broke out off his trance and shook his head in disbelief.

He said, "I'm sorry; I don't know what came over me. I heard that song and it brought back memories. Sorry if I have embarrassed you and your friends."

"It's okay; no harm done," said Cynthia as she and Lisa coaxed him back to their table.

"What's happened to Paresh Miss?" whispered Lisa tearfully.

"Nothing love, nothing at all. He was just wrestling with demons from his past."

The idiom was lost on Lisa, as she looked wide-eyed towards the dance floor expecting to see a whirling dervish or some such monstrosity!

Miss Bolly filled a cup of coffee and presented it to Paresh. He sat with his elbows on the table and held his head between his hands.

"Here… have some of this. It might make you feel better," said Miss Bolly sweetly.

Paresh stared at her. His eyes narrowed and he bared his teeth. The muscles on his neck tensed. He jerked his head towards her. He made a monumental struggle to avoid saying something to her. He choked and coughed. Miss Bolly looked alarmed and confused wondered what she could have done to upset him. In his frustration, Paresh knocked the coffee cup over in her direction.

Miss Bolly stumbled backwards, almost tripping over a chair.

There was a collective gasp from the guests. Michael rushed in and Murphy who was closest to Miss Bolly pulled her away from the table and stood between her and an angry looking Paresh. He glared at her and gripped the edges of the table until his knuckles had turned white.

"I think you should leave now," said Michael firmly to Paresh.

Cynthia stood up and pressed Paresh's arm.

"Let's go," she said to him and then nodded to Lisa.

"Oh, you should stay on a bit. I haven't had a chance to talk to you," said Michael disappointed that Cynthia would be leaving so early.

"It's best that we leave. I'll give him a lift home. He is in no state to drive," said Cynthia.

Cynthia dropped Lisa home first and then proceeded to drive Paresh home. She had not been in a vehicle with Paresh since the first time they met, almost a year ago, when her car broke down on the highway. She felt a strange sense of déjà vu, with the same feeling of discomfort and awkwardness. This time however, he seemed to be in a lot of trouble. He was a brilliant scientist with a deep and troubled past and some of the past had shown itself this evening. He was more approachable and vulnerable and needed help. They drove in silence apart from occasional directions from Paresh. She parked on the curb outside his home and switched off the engine. She looked expressionless in his direction.

He broke the silence by asking sheepishly, "I suppose you would not want to have anything to do with me now?"

"Well, let me put it this way; this is not the worst date I have ever had. However, you intrigue me. I didn't know you could dance then I find you dancing with an imaginary woman. Who was your ghostly partner anyway? And why were you so nasty to Bolly? She was flirting with you all evening," remarked Cynthia.

"I had a vision that I was dancing with my fiancée who later became my wife," answered Paresh.

"What? So now you tell me you are married!" snapped Cynthia.

"My wife and our two children died tragically almost two years ago," said Paresh.

Cynthia felt her mouth drop, and the blood drain from her face. She had assumed that he was divorced, but she could never have imagined this. Paresh opened the passenger side door and stepped on to the pavement.

"Wait!" pleaded Cynthia, "Can we talk some more? How did this happen?"

"There is nothing more that I care to say on this subject," said Paresh as he walked briskly towards his front door.

"Wait! I want to help you," cried Cynthia.

"I am beyond help. Besides, you have helped me enough," said Paresh turning back just before entering his house and slamming the door behind him.

Cynthia sat in silence for a moment. It all seemed to make sense. Part of the mystery surrounding Paresh had unravelled itself. So, he'd lost his family in some tragedy and came to England to forget and get away from it all. She felt a tear roll down her cheek as she knew that she had misjudged him to be a self-absorbed technocrat and the whole VR lab research being an attempt bolster his own ego an publish a few more papers. No! He really cared for her kids and wanted to help them because he could relate to them as a parent.

When she reached home, Noby opened the door and asked, "What's happened? Lisa is very upset. The mad scientist didn't screw things up, did he?"

"Well, he's not as mad as people think he is," retorted Cynthia "but I don't want to talk about it any more. I need to soak in a warm bath before going to bed. It's been an eventful evening."

Uncle Noby had known Cynthia since childhood and knew better than to pursue the matter any further. He had never seen her so agitated, and rarely did she make time for herself to soak in a bath. Something was up. Could it be, he mused to himself, that his niece was in love?

Chapter 19: Whatever Happened to Murphy?

On the morning, following Veronica's Party, the Evergreen Estates Administration office that doubled as a model unit, called Michael to inform him that LEPA volunteers were wandering around the Estates requesting water samples. Michael immediately called Inspector Paradis to remind him that the court order, banning LEPA from the Estates, needed to be enforced. Jim Paradis said he was short staffed that morning.
"When can I expect to see a squad car in the area?" asked Michael.
"Young Constable Watson would have been in that area, but interestingly enough he has gone to see your friend, Murphy," said Inspector Paradis.
"What's Murph been up to?" asked Michael.
"Haven't you heard? My officers found him badly beaten. He was wandering aimlessly near your pub. Good thing he was not driving because he was as drunk as a sailor. They took him to emergency to fix a broken nose. Someone seems to have also hit him with a karate chop. I suspect an attempted coup de gars. He will wear a neck brace for a while."
"Any idea who could have done this?" asked Michael.
"Murphy claims temporary amnesia and suggested that someone mugged him and emptied his wallet. I suspect he is holding something back. Do you know anyone who would have a grudge against Murphy?"
"Murphy?" chuckled Michael, "No, Nooo! He is the most out going and friendly person I have ever known. But I would like to get my hands on the guy that did this to him!"
"Now you leave that to us, you hear," said Paradis firmly.

They exchanged further pleasantries and then hung up. Constable Watson finally got to the Estates and patrolled the circles and crescents of the Estates but found no LEPA trespassers. He was too late. LEPA volunteers had a free run of the Estates. They collected water samples from residents who eagerly gave them what they required. They also collected samples from the artificial lake.

The first signs of the impending CANDO Conference began to appear. The hotel rooms and private accommodations, that homeowners rented, were booked well in advance. The delegates, from NGOs to service providers, were eager to get work on contracts with CANDO as soon as the Indian Government signed the anticipated Nuclear Escrow agreement. Delegates from North America, Europe, the Middle East, China and South Asia registered in large numbers. CANDO contracted the University's Political Science Department to administer and manage the conference. They also awarded the City with an infrastructure grant and a generous discretionary allowance. The renovation and reconstruction of the Lincoln City Conference Centre, also owned by the City, was almost complete.

The regulars at the Saracen's Head sensed a sudden change in the atmosphere at their favourite pub. This occurred soon after Veronica's birthday party. It wasn't so much as what had changed, but rather who was missing. Murphy O'Neal was a long-standing feature at the Friday afternoon gathering. His heavy drinking, boisterous behaviour, enthusiastic dart and billiard playing, came to be an expected feature. Now with him missing, the place was almost silent during the Friday lunch hour.

"Whatever happened to Murph? We haven't seen him for weeks ever since the big party, and when he was mugged," the pub regulars often asked.

The mystery was solved when Veronica visited Patel Printing with a pile of Conference related documents that needed to be urgently printed and bound. When she entered the printing store, she noticed a big difference in the ambience. There was a faint smell of paint in the air. The business looked brighter and more inviting. There were new high-tech digital printing machines and computers. Veronica took all this in as she cast her eye across the store. She saw someone, who had his back to her, at the far end of the print shop.

She wasn't sure so she called out, "Excuse me!" to get his attention.

The figure turned around and replied, "Oh, Hello Veronica!"

It was Murphy, but he was unrecognizable in his smart tweed jacket and tie to match. The shoulder length hair and beard, the "George Best" look, were gone. He was now clean-shaven and well groomed.

"Wow, Murph! You look years younger and so handsome! What brought on this change?" asked Veronica.

"After I was mugged and narrowly escaped serious injury, I took stock of things and thought about the future. Mr. Patel has been after me to mend my ways. We expanded and updated our software and hardware to be ready for the conference. He offered me a full time position. If I perform well, I could manage this store one day. So, here I am, the new assistant pre-print manager for Patel Printing," said Murphy waving to the surrounding office.

"Congratulations! But what about your work with Michael?" Veronica asked.

"Michael and I have parted ways. I will no longer be working for him. I am sorry to let your guy down particularly because of the work that needs to be done on the Estates in preparation for the conference."

"Well, he's not my guy for starters," said Veronica, "My mother likes him, and since she thinks I am with him, she has stopped pressuring me to settle down and produce grandkids. Besides, I suspect the rascal has been sneaking behind my back and seeing Miss Bolly."

Murphy broke out into laughter, which he tried hard to stifle by covering his mouth and turning his back on Veronica by walking instinctively to a shelf to pick up an order form. However, he remembered that their print shop had installed a point-of- sale system. He logged-on to a workstation to enter Veronica's order.

"What's so funny?" demanded Veronica thinking he laughed at her naivety.

"Sorry ... Sorry," apologized Murph. He avoided eye contact as he looked at the keyboard and created an invoice.

"Well?" persisted Veronica.

"It's … It's just that I think our Michael has finally … met … his … match!" said Murphy, trailing into more uncontrolled laughter.

He wiped the tears from his eyes and looked straight at Veronica and said, "I'm glad all this is out in the open Veronica. I don't have to lie about his whereabouts, as I did, when he was with Cynthia. Michael is a fool to cheat on a fine woman like you."

"Thanks" said Veronica softly. They gazed at each other for a while when Veronica broke the awkward silence and asked, "Should I return later today to pick up the printed material?"

"Oh don't worry. I will drive to the University and leave it at reception for you. From the looks of it, the order will be quite a heavy load."

"Better still why don't you come to my office and hand it to me," suggested Veronica.

"I'll be glad to do that," agreed Murphy.

Veronica turned and walked towards the exit. As she looked back to wave goodbye, Murphy finally summed up the courage to say, "I'm glad you dropped by. I … I… er …need your advice and was planning to see you anyway."

Veronica had the door half open as she asked, "Advice? About what?"

"Well, I have taught myself computer aided design, CAD, when I did the drafting work on Michael's remodelling projects. But I think I need formal training on computer graphics to deal with all that conference marketing material that's coming our way."

"You know, that's a smart thing to do Murph. When you drop by tonight, I'll have the course brochures for you."

"I'll trade that, and any advice you can give me for a drink, if you like," ventured Murphy.

"I'd like that very much," she said with a smile and then hurried on her way.

When Mr. Patel returned, he found Murphy working on Veronica's order and smiling to himself while he hummed a tune.
"You're looking very pleased with yourself young man," he remarked.
"What can I say Mr. Patel. I finally got a date with the girl of my dreams," he said.
"Indeed," said Mr. Patel, "What did I say to you some time ago? If you stop your needless boozing, clean up, work hard and focus on things that matter, good things will come your way."
"You are my guru Mr. Patel. From now, I shall always obey you!" said Murphy, as he feigned reverence, held his hands together and bowed to the bemused Mr. Patel.

During the months leading up to the conference, the vendors staged product demonstrations in a square, adjacent to the City Hall. Office workers enjoyed free lunch time BBQs where vendor booths and tents were setup. Those that sat through the presentations were rewarded with door prizes such as tablet computers, gift cards, mp3 players and colourful thumb drives.

A well known a water purification vendor claimed to purify, to a potable state, contaminated water from any part of the world. Their displays show photographs of successful projects in disaster areas from war torn regions to tsunamis, earthquakes, forest-fires and floods.

The public, including girl guides and boy scouts brought water samples taken from local ponds, streams and rivers. They stood in line and waited their turn with a sample number. Each sample was analyzed and a few minutes later, a large LED screen would display results along with the sample number. The results were displayed in a bar chart. The first set of results showed an analysis of the original sample in terms of the major contaminants ranging from heavy metals such as lead and mercury and most carcinogens. Another set of green bars would show the acceptable levels of contaminants as specified by the UN and the EU. The final set, in blue, showed the analysis of the filtered and decontaminated sample. As expected, the purified sample showed a remarkable reduction in most impurities. Unbeknown to the attendees, the exhibitors had exaggerated the vertical scales to emphasize the differences between the results, expressed in parts per million.

Most of the original samples only marginally exceeded the UN and EU compliance in a few chemicals and carcinogenic compounds. However, the purified results were always comfortably below the required upper limits. The crowd clapped and cheered when they saw the results. What is more, a member of the exhibitor's team would always take a sip from the beaker of the cleansed water. This gesture would impart a final vote of confidence in their purification system.

A contingent from LEPA, that had earlier collected samples from the Evergreen Estates, took their turn in the line up. When the LEPA's samples were examined, the screen flickered and flashed as if there had been a power surge! The system finally settled down, but the results were indiscernible. The original sample, plotted on the exaggerated scale, dominated the display. It exceeded the compliance levels by almost an order of magnitude. Hence, the compliance and the processed data could barely be seen when presented on the same stretched scale. The crowds gasped when the LEPA representatives told the crowds that the sample was taken from the Estates' tube wells.

The crowd noticed that the exhibitors sidestepped the ceremonial sipping of the processed LEPA sample. There were no cheers, instead a hushed silence greeted the sombre analysis. Many attendees lived on the Evergreen Estates or knew people who lived there.

It turned out that a reporter from a local newspaper, the Lincoln Chronicle, was in the crowd. He was on a special assignment to report about the CANDO Conference. Normally he dealt with City Council business and was familiar with the work of Councillor MacMillan. He had covered the sale of the City property to Michael Caruthers years ago. There were unsubstantiated rumours of shady goings on, and the way the deal had gone through. This included the fact that Councillor MacMillan had, through a strange coincidence, inherited a large fortune that paid for an enormous luxury home on the outskirts of the City.

The reporter's instinctive reporting antenna was up as he sensed an important story was brewing. He was later seen interviewing the LEPA representative. However, Michael refused to return his calls. The next morning the Chronicle reported that the Estates water was undrinkable and the City's original environmental assessment needed to be reviewed. The Chronicle demanded to see the original document. The City clerk said that the company that did the testing had long since gone out of business. The original owners could not be traced. The Chronicle then turned its attention back to Michael and finally got an interview with him. Michael turned the tables on the City and claimed that he purchased the land in good faith. He had relied on the City's environmental assessment, and their assurances before converting it to the Evergreen Estate and gated community. The City appointed Councillor MacMillan to be their spokesperson.

The interest in the Evergreen Estates' environmental debacle had begun to travel far and wide in UK. This was because the Chronicle's Web portal offered free access to local news. In addition, the impact on the much-anticipated CANDO conference also made big news. To make matters worse, there was a video recording of the water purification vendor's testing of the Evergreen Estate water samples. This appeared on the Chronicle's Web site and other popular social net working sites. It wasn't long before legal "ambulance chasers" from London drove into the City to contact the Estate's ratepayers' association in order to develop a class action lawsuit against the City.

The City's lawyer bent over backwards in an attempt to stifle the impending public relations disaster. He agreed to settle with the residents out of court with the proviso that all proceedings were to be kept secret until the end of the CANDO Conference and all visitors had left the City.

The Lincoln County Health Department set up a mobile clinic in the shopping mall within Evergreen Estates. Blood samples were taken from each resident and further water analysis confirmed the contamination.

The City's Conference discretionary funds now went to compensate the estate residents and to divert the City Municipal water to the Estate. The councillors had voted earlier to use the discretionary funds to bolster their pension fund. Many had planned to retire early. These plans were cancelled. In their anger, they blamed Councillor MacMillan, who resigned.

Michael's problems were only just beginning to surface. The intrepid Lincoln Chronicle reporter had managed to find an old microfiche. This contained the laboratory tests for the environmental assessment.

Chapter 20: Rama Flexes Its Muscles

Patelji and Lisa made regular visits to the Ramanujan Lab. They also continued with their dance and music classes at Miss Bolly's studio. One Saturday afternoon, Cynthia waited, in the circular driveway in front of the studio, for them to emerge. The door opened and Patelji, Lisa and some of the other girls hurried out, giggling and laughing amongst themselves.

Later on the drive home Cynthia asked Patelji what they were laughing about.

"Oh Miss it was dead funny," he started to say.

"Yeah, it really was," interrupted Lisa, "Miss Bolly was demonstrating some new Bharatnatyam dance steps and then asked us to practise them while she visited the washroom. When she returned, something seemed to be wrong with her eyes. As she got nearer almost everyone pointed to her face and started laughing. One of her eyes was blue and the other was her normal brown colour. I guess she must have experimented with blue contact lenses and then forgot to take one off. She looked at herself in the studio mirrors and rushed back to the washroom with her handbag."

"That's strange. Miss Bolly has such beautiful brown eyes. Why would she experiment with blue contacts?" she asked rhetorically.

She thought about Paresh, as he was the only blue-eyed South Asian she knew. It was two weeks since their emotional separation after Veronica's Party. She yearned to hear his voice again. Her email and voice mail to him was left unanswered.

The phone rang late that afternoon. She could almost guess that it was Paresh. He would always call late on Friday afternoons.

"Hello Cynthia, how are you?" enquired Paresh.

"Hi stranger. So you finally got around to returning my calls," scolded Cynthia.

"We've been busy but we have accomplished quite a lot in the last few weeks," said Paresh. "The University's Board of Governors wanted a progress report and the marketing department needed an article on the application of virtual reality concepts to special education. We've made headway with both the modules. I had intended to call you earlier."

"The road to hell is paved with good intentions! Or in your case, could it be the road to incarnation? I hope you return as some soon to be extinct creature!" said Cynthia moodily to punish him for neglecting her.

"I think you'll forgive me once you've seen what I have to show you," said Paresh apologetically.

The next day, Cynthia visited the laboratory with the kids soon after school. The dimmed lights gave the whole place an eerie look. The lab was bustling with activity and looked like a space launch control

centre. Many student volunteers sat facing a bank of computer monitors. They focused on the graphical images that flashed by on the screens and listened to sound through their headsets.
"What are you folks up to here?" she asked.

The undergrad closest to her turned, somewhat startled. He removed his headset, smiled and said, "Sorry, I didn't notice you come in. This is the control centre for the VR simulation lab. I am responsible for monitoring the supercomputer's environmental parameters."
He motioned to adjacent colleagues. They turned and waved.
He then continued, "Jenny is responsible for loading the avatars on demand and managing the simulation. Natasha is supporting Patelji's and Lisa's avatars while Henry, back in the corner will be monitoring the other avatars that represent other students and staff from St. Cuthbert's School."
"Wow, quite a sophisticated set up. It's really exciting!" remarked Cynthia.
Just then, Vivienne stuck her head round the corner and beckoned to the kids. She ushered them into the Virtual Reality lab while Paresh waved to Cynthia to join him in his office.
"Hi Cynthia," said Paresh as he motioned wearily to a seat.
"Looks like you haven't slept in days," said Cynthia as she observed Paresh's dishevelled appearance and the dark rings below his eyes.
"What can I say? It's been really a busy two weeks around here," said Paresh waving to the laboratory. "We should sit in here and watch the simulation unfold. We have access to several vantage points. We could view the show through Lisa's eyes or Patelji's eyes or any of the other school yard avatars' vantage points or observe from a spectator's point of view."

Paresh gave Cynthia a spare headset and donned one himself. He adjusted his microphone and called out to Vivienne, "Viv, lets start with the School Yard Bullying simulation."
Vivienne called to the control room, "CR, load up the Beagle Boys Gang."
Paresh explained to Cynthia that this was a fictitious gang of bullies at St. Cuthbert's. They behaved and resembled a gang of older kids who played truant from school, indulged in petty theft, stole from and bullied Patelji at every opportunity.

The simulation started with a scene from the schoolyard at St. Cuthbert's. It was late evening, and the yard seemed deserted. Oak trees lined the eastern perimeter. The yard bordered the football field. A gentle breeze blew across the field. The late afternoon sun caught the leaves on the upper branches shimmering in the breeze. One of the large swing doors, at the rear of the school, opened and out walked Patelji's avatar with his MP3 earphones fixed in each ear. He seemed contended and immersed in his own thoughts. He walked towards the line of trees in order to take a shortcut to the Patels' residence. A dog, it turned out to be Bandit, scampered across the field. It trailed a leash and Lisa's avatar followed closely. She tried to catch the leash and bring Bandit to heel. She waved to Patelji and he smiled back. Just then, the Beagle Boys, who were sitting on the ground smoking but not yet in camera sight, made their presence felt. They stood up and started to walk briskly in the direction of Patelji.

Cynthia was intrigued with what she saw. She clicked on her computer's monitor to get to the operators console. Here she noticed the intercom button that allowed her to talk directly to Paresh.

"Paresh, I don't understand what I am seeing. Is this a recording? When did you record all this?" she asked.

"Everything you see is digital and virtual. We did make up the background from photographs of the school and the surrounding areas. The software is used to morph from planar views to 3-D," remarked Paresh.

"But you are simulating incredible amount of detail. Just look at the shadows and the leaves and as for Patelji, if you hadn't told me I could have sworn it's just a video of him leaving school," said the awestruck Cynthia.

"That's why a supercomputer is needed in order to capture that level of resolution and detail. RAMA also calculates the avatar's real time movements. These gestures, postures and hand-eye coordination are calculated by an algorithm based on a database of individual characteristics and skills. The avatar not only looks like the person but walks and talks like him or her. These are not artistic cartoon characters. They are very close digital replication of humans. However, the best is yet to come. We'll switch to Patelji's and Lisa's viewpoint and you will be prompted to don your 3-D visor," said Paresh.

"Oh yes, I remember the scary red button!" said Cynthia.

"If you look into the VR lab you'll see them with their VR helmets as they control their own avatars," said Paresh. Cynthia turned on an option that read, "Video link to VR Lab". She saw Patelji and Lisa, each with a VR Helmet on and engrossed in the simulation. They made comical movements with their arms and feet to control their avatars. They also used their wireless handheld control panels.

An icon offered Lisa's vantage point and another offered Patelji's view of the surrounding. As the simulation moved forward, Cynthia donned her 3-D visor and switched from one view to another as required.

The Beagle boys soon caught up to Patelji.
"Give us your loose change mate!" demanded the leader.
"I don't have any lunch money," said Patelji nervously. The leader grabbed Patelji's backpack and started to unzip and rifle through its compartments looking for cash. One of the other three bullies snatched Patelji's MP3 player saying, "Cool! I'll borrow this if you don't mind." The third bully insisted on listening to the MP3 player himself and soon the two began to quarrel over the spoils.

The leader didn't find any money in the backpack. He threw it on the ground and yelled, "Empty your pockets you son of a bitch."

Patelji turned to flee but the other two squabbling bullies blocked his path. The leader grabbed Patelji by the back of his collar, swung him around and punched him. Patelji's glasses were knocked off as he was thrown backwards.
Just then, a female voice shouted from behind, "Leave him alone!" It was Lisa.

The lead bully chuckled and glanced at his friends and said, "Who does she think she is? This Paki's bodyguard? Be off, or I'll pull your knickers off, bitch!"
"Lets do that anyway," urged one of the others. He turned towards Lisa who had arrived dressed for football practice. As he approached, she hopped on to her left foot and kicked him with her right boot, with the motion that resembled a goalie kick. However, it wasn't quite a football she made firm contact with.

He screamed and fell to the ground. He clutched his groin and rolled in agony. The other accomplices looked on with horror. They turned tail and ran back to the school building.

Bandit, distracted by a squirrel he had been chasing, decided instead to chase the two departing bullies. He out paced and then ran circles round them, occasionally giving their heels a gentle nip as if to corral them, like lost sheep, towards the school building.

Cynthia was in stitches and was just recovering from her mirth, when a wizard appeared and waved an admonishing finger at Patelji and Lisa. What's more, the wizard looked suspiciously like Paresh. He sported a white beard and wore a silver turban studded with rubies and diamonds.
Cynthia laughed as he started to speak, "Now, now boys and girls, resorting to violence is never a solution. Use your innate social and communication skills to negotiate! Do you remember the three cornerstones of negotiation?"
"Power and ... and ..." struggled Lisa.
"Information, time and power," blurted out Patelji smartly.
"Veeery, goood, Veeery Goood!!" said the wizard with a roll of his head.

"The whole idea or strategy is to get out of this situation without anyone getting hurt. It is better to negotiate with material things that can eventually be replaced. Watch how these two smart young people use their negotiating skills, firstly on the control of time. The bullies don't have time since they are on a hit and run mission. Secondly, they have a better knowledge of what the bullies want and what they have to offer in return. Finally, these smart people have the power to influence the subsequent steps by using their communication skills."

The wizard snapped his fingers and disappeared from the scene. The plot rolled back to the frame where the lead bully confronted Patelji.

"If you want money, I have 10 quid in my locker that I could let you have," said Patelji.

"You'll have to do better than that," said the bully.

"If you let him go, I'll throw in my iPod," said Lisa.

"Give it to me!" demanded the leader.

"It's in my locker too," said Lisa and then looking slyly across to Patelji she added, "You know the one near the CCCs."

The abbreviation was missed by the bullies. Lisa was gambling on the hope that the coded message would get to Patelji but the hooligans, too intent on their intended booty, would overlook that detail. Patelji smiled and nodded.

"You're sure you want to give that away? You've got loads of music and videos stored on it," he said as he embellished the prize even more.

"Yeah we'll take that too. Nothings too good for us," sneered the brat who already had Patelji's MP3 player in his hand.

The group walked back towards the schoolhouse door with Lisa, Patelji, Bandit in front, and the Beagle Boys behind them. The hostages meandered forward at a slow pace until the lead bully pushed Patelji forward and said, "Come on! Get a move on! I know what your game is. You think some one will come and rescue you." However, all this earned him was barred of teeth and snarl from Bandit. Cynthia gasped in amazement at the intricate detail of Bandit's face that the digital simulation had reproduced.

The Group entered the school building and Lisa headed straight to her locker, opened it and gave the leader her prized iPod. There was a pitiful doe like sadness in her expression that moved Cynthia. In the mean time, Patelji returned with a ten-pound note and handed it over.

"Sure this is all you have? Let's take another look at your locker," said the leader who pushed Patelji aside. As Patelji fell backward barely maintaining his balance. He recovered and said to Lisa, pointing anxiously to the Closed Circuit Cameras (CCCs).

"Oh no! We are in trouble! The janitor will report us and we'll be in detention tomorrow. We shouldn't be in this area so late," exclaimed Patelji.

The Beagle Boys looked up at the cameras in dismay. The small red lights flashed that showed that the CCCs had recorded everything. The leader realized the game was up and to save themselves from a date with juvenile court said, "Hey guys!! We were only taking the micky! Right? We fooled you anyway. Scared them didn't we?" he said playing to the cameras. The hooligans returned the loot and quickly left the building.

Patelji and Lisa gave themselves a high five and said triumphantly in unison, "Negotiate! Negotiate! Or else you won't live to procreate!"

Cynthia fell back in her chair and said, "Wow, this tool is truly amazing. It could have far-reaching applications in special education. However, I have reservations about the cost of producing these VR simulations. You would need to have quite a significant hardware environment, supercomputers and eventually professional staff in order to reproduce this quality of work."

Paresh remained silent for a while as he thought through a careful response.

"Not really Cynthia," he said. "If you recall the Lab was originally designed for business simulations. Due to the generosity of our anonymous benefactor, we were able to divert our attention to support children with learning challenges. The technology was originally directed to create industrial strength simulations for the business world where the market is more lucrative. In the world of primary and secondary school education admittedly all this is an overkill."

"So, how do you plan to keep the costs down to make it affordable?" asked Cynthia.

"Actually one of my Masters students has already done this. He has shadowed the work that Vivienne and I have been doing. He has used simple, Commercial Off The Shelf (COTS) software, to recreate the entire Beagle Boys simulation. The animation software he used, on a laptop, only costs a few hundred pounds. To save time he has used the same audio that Vivienne uses, but his avatars are based on library models, and some he downloaded for free over the Internet. Granted the characters have a cartoon like look and feel. The entire simulation is nowhere nearly as realistic as what you have just seen, but the message still gets across at a fraction of the cost. You could use these modules in special ed. Nevertheless, note, in the fullness of time even the high-end simulation will reduce in cost as it usually does when this research is commercialized. Moreover, global competition will reduce the cost even further. This research is still in its early days."

"Marvellous, my genius!" said Cynthia as she stood up to leave and patted the side of his arm, "You've thought of everything."

"Thanks," said Paresh as he typed in a few closing commands, "But I've thought of you a lot lately."

"I am surprised that you would have the time to invest is such a wasteful un-intellectual activity such as occasionally thinking of me," responded Cynthia.

Paresh stood up and turned towards her. She stood her ground so they were uncomfortably close to each other. He looked into her eyes and moved closer to her when the children ran in excitedly. Cynthia turned to face them.

"That was such fun," said Lisa.

"Uncle, Uncle I'll never be frightened by those bullies again. Now I know how to deal with them," said Patelji excitedly.

"My work here is done," said Paresh.

Lisa looked over her shoulder, as Patelji excused himself to go to the washroom. She whispered something in Cynthia's ear.

Cynthia nodded and turned to Paresh and said, "We have good news to share with you but it's still a secret. A few months ago, I had sent in adoption papers for Lisa to Family and Social Services. Yesterday someone from the department visited us. The meeting went very well so I am sure my application will be accepted."

"That's excellent news," said Paresh and turning to Lisa remarked, "Adoption is the most wonderful thing that could happen to an orphaned child."

"Why do you say that?" asked Lisa who was still struggling with the concept.

"Well, because there are so many children coming into the world to parents who don't even want them. When someone chooses to adopt, it's because that person commits to love and care for that child unconditionally, forever, even if it's not his or her own flesh and blood."

"That's quite profound coming from a nerd like you," said Cynthia smiling at him.

"I am happy for both of you. You at least have each other. You are now a family," said Paresh. Cynthia detected sadness in his voice and even a bit of envy.

Chapter 21: Yesterday Once More

June the 23rd was a day Cynthia looked forward to for a long time. School was out! She had planned a long summer of golf, trips around the country with Lisa and Patelji. She hoped to entice Paresh out of his lab to join them occasionally. She never dreamt that she would have to compete with the likes of a supercomputer for a man's attention. Time had flown by. Just a year ago, they had met, by the roadside, on the A57.

Lisa had never been to the Lake District and neither had Patelji. She wanted to book a round trip with a local bus tour company. She realized that she needed to check with Paresh if he was available since she had decided to travel on a weekday to avoid the weekend crowds. She called the lab with his number on the speed-dial of her home phone. Vivienne took the call and asked if she wanted to speak to Lisa who was busy with the dyslexia module. Cynthia asked to speak to Paresh, only to learn that he was still not at work but Vivienne expected to see him.

Cynthia telephoned Paresh's flat but got an answering service, so she left him voice mail. An hour later, there was no call from him so she called the lab again but he still hadn't shown up. Cynthia got an uneasy feeling about all this and decided to drive to his house. He lived a 10-minute drive from her home and yet, apart from the night of Veronica's party, she had never been to his residence. She recalled from memory where he lived and drove to the right street but couldn't recall the house number. She drove uneasily along the street and spotted his Volvo parked in the driveway.

Cynthia walked up to the door and knocked tentatively at first and then harder but there was no response. She turned the doorknob and was surprised to find the door open. She walked in and called out, "Paresh are you in!"
After a brief delay, a hoarse response followed, "I'll be with you in a moment. Please come in."

She walked through the hallway and passed what she thought was a coat closet. The room was more like a walk-in closet. As she passed the partially open door, she was hit by a current of warm air and heard a low-pitched collective electronic hum. She turned to look at what was inside and was startled to see row upon row of rack mounted Internet servers. The server racks were similar to what she had seen at the Ramanujan Lab. A large window mounted air-conditioner blew cooling air towards the server rack. What on earth is this stuff doing here she asked herself. She was lost in her thoughts as she went into what looked like a living room, only to be confronted with another enigma. The living room had a black leather sofa, a glass top coffee table that faced a wall mounted TV. The

TV had an image frozen on it from a DVD, which had been paused. It showed a beautiful golden retriever leaping into the air and catching a Frisbee in its mouth. She sat on the sofa transfixed by the image. Soon she heard a shuffle of feet from the other end of the corridor and Paresh walked in.
"Good grief!" exclaimed Cynthia and continued impulsively before she could check herself as she took in Paresh's dishevelled appearance, "You look like shit!"
"I am sorry. I wasn't expecting visitors today," explained Paresh.
"They are expecting you at the lab. Are you not well? What's up with you?" enquired Cynthia. He was unshaven and still in his pyjamas. His eyes seemed blood shot and his hair was tousled as though he had just woken up.
"I'm fine. It's just..."
"It's just what?" asked Cynthia as she moved further along the couch and motioned to him to sit.
"This day gets me down, every year."
"This day? You mean the 23rd of June. What special about today?" pressed Cynthia.
"I…I don't want to bother you about this," said Paresh. Cynthia noticed that he looked anxiously at the image. It appeared to embarrass him. He reached out to the remote control on the coffee table but Cynthia instinctively snatched it away.
He tried to retrieve it from her, but she playfully moved away and hung on to it.
"There's something on this DVD that's bothering you isn't it? I'm going to get down to the bottom of all this," she said resolutely.
"No, No please don't," pleaded Paresh.
"Well, let's face your demons together shall we?" she said and promptly restarted the DVD from the beginning.

The scene was a residential backyard. To Cynthia it seemed enormous and not the sort you would typically find in England. She noticed the tall light green coloured compressed wood fencing she had often seen on North American TV shows. There was a large shady blood red maple tree in the foreground and in the distance towards the far end of the yard was a pine tree. The lawn was freshly mowed, lush but light green. No sign of any nitrate laden fertilizer here. The camera panned towards a large deck. A tall North Indian woman, with light brown complexion and beautiful waist length jet back hair was busy at the barbeque. She had an almost perfect oval face. Cynthia noticed she wore an intricate black and gold beaded necklace. She smiled at the camera and said, "Meena's friends are staying over for lunch. It's her birthday treat. You should see them; they look so cute in their little bikinis. Take some good shots of them when they come out."

Hardly had she said that, than the patio door slid open and three pre-teenaged girls, a blonde, followed by what looked like Paresh's daughter Meena and the third girl, with dark brown hair and braces, ran across the deck and headed straight for the oscillating sprinkler in the middle of the lawn. They all shrieked as the cold spray caught their bare backs as they skipped in and out of the spray.

The lady at the barbeque, Cynthia surmised was Paresh's wife, looked up and said "Meena darling, get everyone to sing that song you kids have been practising all morning. They've been driving me crazy, I tell you!"

Meena whined, "I don't think we are ready, Mom."

But the girl in braces said, "Lets try it; look your dad's videotaping us. We could put it up on YouTube."

"Yeah, let's do it Meena," urged the blonde. After some urgent whispering, the three girls straighten up and sang in near perfect Hindi, gesturing correctly with their hands,

"Mera Joota hai Japani
Yeh Patloon Inglistani
Sar pe lal topi Rusi
Phir bhi dil hai Hindustani."

Cynthia immediately remembered it as the song that Lisa sung for her a few weeks ago and that Paresh was so overjoyed at hearing. It seemed to be quite a musical icon for the South Asian diaspora.

The girls had hardly got into the second verse of the song when they looked anxiously at the backyard fence door as it flew open, and they screamed in unison as a boy in swimming trucks ran into the backyard, followed closely by a golden retriever. The source of the girls concern was the pump action water cannon that the boy used to spray each girl in turn while they tried to disperse in different directions.

The lady called out to her son, "Mukesh darling! Leave the girls alone! Be nice to your sister. It's her birthday today. Your hot dog is ready."

"I'm not eating that yucky, smelly Goa sausage thing," warned the young lad.

"Not to worry, I've got a nice Canadian Sausage well done and ready for you Master Canada," said his mother.

The girls regrouped at a safe distance at the far end of the backyard and started to play with a Frisbee. They called out to Micky, the retriever, and then teased him by throwing the Frisbee to one another until one got careless with a low trajectory. This allowed Micky to jump

in the air and catch it in spectacular fashion. The video taping ended abruptly at this point and showed Micky transfixed in midair with the Frisbee in his mouth.
Cynthia sat for a while in silence while she collected her thoughts. She then turned to Paresh who was looking at the screen with an empty stare.
"Wow, what a lovely family you…"
"Had!" prompted Paresh bitterly "They are all gone! The DVD is all I have of them; Just memories of yester year."
"I'm so sorry to intrude. I had no idea what was on the DVD," said Cynthia genuinely remorseful, and shaking her head.
"It's okay. I only get this way on this day. I've been on my own until now. It's nice to have you around to lower the burden. I should have been with them on that day, the 23rd of June. Then we would have all gone together."
He paused for a moment and asked, "Did you want something?"
"I came around to see you because I needed an answer regarding something but in light of all this, it can wait."
"Tell me what it is," insisted Paresh.
Cynthia told Paresh about her plans for the trip to the Lake District. He consulted his calendar and found that he had an early morning budget meeting with the accountant representing the donors' family. He agreed to come. After his meeting, he would drive to the Lake District to join them there.

Chapter 22: The Picnic

The bus ended its journey in the parking lot adjacent to Lake Windermere at the lakeside town of Bowens-on-Windermere. It emitted an annoying series of snorting sounds as the compressed air driven doors opened. Cynthia, Lisa and Patelji were placed at the back because of Bandit, who much to his credit, behaved well. Although their journey started with a drizzle, it had evolved into a beautiful cloudless day. The trio and dog finally emerged from the bus. The vast expanse of blue water ahead of them seemed to take them by surprise.
"Look at the lake Miss! Just look at the lake!" said the excited Patelji tugging at Cynthia and pointing to the lake.
"It's lovely isn't it," said Cynthia almost tripping over herself, with a large picnic hamper in one hand and Patelji tugging at the other. Lisa had Bandit on a tight leash. Cynthia spotted an empty picnic table under the shade of a large oak tree. She told the children to go to the wash room and meet her there. She set up the hamper's contents on the park bench and placed a rug in front of it. They could sit on it or take a nap.

Bandit, who never let the children out of his sight, was overcome by a sense of divided loyalty. He paced the distance between the men's and the ladies washroom and whined as he waited for one of them to come out. Patelji appeared first and promptly raced Bandit to the picnic table. He led the way with his arms out stretched out like an airplane. Cynthia smiled as he ran towards her. She thought to herself, away from his computers, disciplinarian aunt and uncle, who were never content unless he brought home straight As, he was a carefree fun loving child again.
"Here's your cheese and tomato sandwich, love," she said. She knew the Patels were strict vegetarians.
"When Lisa comes back, I'll go over to the concession stand and get us something cold to drink," added Cynthia, which she soon did and noticed a flyer that indicated that the boat tours left by a nearby dock every hour. She rushed back with the drinks and called out to the children as she approached with the drinks, "Do you kids want to go for a boat trip?"
The answer was an all round affirmative.
"When you finish your lunch we'll walk over to the dock," she said.
"May I have another Salami sandwich Miss?" asked Lisa.
"Sure sweetie," said Cynthia and continued saying, "But you can call me Mummy now, Lisa."
Lisa grinned at Cynthia. Cynthia noticed Patelji had a glum look on his face.
"Can I call you Mummy too?" he finally blurted out.

"No you can't!" rebuked Lisa who wasn't willing to share her newfound status.

"Some one has to adopt you before you call them mummy or daddy," she added.

"How much does it cost to get adopted?" asked Patelji innocently.

"You can't buy an adoption silly. A big person goes to a lawyer and signs papers and stuff. Isn't that so Mom?" asked Lisa.

"Yes, there are papers to sign," said Cynthia in a flat tone of voice. She hoped to keep out of the discussion.

"But my uncle said if you have enough money you can buy anything. It's not fair! Lisa gets to call you Mom and I don't have anybody," whined Patelji.

"You have your wonderful aunt and uncle. What more do you need?" consoled Cynthia.

"They are more like my grandparents," argued Patelji.

"Okay, then I'll tell you what. When we are not at school, you can call me Mom. It's our little secret," offered Cynthia.

"Eeuuu!" exclaimed Lisa. "That would make him my brother!"

"And I don't need a sister!" retaliated Patelji. "All I want is a Mom!"

"A dad would be nice too," said Lisa.

"Now, now kids," said Cynthia who was beginning to tire of the bickering over her ownership, "Let's get to the dock before the boat leaves."

Patelji was disappointed when he learned that Cynthia wasn't accompanying them on the hour-long trip. Cynthia and Lisa, much to her credit, conspired to elevate him to chef de mission for the duration of the boat trip. Happy with his promotion, Patelji marched up the gangway on to the tour boat and presented the young peak capped attendant with the tickets saying, "These are for my sister and me but my mom isn't coming."

The attendant looked curiously at the South Asian boy, then to his alleged Trinidadian sister, nodded in the direction of his claimed Yorkshire mother and promptly rose to the occasion and said, "If this is your sister and that's your mum, mate, then I'm your second cousin Hector once removed; welcome aboard!"

The boat pulled away from the dock and the children waved to Cynthia. Bandit, snuggled between them, put his paws on a lower railing, and barked at their reflection. As the boat drifted further, Bandit whimpered as he realized they were moving away from Cynthia.

Cynthia looked at the smile on Lisa's contented face as she waived.

Minutes earlier, she had drawn Cynthia aside and whispered, "You are not coming with us because you are hoping Paresh will show up aren't you mom?"
Cynthia just nodded and winked at her. She reflected on the year that had past by. She marvelled at how perceptive Lisa, who just turned 15, had become. She was growing into an empathetic young woman. This in itself was no mean feat since the ability to show empathy is a major issue for some autistic persons. Her academic struggles were not over and it was clear that she would need much more time to attempt a few subjects for the General Certificate of Secondary Education (G.C.S.E.) at Ordinary or "O" levels. At least she was learning at a pace that suited her. Patelji, who was 2 years younger had already passed 8 "O" levels and was ready to enter a 6th form college in a year. At this rate, he could be entering university at 15! However, academics aside, both children had made tremendous strides in their social skills.

Patelji had learnt to stand his ground and seek help if bullies bothered him. He now knew where to go for help. School had become a safe place that also challenged him. He did not have the urge to skip class anymore. His project with the school's Astronomy Society was a grand success. He published shots of Saturn with its rings in the school's newsletter and on their Website. His self-esteem had increased as he continued to assist others in maths and science. Yes, they had come a long way. Cynthia knew she could not have managed on her own. However, the man, who had made such a big difference, still perplexed her.

Cynthia walked back to the picnic bench and cast a hopeful glance at car park but the forest green Volvo station wagon she longed to see was nowhere in sight. She sat with her back against the bench and buried herself in a Toronto University based novel about the exploits of a malicious woman who interfered and ruined the love lives of her girl friends. Ever since Paresh had come into her life, she took an interest in most things Canadian: politics, ice hockey, the prospects of Canada's Aboriginal people etc.

Cynthia nodded off to sleep. She woke with a start, to laughter and Bandit licking her face. The children competed with one another to tell their version about the trip. Finally, Patelji got a word in to tell of his adventure with 'cousin Hector' who allowed him to visit the wheelhouse and look at the navigation equipment. They settled down to some tea, and Bandit decided to take a nap on the rug.

The children worked up quiet an appetite on the boat trip. They were so engrossed in the scones and cakes that no one noticed that Bandit had woken with a start and cocked his ear. He then uttered a muted whimper, which turned into an excited bark. Bandit bounded towards the car park.

"Get him, quick!" yelled Cynthia.

Lisa sprinted after him with Patelji close on her heels, in hot pursuit. She watched as they slowed and appeared to wave their arms furiously. They were looking at Paresh who eventually noticed them. He seemed embarrassed as he walked towards them with the uncertainty of a person who wasn't sure what he was doing there.

"Hello, Infant Phenomenon and Pretty Brain," he teased them.

"Uncle, Uncle we went on the boat, and watched the radar," said Patelji.

"Paresh!" said Lisa "Cynthia has been looking out for you ever since we got here."

The children led Paresh by his arms, like a captive, towards the picnic area. Bandit ran circles round the group, barking excitedly. Paresh, dressed in a black jeans and a white tee shirt with the slogan of a software company on it, was relieved that his jeans had no turn-ups.

"Welcome to the Lake District. Voila, Lake Windermere," said Cynthia beaming at Paresh and pointing with a flourish to the lake.

"Well," said Paresh, as he struggled to continue the conversation, "I see the opposite shoreline. It looks like a large river!"

A couple, who happened to walk by, whom Cynthia recognized as fellow passengers on their bus, cast a stern glance at Paresh.

Paresh, realized his undiplomatic gaff, lowered his voice and said, "What I meant to say was that the rolling hills on the opposite shore give it a sense of scale. In Canada we are spoilt by large expanses of fresh water as far as the eye can see."

Cynthia came to his rescue and said, "Lake Windermere is longer than it is broad, I suppose."

Cynthia giggled at the inadvertent sexual inference while Paresh did his best to ignore it but not fast enough for Cynthia to notice a shy smile before he looked away from her.

"I come bearing gifts; a small token of my thanks to you guys for volunteering your time in the lab. Vivienne and I really appreciate that," said Paresh reaching out into his pocket. He produced a new smart phone and handed it to Lisa. Lisa's eyes grew as large as saucers.

"Wow Paresh! That's fabulous! I always wanted a cell phone. Just look Mom," said Lisa waving it in front of Cynthia.

"It comes loaded with Internet service and has a built in video camera. You should be able to surf the Internet, send email or text messages".

He then turned to Patelji he said, "As for you young man, I've got you a telescope that will help you take great shots of the Solar system. It's a six-inch reflector with a motorized mount, which automatically tracks your target. I'll give it to you when we meet again in the Lab".

"Thanks, Uncle Paresh! Will it interface with my laptop?" asked Patelji eagerly.
"Yes, yes ... it can do all that," assured Paresh handing Patelji a tri-fold glossy flyer.

Patelji glanced over it and then handed the brochure to Cynthia, which she put away at the bottom of the picnic hamper. He sat next to Lisa and helped her navigate her options on her new cell phone.
The children huddled together engrossed with Lisa's cell phone. Paresh sat awkwardly on the park bench and avoided eye contact with Cynthia but turned to her to reply in monologues. She asked about how he managed to get away from work and the long drive to the Lake District. Cynthia realised that, although they had known each other for over a year, this was just their second date.

The children decided to play with the Frisbee and tossed it to each other as Bandit leapt up, barely missing it. Paresh turned to watch them play.

Patelji pitched it in a low trajectory but Bandit caught it in mid-air. Just then, Paresh jumped to his feet and shouted at the kids in Marathi. He then continued to address the bewildered children, in a loud voice in English,
"Meena! Watch Micky doesn't run into the salad bar! Mukesh, son, careful you don't knock the barbeque over! Careful, careful…"
Cynthia looked about her, but there was no salad bar or barbeque in sight. Besides, who were these children and dog called Micky?

Paresh had adopted a Lenin like stance, with his protective right hand stretched above him. His voice tailed off saying, "Careful, careful, careful…"

Cynthia stood up and walked around him to face him. His glazed over eyes stared into the distance. He seemed oblivious to everything around him. She was overcome by déjà vu and then it came to her. The DVD that they viewed at his house showed his children also playing with a Frisbee and the family dog, a golden retriever, which she concluded must be Micky. When Paresh saw Patelji, Lisa and Bandit playing with the Frisbee, it must have triggered a painful flashback to past events. This also explained his strange behaviour at Veronica's birthday party. Some awful event, in the past, had traumatized him so much that he experienced flashbacks, triggered by similar current events.

Paresh's hand fell to his side as he gradually recovered his composure. He seemed to be embarrassed and shook his head as he started to say, "I am sorry, I was watching the kids and just lost my presence of mind…"
Cynthia cut him off and said, "It's okay, let's sit down love."

She realized that she had addressed him using an endearment for the first time. She took him firmly by the arm and sat him down on the park bench. The children rushed towards Paresh and sat beside him.
Lisa hugged him and rested her head on his shoulder and asked tearfully, "It's that demon from Veronica's party again isn't it Paresh?"
She looked into his eyes and added, "Just say three Hail Marys and it won't bother you again!"
Patelji, not to be outdone by Lisa, put his arm over Paresh's neck and said, "Don't worry Uncle Paresh, when we get back to Lincoln, I will ask my Uncle and Aunty to offer a special puja for you at the temple. That will surely drive the demon away."

The children's concern moved Paresh. He surprised Cynthia by kissing them on the cheek and forehead. Cynthia watched the three huddled together on the park bench. She would have loved to been part of that support group for Paresh.
"Fancy a cup of tea?" asked Cynthia.
"That will be nice, thanks," said Paresh.

Then Paresh sat up and said with a chuckle, "Please no more prayers to the Madonna or visits to the temple on my behalf. I'm okay, I'm okay... really! Come on; let us go play with the Frisbee. I came here to get away from the office and have fun."
With that, the three ran off towards the lake and tossed the Frisbee to each other. Bandit had to work harder as he ran and jumped between them.

About ten minutes later, when Cynthia appeared with two Styrofoam cups, the Frisbee lay abandoned and the children were now engrossed in a pickup five a side soccer game. She sat, on the grass, beside Paresh and handed him a cup. Paresh explained that a group of young men came over to Lisa and asked her if she would like to join them, which she agreed as long as Patelji could be their goalie. Cynthia arrived to see Lisa sprint down the right wing, chasing a long pass from centre field. Her speed surprised her opponents as she caught the ball chest high in mid-flight and proceeded to dribble it deftly past a bewildered defence and effortlessly scored a goal.
"Wow! She is amazing!" exclaimed Paresh.
"Well, Dr. Naik that young lady can do a whole lot outside your lab that you don't know about!" said Cynthia with pride.
"May be the lab is not the best place for her. She needs to focus on what she is good at and that's soccer. Just look at her."
"No, no, no… my friend lets not get carried away here," replied Cynthia, as she waved a finger at him. "You're not getting away that easily! She still needs a basic education. Sports will not sustain her forever. The

ability to read, write, comprehend and paraphrase will allow her to pursue further education and develop employable skills after she hangs up her boots."

Paresh stood up to stretch his legs and appeared to be suffering from cramps.

"Would you like to stroll along the lake front?" he asked Cynthia.

"I would love to," she replied. He leaned over and helped her up.

"You've never been to these parts before have you Paresh?" she asked.

"Never had the opportunity, so you can be my tour guide," he answered cheerily.

After they walked along the rocky shoreline he asked, "By the way, what career do you think Lisa should pursue?"

"Oh … I think she'd be good at sports news casting where she could give a verbal report on what she sees. There are no shortages of TV and film celebrities who are learning challenged."

"And Patelji?" asked Paresh.

"Now there you have so many options. It would be up to him. Our infant phenomenon is so talented. The world is at his feet," said Cynthia.

"Yes, he is so smart you would think he was Jewish," suggested Paresh.

"Or Gujarati!" interjected Cynthia. "Well, it will not be long before he goes up to Cambridge University. We need to keep his mind occupied and that's why his astronomy project and a planned computer chess contest are so important. Thanks to you, he looks forward to going to school."

"What's all this about Cambridge?" asked Paresh.

"Oops!" said Cynthia, "I shouldn't have revealed this to you. It's confidential material between the special ed. department and the Patel family. Please keep all this to yourself or I'll get into more trouble with the school board."

"I am hoping we can trust each other to be discreet and put the children's interests first," said Paresh.

"My thinking too," said Cynthia as she reached to squeeze his arm and continued saying, "Well, I've had a running battle with the Patels who, as you know, have been pushing us to do more for Patelji. Since the board failed to do anything at the special ed. Annual Review, the Patels have been advocating an early entry into Cambridge. They got Patelji to take the Cambridge scholarship exams, which to nobody surprise he passed with flying colours. But he still needs three A levels, and if he does well there, they will call him in for a interview. The Patels plan to bypass the school system by getting him to take his A levels earlier, but privately."

"I detect some concern on your part. Do you appose this?" asked Paresh.

"Yes I do, but we have come to this impasse only because the school board, mainly Dr. Hodicroft, refused Patelji's application to Surrey Place.

However, I agree with them that sending him off to University in a year or two would be a big mistake."
"Why is this?" persisted Paresh.
"Because, he is just reaching puberty," said Cynthia showing some impatience in her voice and an interest to move on to another topic, "the kid needs time to adjust and make the transition from boyhood to manhood. Besides, smart as he is, he hasn't yet developed mature social skills. I don't want him packed off to an adult institution in order to satisfy the high academic aspirations of his South Asian guardians!"

Cynthia regretted her outburst. It did not set the mood for the more personal conversation, which she had hoped to have with Paresh. There was a long silence as they picked their way along the shoreline. Cynthia struggled with an idea to rekindle the conversation. She picked up a flat stone and skimmed it across the water.
"Four hops!" she announced, "I bet you can't beat that!"
"Hey, you're a lefty," observed Paresh.
"You've known me for about a year, and you just noticed that," admonished Cynthia.
"What I know about you impresses me beyond measure," replied Paresh.
"Thank you, kind sir," she said and asked, "So, what do you think about the Lake District? I suppose it's not quite as beautiful as the mountains, lakes and pine forests of Canada."
"Oh come on, the scenery here is just as nice. I don't blame you for having a picture postcard image. You visualize scenic train rides through the Rockies, the mountains and forests of Banff National Park, the lakes and forests of Algonquin Park and the scenic splendour of the ski slopes of Mount Tremblay, in Quebec. Yes, yes we have all that. However, the best part of Canada is the purity and innocence of its indigenous people."
Cynthia furrowed her brows in polite enquiry and asked, "Why do you put them on such a high pedestal?"
"Canada has its areas of technical and business excellence," said Paresh and adopted a didactic tone as he added, "But the economy still relies on land based resources. Most of this belongs to the Aboriginal citizens. Canada's moral dilemma is a tight rope-balancing act between exploitation of non-renewable resources and the fair treatment of these beautiful people and the protection of the environment of which they are an essential part. Take, for example, the plight of the Porcupine caribou herds. Only our native folk know what is best for the herds since they have lived in a healthy symbiotic relationship with them for millennia. Now oil wells and access roads could threaten the herd's very existence. For Canadians, what matters is how the North is won, but at what price."

The eco-political diatribe took Cynthia aback, but her experience with dealing with challenged children allowed her to recognize the use of a red herring, to avoid talking about a difficult issue. She nevertheless persisted relentlessly. It was now or never. She needed to find out for herself who Paresh Naik really was, and what a person of his professional depth was doing in Lincoln, of all places in England.

"Well, Paresh, you seem to be on a mission to save the world. Shouldn't you be trying to save yourself? Let's face it you have these strange episodes – flashbacks that are scary. If I didn't know you any better, I would have concluded, as some others have already, that you are mentally deranged. Besides, you see how you have upset the children. I … I mean, we are concerned about you. I don't mean to pry, but you owe us an explanation."

Cynthia turned to Paresh and looked him in the eye. Just then, they came to a change in terrain. A hillock loomed ahead of them with a torturous but well trodden uphill path. Cynthia accepted Paresh's hand as he led the way.

The walk up the steep incline offered a respite from the conversation. She waited as he prepared his response. When they got to the crest, they were rewarded with a pleasant view of the shoreline, the surrounding area to the dock and beyond. Cynthia released her hand from his grip but instead hooked her arm under his and leaned against his shoulder.

"Well?" she persisted and looked into his eyes.

Paresh took a deep breath, placed his hands on her shoulders and said, "Believe me I was much worse off when I first met you. I was going down a path of self-destruction. You and the children saved me from myself."

"What destruction? What are you talking about?" asked Cynthia in bewilderment and added, "You helped us for goodness sakes."

"No, no my dear," said Paresh, "I am overwhelmed by your dedication towards those you serve. The education system does not deserve a wonderful person like you. I was lost but you involved me with Lisa and Patelji. This gave me a purpose and direction. Take Lisa, in spite of all the systemic discrimination, neglect and sexual abuse, she has risen above it all and succeeded. Her smile brightens my day. Patelji, under your guidance has found the courage to be a man and fight for his rights. He is no longer timid and introspect. It occurred to me, if the children with all their challenges can do all this …. may be, may be there is hope for me yet?"

Cynthia put her arms around his waist and buried her head in his chest.

"You are probably suffering from Post Traumatic Stress Disorder (PTSD). Why can't you tell me about the accident that took your family away from you?"

"It is too painful for me to even think about it not only because they are gone forever, but also for lost opportunities when we were together. I was pre-occupied with my satellite image processing business. I worked long hours and attended conferences when I should have spent more time with my family. Now, how I wish I could have taken time off to camp and fish with them, on some pristine lake, somewhere out West, perhaps with a snow peaked mountain reflected in it."

"But … but, Paresh, Paresh," consoled Cynthia, "it's not too late. Don't make it sound like a lost cause. We can still do all these things. You need to confide in me and let it all out. That's the only way you will get rid of these flashbacks. Why did you come to Lincoln and what are you really doing here? Please explain what that closet full of computers and electronic wizardry is doing in your house. Even I could figure out that set up is too sophisticated to just receive email and browse the Web."

Paresh put his hands on her cheeks, raised her face toward his, and said, "I have never told you anything because I care too much for you to ever lie to you. Could you please give me some more time? A week or two maybe? Then I will reveal it all. I warn you, once you know the truth about me, it will not be pretty. I'm afraid our time together is rather limited."

"Paresh you are the most enigmatic person I've ever met. However, this I am sure that as far as the children are concerned, you are sincere. I don't know what the future holds for us in this crazy world. I'm grateful for whatever time we have together."

In his arms, Cynthia felt a fulfillment she longed for, ever since he had visited her home. She looked into his light blue eyes. They seemed to shine like beacons in the backdrop of the dark blue lake. She saw a fire in his eyes but these were not of Indo-Aryan arrogance but instead these flames seem to dance with millennia of wisdom and kindness.

"Thank you for you patience and understanding," he said.

"Take care of yourself," she said softly.

He moved his lips closer to hers as she tightened her grip around his shoulders. Just then, a sound and some movement in their peripheral vision distracted them. There was someone running, shouting and waving. It was Lisa.

"Mom, Mooom!" she shouted. It sounded urgent.

"Good Lord, something's wrong," sensed Cynthia.

Paresh instinctively turned and started to walk briskly down the hillock. He hesitated and stopped to wait for Cynthia.

"Run ahead. I'll catch up," said Cynthia.

Paresh met Lisa as she ran towards him.
"Paresh, Patelji almost drowned," she gasped breathless with anxiety. "I think he's going to be okay."

It turns out that Patelji let a ball get past him at the goalmouth. He was annoyed with himself and chased after it as it bounced into the lake. He thought the water was only knee deep, so he ran after it. He found himself out of his depth in an unseen shoreline trench. He was under water for almost 20 seconds as Lisa and her team mates frantically searched for him in the murky depths. Bandit pounced into the water with her and circled the area where Patelji was last seen. Lisa reached down, grabbed Patelji by his collar and pulled him towards the shallow water. Then she dragged him onto the grassy bank. A crewmember from the dock, who had witnessed all this from a distance, came to help just as they lay Patelji on the grass. She administered CPR and turned him on to his side as he coughed up water and started to breathe normally again.

By the time Paresh and Lisa arrived on the scene, a number of concerned onlookers surrounded Patelji. A woman was helping him to wash is face and rinse his mouth with bottled water. Another was drying him with a towel. He was delirious and spoke incoherently in his native Gujarati, much to the confusion of his well-wishers.

Paresh and Cynthia decided to go home in Paresh's station wagon rather than wait another hour for the bus to leave. Besides, dark clouds approached, and Patelji looked rather green having drunk several mouthfuls of dirty lake water.

The drive home was uncomfortable for Patelji. He was sick quite often. Paresh had to pull over so he could rush out of the station wagon and throw up. Much to Lisa's disgust, on one occasion, he threw up inside before Paresh had time to pull over. Paresh and Cynthia became concerned with Patelji's condition. They decided to take him directly to Lincoln General. Cynthia phoned ahead to the Patel's residence and asked them to meet her at the hospital.

Chapter 23: The Target

It turned out that Patelji had nothing more serious than gastroenteritis. The doctor in Emergency recommended an overnight stay as tests showed that he had lost fluids and was dehydrated. Mrs. Patel stayed behind with Patelji. It was very late and the rest of the party decided to go home. Cynthia and Paresh agreed to meet at 10 am at the hospital the next day.

The next morning, Paresh arrived at Lincoln General a quarter of an hour late and presumed Cynthia had gone ahead to Patelji's room. He walked to the reception carrying a long tube like cardboard container that housed the six-inch reflector that he had promised Patelji. This would certainly brighten his spirits and return him to this lively intellectually inquisitive state thought Paresh. As he approached, a young lady at the large circular reception desk, eyed him curiously and greeted him with a smile.

"I am looking for the room of a young lad called Susheel Patel," inquired Paresh.

"Could you spell that for me please?" she asked.

Paresh spelt out the name. The lady looked at the monitor ahead of her and frowned.

"Sorry, I can't find anyone by that name."

"I was here with him last night in emergency," insisted Paresh.

"There is usually at least a couple of Patels on my list, but today nothing is coming up," said the young lady.

Paresh thought for a moment and then said, "Could you do a wild card search?"

"A wild what?" asked the confused receptionist.

"In the search form, just type in *Patel* and see what comes up. I suspect all names, with the character string Patel in them, will be listed," suggested Paresh, thinking due to the previous night's urgency, he may have been registered as Patelji.

"Oh that's interesting. I learnt something new today!" she said cheerfully. "Here sir!" she said as she pointed to the screen triumphantly, "Susheel Patel-Gandhi. He's in the paediatric ward, room 131."

Paresh almost dropped the telescope container. His jaw fell as fear griped him. His mouth went dry.

"Patel-Gandhi, Patel-Gandhi…" he murmured to himself. Of all the places in Europe, they could be operating from, this is why the Deccan Dhaku is in Lincoln. By strange coincidence a distant relative of the great Mahatma, had sought refuge and anonymity in an inconspicuous city in the British Midlands and now this same city was going to host a world wide conference, which could eventually lead to nuclear disarmament. Of course! It now became clear. They plan to assassinate Patelji, a symbolic

link to the grand-prince of non-violence. The CANDO Conference would be doomed!
"Are you okay sir? …The paediatric ward is in the West Wing," said the receptionist, pointing to the direction. However, Paresh headed hastily to the exit.

As he approached the revolving door, he saw Cynthia. She had overslept after the previous late night.
Cynthia rushed towards Paresh and greeted him cheerfully, "Hi ya! What the jeepers is in the big box?"
"It's the telescope for Patelji. Could you give it to him, please?" asked Paresh.
"Sure, but aren't you coming in too?" asked Cynthia.
"No, I must go and finish my mission. Now I know the intended target. That was the last piece of the puzzle."
"What mission? What target? What puzzle?" asked Cynthia.
"This is what I tried to explain to you yesterday. I wish I had acted earlier. It may be too late. Please don't leave Patelji's side, he is in grave danger," said Paresh as he handed the long box to Cynthia and rushed towards the exit.
"Good grief! Has Patelji taken a turn for the worse?" she asked after him anxiously, but he just waved back and was gone.

Cynthia thought to herself, she really knew how to pick them. First, it was that womanizer, and now she is hung up on an eccentric computer scientist.

Paresh drove through the hospital's multi-levelled parking garage. As he spiralled down through to the ground level, he reflected on the name Patel-Gandhi. He recalled during his earlier years in England, students in Grammar schools and Public schools rarely used first names. They called each other by their last names. He thought about Patelji and Patel-Gandhi. It came to him in a flash out of the blue. The Patels didn't want to attract attention by using his original last name of Gandhi, so they must have changed it to Patel-Gandhi. Patelji's English classmates and teachers called him Patel-G, a short form of his registered last name of Patel-Gandhi. When his friends came around to the print shop or their residence above it, the Patels interpreted their use of the name Patel-G as Patelji. Since the appendage "ji" is a sign of respect or familiarity on the Indian subcontinent, the Patels accepted this as appropriate for his friends. Hence, in the future he was always introduced by his nickname, Patelji.

Chapter 24: Commander Gill Closes on His Prey

With the Conference only two months away, Anwar Khan called an urgent video conference. Both Tiru and Jeevan watched a large monitor in a secure location within the Indian High Commission in London. Jeevan introduced Tiru to members of the RAG team in New Delhi.
"It's an honour to finally meet with you Sir," said Anwar Khan.
"Likewise," said Tiru, "Lieutenant General, the situation is precarious. I have spent the last 18 months with the conference committee, with London as my base, to build trust and confidence. NGOs and Government officials from Europe and South East Asia are converging on Lincoln. About a hundred Requests for Proposals (RFPs) were sent out and we received over a thousand proposals. These came from organizations all over the world, for various humanitarian projects, destined for the Indian Sub-Continent. The first round of funding amounts to 5 Billion dollars (US). In order to ensure impartiality and total transparency in the selection process, the conference attendees will select the winning bids. Everything hinges on whether those that have registered for the conference, online, attend and are not frightened off by terrorist threats."
"I am aware of your predicament Mr. Krishnaswamy, Sir," responded Anwar Khan, "but please understand that we have limited resources committed to this project. We cannot compete with well-heeled and unscrupulous arms dealers, which secretly fund the Deccan Dhaku. It is the duty of local law enforcement agencies to deal with this issue."
"Local law enforcement, here in UK, is too pre-occupied with their own security issues. They struggle to acknowledge that a threat exists. We need to take unilateral action ourselves to protect our own interests or else the Toronto fiasco will repeat itself," said Tiru and continued to say, "I have recommended to Mr. Alfred Pinto, the Defence Minister, that Commander Gill apprehend Anil Godsé."
"Great!" said Khan, "We hoped for this timely initiative. Up to now, we had to lay low in England. But as you implied, it is urgent..."
"It is not just urgent! It's a political crisis!" interrupted Tiru. "If the conference should fail, it could have dire consequences for the Asian Global Alliance party and all who work for them, including your department, my friend. What is more important," continued Tiru with a statesman like tone, "our failure will allow the opposition to take over and return us to large scale defence spending. This will reverse rural development with micro business loans, infrastructure initiatives, alternative energy projects etc. The Nuclear Escrow Treaty will have a major impact on nuclear proliferation in Asia and eventually disarmament. It will release much needed Federal funding. The

Government has agreed to match dollar per dollar any funds raised by the Mano Foundation. The CANDO conference cannot be allowed to fail. Too much is riding on it."

Tiru paused to catch his breath.

"Commander Gill," said Anwar Khan, taking advantage of the lull in conversation, "You are going to have to get off your butt and move your base of operation north to track down Godsé. We discussed various options earlier. Bring us up to date on your latest strategy."

"I will keep gay bars, in the Lincoln area, under surveillance, and see if I can spot Anil Godsé. There can't be that many gay bars. A blue eye male South Asian should stand out in a crowd of Englishmen," responded Jeevan.

"You are not a bad looking guy yourself Gill. Make sure you don't get picked up!" remarked Anwar, which was followed by a ripple of laugher from the Delhi contingent. In the past, Tiru would have joined in and added his ten cents worth to the humour, but he said nothing. The Kashmir Princess disaster still affected him deeply.

"Gill, what do you think Godsé's modus operandi would be?" asked Tiru.

"The Deccan Dhaku specializes in assassination. They can make people disappear without trace. The British Government views the conference as a low-key event. A junior Minister from Foreign Affairs will attend on the first day and deliver a keynote address. He will be surrounded by adequate security. The Deccan Dhaku is smart enough not to risk failure with fewer resources in a foreign country."

"I think that a few well placed bombs will cause considerable death and destruction. If this happens, those NGOs will scurry back to where they came from, and the conference will be cancelled," interjected Anwar Khan.

Jeevan Gill reflected on Khan's viewpoint and said, "They may have developed a taste for bombing but they have found it too messy. They prefer working with targeted individuals. Their operatives like to develop a relationship with victims before they kill them; a black widow like syndrome. This is why I found the Lonavala and Kashmir Princess bombings uncharacteristic of Dhaku. They needlessly killed hundreds they did not know. They realized their strategic blunder. The entire Nuclear Escrow team, you (Tiru), the Minister and I were the intended targets. The honest answer is that I don't know what Godsé will get up to because I cannot visualize an obvious target."

"It is best to end here. We will reconvene in a few weeks time when you (Gill) settle in the Lincoln area and report back from there," said Tiru.

"Good plan Sir," said Anwar Khan and that ended the conference call.

It took a week to prepare for his trip to Lincoln. Jeevan did a quick Internet search to find most of the gay pubs in Lincoln City. One pub, called The Groomsman, attracted his attention, since it was located near the city centre. Temporary digs were more of a challenge. All the hotel rooms were booked for the conference by advanced teams of vendors who were sent ahead to develop marketing contacts and publicity. Moreover, even the bed-sitters in the city were taken. He eventually found accommodation in the nearby suburb called Birchwood.

Chapter 25: Hunter and Hunted

Jeevan spent his first week at Lincoln visiting the tourist attractions like the Cathedral. He went to the library where he caught up to world events reading the newspapers by using the free Internet service. Once a librarian, realized that he was a conference attendee, she brought him up to date on the vendor exhibits. Jeevan followed her recommendations and found himself in the midst of Low Carbon Footprint Week, a featured pre-conference event. The vendors represented solar array manufacturers, wind turbines and biogas generation systems. The exhibit also featured a subcompact vehicle called Chota, designed for the South Asian market. It was a collaborative effort by an Indian manufacturer and a UK automobile electric vehicle company. Another company advocated lunar mining. It promised an end to global warming with nuclear fusion reactors. These would provide an unlimited source of pollution free energy using small amounts of Helium 3, only available in significant amounts on the Moon!

Jeevan found it difficult to concentrate on the exhibits. A strange email that he received earlier distracted him, it read, "The Deccan Dhaku is on to you. If you value your safety, leave Lincoln immediately!"

Jeevan forwarded the email to RAG HQ in New Delhi. Anwar Khan's team could not trace the origin of this message and annoyed Jeevan further with the admittance that their security network had been breached, not by the Deccan Dhaku, but by another unknown source in the UK; an independent third party. The trail went dead when the investigation tracked the intrusion to the outer perimeters of UK's vast Internet. Moreover, MIQ and Scotland Yard both vehemently denied any mischief. Jeevan's cover was blown. He needed to act fast. He was the hunter and now the hunted. In face of all this uncertainty, Anwar Khan issued a final order to Jeevan.

"Terminate Anil Godsé on sight. The High Commission will make arrangements for you to be escorted out of UK under diplomatic immunity."

Jeevan doubted the credibility of this assurance and fully expected to be disowned by his diplomatic mission should he find and kill Godsé. However, it pointed to the desperation of RAG. He was nevertheless prepared to sacrifice himself and morally justify his action as a means to an end. The noble Sikh knew that the conference could not be allowed to fail. He would kill this beast, if he could only find him and then give himself up. The diplomats would be free to squabble over his future.

The mysterious email puzzled Lestrade and his colleagues at Scotland Yard enough for his team to take at least a passing interest in the illusive Canadian Visitor. Jeevan's cell phone rang early in the morning.
"Hello, Gill, it is Chief Inspector Lestrade here," said the voice.
"Oh, Good Morning!" said Jeevan somewhat surprised.
"Now, look here Gill old chap, that email that you forwarded to your people at India House has caused quite a stir. I wish you had checked with me before you did that," said Lestrade sounding agitated.
"I apologize," said Jeevan, thinking that at last, Scotland Yard had renewed its belief in the existence of Canadian Visitor and reinforcements were on the way.
"After your visit here we researched the information you gave us and found no evidence that Canadian Visitor is in the UK or that such a person exists at all. Frankly, this is a storm in a teacup. The Indian High Commission has friends in White Hall. With all these multi-billion dollar defence contracts being signed, White Hall doesn't want to upset the Indian Government. So, I'll do this for you...," said Lestrade reluctantly, while he shuffled some papers.
"Ah, here it is... Inspector Paradis in Lincoln. He's the chap you need to meet soon. Please let him deal with your concerns. He has the Air Kanishka file and will contact you shortly."
"Thanks, Chief Inspector Lestrade. I look forward to meeting Inspector Paradis."
"Good-Luck!" said Lestrade and hung up.

Jeevan looked gloomily at the flowery wallpaper in his digs. He wondered if there would be any purpose served in meeting Inspector Paradis. His file had been passed on to a lower authority. The bureaucracy reminded him of India. At least in the old country, he thought to himself, you could grease a few palms to get things done but here in England it's more like who you know rather than what you know. Tiru must have done a good job persuading the High Commissioner to make a few persuasive phone calls or else he would have never had heard from Lestrade. He felt an immense burden on his shoulders. He was in the UK with no backup, to hunt down a murderous enigmatic figure that he was not sure existed.

Later that afternoon, Jeevan returned to the public library and searched the conference Website for all available information. He was convinced that the clue to Deccan Dhaku's target lay in the attendance list. A person of prominence, a strong advocate of or associated with nuclear disarmament, non-violence and peaceful co-existence, would be an ideal target. Jeevan was deep in thought when his cell phone started to vibrate. He walked away from the computers and went towards the entrance steps where he sat down to take the call.

"Is that Commander Gill? I'm Inspector Jim Paradis from Lincolnshire Police."
"Yes, I'm Commander Gill. I was expecting your call."
"Sir, we have your file from the Yard and I was wondering if we could meet. I have someone here who could help us in our enquiries."
"I would like to meet you as soon as possible."
"Where are you?"
"I'm in the Lincoln Cathedral library on Priory Gate. I am sitting on the steps at the entrance."
"Great, I'll send my constable right away."
Constable Watson found Jeevan and drove him to the Lincoln City Police Station. Inspector Paradis greeted Jeevan warmly and ushered him into his office.
"That will be all Watson," said Paradis. Watson nodded and shut the office door behind him as he left.
"Gosh, you are a long way from your home base in Puné, Commander Gill," remarked Paradis as he opened the folder that Lestrade had passed on to him.
"I've gone through the file and the DVD; frightening business. I can see what all the fuss is about."

Jeevan now found himself face to face with a local cop who had only just realized the gravity of the situation.
"I presume you hold the same opinion as Lestrade of Scotland Yard that the Air Kanishka super jumbo somehow exploded over the Southern Irish Sea and this terrorist is a figment of our imagination," said Jeevan.
"Not true, I intend to keep an open mind on this regardless of what the Yard thinks. This is all new to me so pardon me if I am somewhat slow to pick things up," Paradis fired back.
After a brief pause, Paradis continued, "I have a visitor in the interview room. He has a background that could help us. Let's have a chat with him, shall we?" said Paradis and then led the way.
They entered an interview room together and Jeevan found himself face to face with Paresh Naik.
"This is Prof. Naik from the University," said Paradis.
Paresh, who continued to read his email on his cell phone, did not bother to acknowledge his introduction. He was prompted to do so when Jeevan extended his hand and said, "Hi, I'm Commander Gill, military attaché for the Indian High Commission."
Paresh took Jeevan's hand in a limp handshake and gave him a cold blue stare as he sat down.
"I am looking for a suspect who blew up the Air Kanishka airliner just over two years ago. We believe he is still...," started Jeevan, awkwardly.

"Inspector Paradis has briefed me with the details. What do you want from me?" interrupted Paresh.
Jeevan raised his eyebrows as he glanced at Paradis.
"Where are you from Prof. Naik?" asked Jeevan.
"I'm Canadian."
"What is your country of origin?"
"I'm originally from Puné."
"You look like a typical Puné Brahmin," said Jeevan with a slight smile hoping to break the ice and be more personable. This did not solicit even the briefest response from Paresh who continued to fix Jeevan with a penetrating stare.
"Please briefly describe your research," requested Jeevan.
"My original mandate was to develop Virtual Reality simulations of business scenarios. However, I am applying this technology to develop teaching tools for special needs children."
"His research brought him into contact with my golf friend, Cynthia Amis, who works as a special education consultant at the local school board. I know of Prof. Naik's work through her," contributed Paradis.
"That's interesting. So, you are well known in the community. I hope you don't mind if I change the subject. Have you had anything to do with an organization called Deccan Dhaku in Puné?"
"No," said Paresh.
Jeevan then showed Paresh an image of Anil Godsé on his cell phone.
"Have you ever seen this gentleman, here in Lincoln or elsewhere?"
Paresh glanced at the digital image and replied, "No, I haven't."
His dismissive manner was not lost on either Jim Paradis or Jeevan.
"Just one last question Prof. Naik; when did you last visit India?"
"Five years ago when I attended my father's funeral," said Paresh.
"Then, that will be all. Thanks," said Jeevan and looked at Paradis as if to hand over any further interrogation to him.
Jim had nothing to ask and pressed the intercom button and said, "Watson, please show Prof. Naik out."
Jeevan sat pensively for almost a minute after Paresh had left and then turned to Jim and said, "He is lying about Anil Godsé. There is some connection between the two. I sense it, and I would like to find out what it is."
"Could he be an accomplice?" asked Jim.
"Possibly, but lets not rush to conclusions before some further background investigation. If you excuse me, I need to make a quick call to my boss at the High Commission."
"Go right ahead," said Jim. "For your information, we did a preliminary background check on Prof. Naik but nothing meaningful showed up in our UK database. Perhaps we need to see what comes up in Canada. I'll

make us some tea while you get on with your call." This got an appreciative thumbs up from Jeevan.

"Hello Mr. Tiru, this is Commander Gill," said Jeevan on his cell phone. "I've just interviewed a very interesting person here in Lincoln. His name is Paresh Naik and what is more he admits he came to UK via Canada. Could we do a check on him on his activities in Canada? His physical appearance has many features in common with Anil Godsé, since they both originate from Puné. There is something about him that makes me uneasy."

"I'll get Mavis to investigate this for us and report back. Her security company has been tying up some loose ends for us in Toronto ever since the Kashmir Princess fiasco," replied Tiru.

"Great! How is Mavis doing?" asked Jeevan.

"Well, much better now but she had a tough time starting her new security business. She broke up with her RCMP boyfriend soon after she left the force. I met her on my last trip to Canada when I was asked to appear before a Canadian Parliamentary committee that is investigating the security lapses in the Kashmir Princess bombing. I will email her report to you as soon as I get it," said Mr. Tiru before hanging up.

Jeevan smiled to himself as he speculated on the relationship between Mavis and Tiru. He thought they would make the quintessential odd couple, but miracles could happen!

Jim handed Jeevan a mug of tea and sat down on the table facing him. Jeevan appeared to be lost in thought.

"Should we keep Prof. Naik under surveillance?" Jim asked.

Jeevan took a while before he responded. He finally responded by shaking his head saying, "No, let's wait for the background check to come in first. My instinct tells me that, blue eyes and all, he's still not our man but there is a mysterious connection. He's out of place here. The moment I laid eyes on him, for some reason I cannot explain, I remembered an incident that occurred in Puné on the day of a terrorist attack, which as I had predicted, was a prelude to the Air Kanishka bombing."

"So is Prof. Naik linked to another terrorist incident?" asked Jim.

"Not necessarily," said Jeevan sipping his tea, "but on the morning of that bombing that kill 37 high school students and staff, a wandering sage recited a classical Sanskrit poem, outside my apartment. It was about the futility of revenge. I had the strangest feeling when I heard that verse. Something told me that I needed to communicate this message to someone else. As time passed on, I forgot about the sage and his message. When I walked into the interview room today, more than two years later and saw Prof. Naik, the sage's message came to mind immediately, as if it had only happen yesterday."

"Why didn't you tell Prof. Naik about the sage?" asked Jim.
"I couldn't work it into the conversation. Besides, that would imply that I suspected that he was about to commit an act of revenge. He could be a university professor on sabbatical from Canada."
"Cutting through the South Asian mystique, I surmise that your instinct tells you that Prof. Naik will seek revenge; on whom and why?" asked Jim.
Jeevan shrugged but did not respond.

Paradis and Jeevan made plans to co-ordinate their efforts. Paradis would do background checks on registered participants while Jeevan would continue to stake out gay pubs. Jeevan found working with Paradis a refreshing change from the condescending manner of Lestrade and his colleagues at MIQ. He found English Northerners friendly and jovial. Moreover, Paradis treated Jeevan as a cordial colleague and cooperated with him despite the modest resources at his disposal.

At night, Jeevan visited pubs in the city centre including The Groomsman. He often got into conversation with the patrons and passed himself off as a security consultant. Tradespersons, salesmen and the occasional University academic, visited the pub. The Groomsman was moderately full for a Friday night. With the conference due to start in six weeks, there were not many out of town faces, not at least at this pub.

The City took on a carnival like atmosphere. Conference banners were appearing everywhere. CANDO marketed the conference in UK and worldwide. Their logo featured a multi-racial handshake, with the flags of all the major participating countries, in a circular band around the circumference of a globe. Below the handshake was the conference's slogan, "Grass Roots Abatement of GHG". Storeowners or businesses that displayed the logo offered a ten percent discount on goods and services to all attendees.

Jeevan sat in the Groomsman and nursed his usual Newcastle Brown Ale, which he had taken a fancy to ever since he arrived in England. He gave it much thought and ruled out Paresh Naik being an alias of Anil Godsé. There was some thing strange about Prof. Naik. His physical appearance had many of the features that described Canadian Visitor. One stood for good, the other represented evil. It was an odd coincidence that he appeared soon after the time Canadian Visitor was rumoured to be in the UK. He asked himself, 'What was Prof. Naik doing here? Could his University job be a cover for something else?'

While these questions perplexed him, he knew the search for Canadian Visitor must still go on. He peered over the slight froth that crowned the wide brimmed glass. Jeevan glanced across the pub but could see no South Asian male. He emptied his glass and thought he would call it a day and walk back to his digs. He stood up to leave when a female voice, with a Mumbai English accent, caught his attention. He looked across the length of the pub and saw a tall, rather attractive woman he hadn't noticed before, in conversation with a group seated around a large round table. They seemed to hang on to every word she said. Jeevan pined for female companionship. Apart from a few visits to his family, whenever he could sneak a free ride to Delhi on his Government's Global Express, it had been all work and no play. Tiru kept him busy with many aspects of the conference planning other than security. Now his mission was to kill someone he had never met. He waited long enough. Mr. Godsé was unlikely to make an appearance tonight. Perhaps the Brahmin terrorist was too orthodox to drink alcohol and the intelligence reports on him were wrong.

He needed to let his guard down and relax. He wanted to stay on a little longer and strike up an acquaintance with the lady that had caught his attention. He walked over to the bar and ordered another pint of ale. He looked towards her table, which was now closer to where he stood. He could discern her features better. She wore a white top intricately embroidered with saffron coloured thread, which matched a saffron scarf. It had black patterned borders. Jeevan's heart raced. He felt compelled to meet her. Something about her drew him to her. He had seen that face before. It rung a bell but he couldn't remember where he had seen or met her. Jeevan glanced in her direction and caught her eye but she just looked away uninterested. The barman topped up Jeevan's drink. He glanced at the woman again. This time she gazed at him. He captured her gaze and held it for a few seconds before he smiled at her. She smiled back. A good start thought Jeevan to himself as he walked back to his table to strategize his next move.

Perhaps he could ask for directions and then linger on and introduce himself. As he summoned up courage to do this, Jeevan happen to glance in the opposite direction, towards a dimly lit section of the pub. He had wondered why there were no tables there. It turned out that it led to a stairwell for the pub's cellar. Above the stairwell's entrance a sign read, 4U2P.

He rose and walked slowly towards the sign. He was sure she was watching him. If she was interested, she could excuse herself from her table, to use the washroom, with the hope of running into him. He walked down a first short flight of stairs. This led to a square shaped landing and a left hand turn to another short flight that took him to the cellar floor.

He visited the gents and returned to walk up to the landing. As he turned to walk up the second set of stairs, the lady entered the stairwell. She hurried past him. He had just enough time to say "Hi".

Disappointed, he took one step up when it all came to him in a flash. Her proximity to him gave him the opportunity to take a much closer look at her. This prompted him to recall the conversation he had with Prof. Paranjpé in Puné, over two years ago, about the recruitment of Hijaras by the Deccan Dhaku. No wonder she looked familiar. It all became clear, and yet he hesitated and started to take the next step up, as he thought, no it can't be, not this beautiful woman. He should have known better. He then stopped and changed his mind. He thrust his hand frantically into his trouser pocket to grab his Glock 17. He started to turn and was ready to get the first shot at her straight through his trouser pocket, if required. However, as he completed his turn and looked down the stairwell, he was startled to see her already facing him with her right hand coiled back and adjacent to her torso. She thrust at him with her clenched fist and hit him in the neck, about the level of his Adam's apple. Jeevan sank to his knees, on the landing and clutched his throat. The apparition stepped past him. Jeevan was barely conscious as he felt her scarf wrap round his neck and tighten like a noose. He gasped for air as he desperately tried to stick his fingers under the scarf to loosen its grip. It was only then did he notice the black swastika border on the scarf. The scarf tightened round his neck like a boa constrictor. His assailant pulled back on his neck, with the two free ends of the scarf. She kept his upper body in place by pushing forward with her heeled shoe. Jeevan felt a sharp stiletto heel dig deep into his back. He could barely breathe let alone scream with pain. Jeevan's attempts to wriggle free soon became feebler, and his world got darker and darker; he lost consciousness. Soon the lion of Puné was no more

The Lincoln Chronicle headlined a story about the death of an Indian military attaché, in presumably a drunken brawl, at the Groomsman. Inspector Paradis and Constable Watson were shocked and grieved by the news. The search for Canadian Visitor became a priority but like Jeevan, they were now on their own. In spite of Jeevan's murder there was no national reference or concern about this killer, who was in their midst. This was Jim's first murder investigation. Murders were practically unknown in Lincoln. The county had one of the lowest homicide rates. A set of usual suspects, who frequented the Groomsman, were called in for questioning. The ferocity of the assault led Jim and his team to assume the perpetrator to be a male. None had anything more than petty larceny charges against them. The coroner's verdict, death by strangulation, did not explain the strange circular wound on the victim's back.

The staff, at the Indian High Commission in London, were in a state of shock. Those who worked with Jeevan couldn't believe what had happen. Only Tiru knew of Jeevan's true mission. Tiru and Anwar Khan called a hasty video conference and agreed to break their silence. Accordingly, Tiru informed the British press that a terrorist, code named Canadian Visitor, was most likely responsible for Commander Gill's death and had also sabotaged the Kashmir Princess, which crashed off the coast of Southern Ireland. He belonged to a UN banned terrorist group called the Deccan Dhaku whose sole purpose was to disrupt the CANDO Conference. Tiru claimed that Scotland Yard and MIQ had done little or nothing to catch Canadian Visitor who roamed freely in England for the last two years.

Scotland Yard retaliated by issuing its own press release. They claimed that their investigation had revealed that there was no one in the Lincoln area that matched the description of Canadian Visitor. They offered a grainy picture of Anil Godsé to the press. It showed a young Indian male, in his late twenties, with light brown complexion. He could easily be mistaken as a Mediterranean or Middle Eastern person. It showed his shoulder length hair with piercing blue eyes. Scotland Yard believed that Canadian Visitor had done his evil deed, that is the Kashmir Princess bombing, and returned to India. To add insult to injury, Scotland Yard opined that the Indian High Commission used Canadian Visitor myth to mask its embarrassment over the death of their military attaché in a gay bar brawl. They reassured the public that the conference was safe and secure. They warned the High Commission not to raise this issue again least it turn attendees away from the conference.

Chapter 26: Trouble in Paradise

Cynthia settled down to her role as a single mother. Her days were very long with special ed. consultations and travel from school to school to deliver seminars on special ed. topics. She often ended the day with parent/teacher meetings. Once at home, she finished dinner and argued with Lisa about homework. Later she assisted with her dyslexia exercises. Cynthia purchased a course based on the Orton-Gillingham method and figured out how to deliver it to Lisa. Lisa's reading and comprehension skills improved dramatically. The regular tutoring made the difference but Paresh's VR lab work had also enhanced her social skills and vocabulary. Lisa found the avatars to be kind, considerate and non-judgmental or anything Paresh could dial in to enhance her learning experience. What's more, Patelji worked with Vivienne to include age appropriate expressions. He used a software application to synchronize the avatars' lip movements and facial expressions with their dialogue. The avatars behaved like teaching assistants, both male and female, each with their own behavioural characteristics, ethnicity and accents.

Patelji made good use of the telescope that Paresh had given him. He spent his spare time on this new hobby and would occasionally skip his music and dance class at Miss Bolly's studio. His digital images of the Rings of Saturn and a small but noticeable object that he claimed to be Ganymede, the largest of Jupiter's Moons, stirred up much debate in the Astronomy Club at St. Cuthbert's. Cynthia was not interested merely in his advancement in science. She wanted him to emerge from his introvert shell and communicate his excitement to others. This opportunity came when he wrote an article for the school's newsletter on the probability of primitive life forms in the Solar system. She encouraged him to simplify his language and explain things in plain layman's terms. Later Cynthia persuaded the Lincoln Chronicle to publish Patelji's article. Patelji was the first St Cuthbert's student to have ever published anything in a newspaper. This boosted his self-esteem, and although he had a wider circle of friends, his best friend was still Lisa. The two argued, shared things and quarrelled just like siblings.

Both the kids fared well in school, and for the first time in years, Cynthia enjoyed a sense of personal and professional fulfillment. Special education support in the school system could improve, but at least with Lisa and Patelji, she saw positive results. Her busy schedule left her mind pre-occupied, however since the picnic, Paresh drifted into her head at almost every free moment. What is more, he trusted her. He was part of her new contentment, but he needed help. She would soon break the invisible barrier between them.

About mid-week, Uncle Noby and Lisa informed her of their plans to watch Manchester United play at Nottingham that weekend and return late at night. Apart from Bandit to keep her company, Cynthia realized she would be home by herself. She decided, on the spur of the moment, to invite Paresh for dinner. Paresh accepted the invitation but she noticed some hesitancy on his part, even when she enticed him with her lemon meringue pie.

Cynthia opened the novel she started to read at the picnic, and hoped she could read herself to sleep. She progressed a few pages, when the phone rang. A distraught Veronica spoke.

"You don't sound too good. Got a cold? What's up?" asked Cynthia sleepily and sat up because she thought it must be urgent or else why would Veronica phone at such an unearthly hour?

A long pause followed before Veronica answered.

"I've lost my baby!" wept Veronica.

It took seconds for Cynthia to grasp the significance of this announcement and longer for her to be filled with a sense of shock and dismay.

"I've lost my b-a-b-y!" she sobbed uncontrollably.

"Baby? What baby?" asked the astonished Cynthia. She didn't know how to interpret this strange news.

"I've known about my pregnancy for six weeks. I called Michael over during the weekend to tell him the news. He flew into a rage and almost struck me. He kicked and threw stuff around and claimed I tricked him. He demanded that I have an abortion before it was too late. He showed his true colours. I really wanted to keep the baby and raise it myself. I didn't need his support. I hadn't even told my parents. Then, earlier today, I got abdominal cramps and bled profusely. I called an ambulance. At Lincoln General they confirmed that I had a miscarriage."

A burning rage built up within Cynthia. That man Michael! Were there no limits to his egregious behaviour?

"I'm sorry to hear this," sympathized Cynthia.

"The strangest thing is," continued Veronica, "that when I informed the nurse that I was from the Evergreen Estates she said that she knew at least another five women who had miscarriages from the Estate. Is it anything to do with the well water? They only switched to the municipal supply two weeks ago."

"I don't know if you've read the latest edition of the Lincoln Chronicle. Aside from a crazy story that some terrorist is trying to stop the conference, the front page is about the Evergreen Estate scandal. It looks like your lover boy is in trouble," said Cynthia.

"For starters, he's not my anything!" yelled Veronica, and then regaining her composure continued, "We've broken up. I knew he has been seeing that Indian woman. Big hypocrite if you ask me, knowing his political views. I tolerated his cheating, thinking he'd come to his senses and see that it would not last. He has serious commitment problems and just wants to play around. I was just his passing fantasy. Anyway, my copy is in the recycling bin. What's this about a scandal?"

Cynthia had the goodness to refrain from saying, "I told you so." Instead, she welcomed the diversion and said, "This is regarding the sale of the air force base property, which is now Michael's Evergreen Estate. Our friend allegedly bribed Councillor MacMillan some years ago. He financed her mansion. The police found no evidence of any ancestral wealth, which she claimed she used to pay for it. Michael allegedly set up a fictitious ground water testing company, which cleared the base land for residential use and certified that the water was potable. This water was contaminated due to leakage from an Agent Orange storage facility, which was on the base. They used this defoliant in Vietnam. All this was hushed up when the sale was rushed through for approval, by Councillor MacMillan, at a City Council meeting. Michael bought the land and resold it to Evergreen Estate residents, like you. He knew it was contaminated."

"Why has all this only just come to light?" asked Veronica.

"The issue resurfaced a month ago when, just by chance, one of the conference vendors, which dealt with water purification, tested random samples from the estate. It was heavily contaminated. The City confirmed this by its own independent investigations. However, the dogged Chronicle reporter established the scandalous link between Michael and the councillor. He unearthed a microfiche of the bogus lab report from the City archives. Moreover, with the City on the defensive, the reporter coerced them into handing over a copy of the councillor's email account. The emails incriminated Michael. He is naïve about email. The Evergreen Estate residents have filed a class action lawsuit against the City, which includes Michael's real estate company. This is on hold, by mutual agreement, due to the conference. Some are calling for him to face criminal charges. Jim Paradis has been very busy."

"Michael will be brought to justice, and it serves him right. I might even join that class action suit," said Veronica with conviction, now sounding more like her usual self. The thought of getting even with Michael appeared to brighten her spirits.

"Oh look!" exclaimed Cynthia, "Jim is on BBC 1. Veronica, turn it on quick! They are probably discussing the Evergreen Estate scandal! I want to listen to this. I'll talk to you later."

Cynthia hung up and focused on the BBC channel to find Jim Paradis and two others, later identified as Inspector Lestrade of Scotland Yard and Mr. Krishnaswamy (Tiru), of the Indian High Commission in

London, in a stormy debate. The discussion concerned the murder of the Indian military attaché in the Groomsman but not the Evergreen Estate scandal. Tiru engaged Lestrade in an intense discussion. Jim Paradis tried not to take sides but attempted to make sense of it all. The BBC anchorman acted as moderator. He was about to question Lestrade when the TV debate drew her attention.

"Inspector Lestrade, I understand that the late Commander Gill sent Scotland Yard a copy of a mysterious but threatening email, and days later he was dead. Are you sure there is no terrorist lurking around Lincoln who goes by the code name Canadian Visitor?"
"Before I answer that question," said Lestrade, "I would like to offer my condolences to the Indian High Commission. I knew Commander Gill. I warned him not to take the law into his own hands but instead work with the Yard on this matter. Now regarding Canadian Visitor, the RCMP informed us that a terror suspect called Anil Godsé had left Canada for UK, and that he was responsible for the Air Kanishka bombing. Our extensive database for all UK ports of entry showed no record of any person that fitted that description. That crank email could have come from anywhere. We don't believe Canadian Visitor is in England."
"You are mistaken," asserted Tiru, "Anil Godsé is in England. What Scotland Yard may not know is that Mr. Godsé belongs to a sect of professional assassins called Dhaku who are masters of disguise. You may recall during the colonial days, there was a murderous gang of stranglers called the Thuggees. We suspect their descendants are alive and well in India, but now they call themselves Dhaku. It's no coincidence that the autopsy on Commander Gill determined that he was strangled. The Dhaku have now joined forces with a Nazi/fascist like right wing group called the Deccan Mandate. On the Indian sub-continent, this deadly alliance is known as the Deccan Dhaku. With encouragement from illegal arms dealers, who want to stifle any peace initiative, they are hell bent on stopping the CANDO conference."
The BBC moderator now turned to Tiru and said, "Come now Mr. Krishnaswamy, do you claim that these 19th century Indian assassins have somehow resurfaced in England and about to commit acts of terrorism here?"
"They are here, and now support a political agenda," remarked Tiru and then turning to Lestrade, Tiru asked, "How many of your staff do you have in position for the Lincoln Conference?"
"None at all at the moment; we have passed the file on to the local constabulary. The investigation is now in their jurisdiction," answered Lestrade nodding in Jim's direction.

"With all respect, Inspector Lestrade," said Tiru, "I would have thought you would dispatch your crack anti-terrorist team to Lincoln to protect the conference. The Deccan Dhaku will strike and ruin the conference. I warn that there will be dire political consequences, if it were cancelled. Billions of dollars are earmarked for a substantial UK supplier base, NGOs and contractors."
"You are being somewhat melodramatic. It's regrettable about Commander Gill but the report from Inspector Paradis's team suggests that he was killed in a pub brawl..." said Lestrade.
"We have not drawn that conclusion," interjected Paradis, and turning to Tiru he continued, "Let me assure you Mr. Krishnaswamy, I plan to keep an open mind on this. We know of only one person that vaguely fits the description that the Yard has sent me. The late Commander informed you that we interviewed this person of interest from Canada, and we will take further action as soon as we receive your Canadian background check."
"While we wait, I recommend that you arrest this person!" exclaimed Tiru.
"Not so fast Mr Krishnaswamy!" replied Jim, "We have our own ways of doing things here. I have a question. The saffron silk scarf, which Commander Gill was strangled with, had a border made up of black swastikas. Does this have a symbolic significance? "
"That's the calling card of the Deccan Dhaku; black swastikas on saffron. Now do we all agree that they are here in Lincoln?" asked Tiru.
"Couldn't you at least bring that suspect in again for questioning?" suggested the BBC anchor.
"We'll keep you all informed," said Paradis with a wry smile. He played his cards close to his chest. Scotland Yard had abdicated its responsibility. This was a great opportunity for Jim and his team to break new ground. If there were any truth in Tiru's concerns then it would be up to his department to find the underlying cause of things.

Cynthia switched off the TV in disgust. She couldn't believe what she had heard. Paresh had now become a prime terror suspect. She assessed him as a wounded genius who needed psychological help, but major pieces of the puzzle were still missing.

Chapter 27: Dr. Naik and Mr. Hyde

Michael's troubles did not deter him from enjoying life. His lawyers could tie things up for months before they even came to the Examination for Discovery. The City's lawyers prepared their own defence, and Councillor MacMillan's lawyer had much to say. With the best legal minds in Lincoln left to unravel the Evergreen Estate case, Michael went about his business without a care in the world.

His major preoccupation now seemed to be to find a way to seduce the beautiful but illusive Miss Bolly. They had been together several times. No matter how posh the restaurant, country club or casino they visited, her poise and charm drew attention and turned more heads than Michael had experienced on any other date. Miss Bolly always dressed fashionably and favoured European based Indian designers that gave her outfits a unique East meets West fusion look. She relished the good life and appeared to fit in seamlessly regardless of the venue. She surprised him with her love of fast cars. When they went out, she would pick him up in her red vintage Mercedes 300 SL. She loved to drive fast and Michael found himself white knuckling an armrest as she raced through the bends and curves of the narrow English countryside roads. Her wide knowledgebase proved that she was well read, educated and widely travelled. She could make conversation with anyone from a doorman to a duchess. Michael often felt like an escort rather than her boyfriend. He tried on many occasions to kiss her good night but she would just keep him at bay. She was cold and detached when it came to intimacy. Her evasiveness challenged Michael even further. He was determined to add her to his trophies. He realized that she was beyond his reach. He needed to change his strategy and try a different approach that would win her over.

One summers evening Michael decided to go to an abandoned drive-in theatre. This was built over strawberry fields. As a teenager, he would take his dates to what was then called the Strawberry Fields Drive-In. The City owned the land. He wanted to make an offer to buy the land and build a shopping Mall. He had to inspect the property and see for himself how much work was involved, as the grounds had not been maintained for years. As he approached the old drive-in, he noticed some activity in the main viewing area. He assumed vandals were at work, and possibly the same ones that disfigured his property with graffiti, he decided to travel past the drive-in and leave his car further along the road. He returned stealthily to investigate this further. Prior to exiting his car, he reached into the glove compartment and picked up his binoculars. He often used these to inspect roof tiling and down spouts. He crept passed the wrought iron gates and hid behind the old box office hut. He trained the binoculars on a lone figure and almost dropped them in amazement. It was Paresh Naik!

Paresh dressed in military styled camouflage fatigues, walked with a crossbow slung across his shoulder. Michael also heard a small portable electrical generator. Two projectors were located about ten metres apart. He noticed another device located about 50 metres away. It looked like a humidifier but it bellowed out smoke. He concluded that it must be a smoke generator, similar to those used in horror movies, to depict grim fog filled graveyard scenes. Paresh tapped the keyboard and both projectors sprang to life. Their overlapped beams created a 3-D image of a person running against the grey-blue smoky background. Another few taps caused the image to run from the right to the left. As the image disappeared on the left, a new, identical image emerged from the right and the cycle would be repeated. Paresh continued to tap the laptop's key board and changed the size of the image and its speed. The images were true lifelike scale and resembled a person jogging at ground level.

Paresh un-slung his crossbow and took up a prone position between the projectors. A thin ruby laser beam radiated from the crossbow. It seemed to penetrate the head of the image and followed it as it moved across the misty background. This went on for a few minutes, as Paresh was content to steady his arm and practise his ability to track the moving target while aiming at it through the crosshairs of its binocular telescopic sights. He then cranked up the cross bow, loaded an arrow, aimed and fired at the moving image.

To Michael surprise, a light emitting diode (LED) illuminated the arrow's base. Its purpose soon became apparent after Paresh finished shooting six arrows in quick succession. Paresh stood up and walked a short distance away to a tripod-mounted video camera. He studied the camera's playback screen. He could see the crossbow's laser beam and observe the arrow's trajectory. He made fine adjustments to the telescopic sight with a jewel screwdriver to ensure that the laser beam and the trajectory of the arrows intersected when they passed through the image's head. The arrows were caught in a fine-meshed net, which he had set up beyond the smoke generator. Paresh repeated the cycle of firing the crossbow and calibrating his telescopic sights until he was satisfied with the accuracy.

Michael realized he misjudged Paresh. He now concluded that Paresh masqueraded as a quiet professorial intellectual by day and turned into a murderous assassin by night. However, who has he planned to kill and why? He then recalled that he had interrupted a heated debate between his lawyers, earlier that day, while they waited for his arrival.

They discussed a newspaper article in the Manchester Guardian about a terrorist called Canadian Visitor; a Canadian with shoulder length hair and blue eyes, and the fact that Scotland Yard denied his existence. Bingo! Paresh was the perfect fit! He matched all the physical parameters as well as being Canadian. Moreover, he was now caught red handed preparing to shoot someone.

Michael never liked the man, particularly because of his close friendship with Cynthia. Just then, a car drove by on Penny Lane, which ran adjacent to the drive-in. Paresh glanced towards the entrance, and Michael crouched low just in time. His euphoria suddenly turned to fear. He knew he was in mortal danger if he were discovered. He had seen enough anyway and so decided to make a stealthy retreat. He pushed his Jaguar further along Penny Lane before starting the engine with the lights off.

Michael was a good businessman and tried to figure out ways in which he could capitalize on his discovery. His preoccupation was still Miss Bolly. Now a unique opportunity presented itself. This could have her indebted to him. He remembered she had told him that her Bollywood Dance and Music studio was undertaken to fill in the time until the start of the conference. She was in Lincoln to cover the CANDO Conference for a syndicate of Indian newspapers. The news scoop he would present her with was a once in a lifetime event for most reporters. He called her right away.

"Bolly, it's Michael. Listen, you need to drop everything and meet me right away!" said Michael with confidence and a somewhat bolder stance from his usual pleading and compromising in her favour, when he would ask her to go out with him.

"Well, I can't come now I am just off for my jog. Can't it wait?" asked Miss Bolly.

"I wouldn't have bothered you this late in the evening if it wasn't very important. I would like to meet you tonight. The information is critical in your role as news reporter for the CANDO Conference," reasoned Michael.

"Give me a hint what this is all about before I decide," said Bolly getting irritated by Michael's persistence.

"You will never believe what I have seen. I have information regarding the so called Canadian Visitor," tempted Michael.

There was silence at the other end of the line, and then Miss Bolly said, "Michael this better be good or else you will be in trouble."

"You won't regret this. It is the news scoop of the century! I'll see you after your jog at the Saracen's Head. Just walk through to my back-office," said Michael.

Chapter 28: The Dance of Shiva

Soon after Michael retreated, Paresh started to pack some of his equipment away into the back of his station wagon. He reached into a box and removed a pair of night-vision goggles. He put them on and adjusted each individually. He looked at his reflection in his station wagon's large rear door window and smiled to himself. The protruding lenses were comical. He looked like an alien creature. He couldn't use the ruby laser to line up his target since its beam, and the source could be visible with deadly consequences. It had served its purpose and allowed him to adjust the crossbows sights. He had just one shot, and it had to be perfect.

Paresh had experimented with a miniature short-range Doppler radar system, which was small enough to snap on to the base of the crossbow's stock. It could isolate and track a target such as a jogger. It could track targets that travelled at speeds between 2 to 35 feet per second, which covered the speed range for walking to sprinting adults. A crossbow arrow travels at about 300 ft per second. A snail's pace compared to a rifle bullet. At a distance of 300 ft, a jogger running at 5 ft per second would have moved 5 feet, by the time the arrow reached him/her. One needed to know the target's velocity in order to aim the shot ahead of it. Paresh resolved these problems by using the best available technology. He linked the binocular sniper-scope to the Doppler radar unit by a visual interface. This visual interface produced a "ghost" image of the moving target, ahead of the real image, by calculating the offset distance. All Paresh had to do is to set the crosshairs on the ghost image and pull the trigger. Furthermore, there was no time to read any scrolled text messages in the seconds that it would take to acquire and shoot his victim. The radar unit would communicate with him via pre-recorded voice instructions heard through his earphones.

Little did Michael know that Miss Bolly would soon jog along Penny Lane, past Strawberry Fields, where an assassin lay in wait. He had adjusted his weapon's sights and fine-tuned his archery skills. He observed her regular jogs and knew to within a few minutes when she would jog by the drive-in. He had selected the best place to set up. There was an ideal spot with a break in the shrubbery. This area had a slight elevation. He looked down the lane with his night vision goggles, and he saw a lonely figure moving towards him. She wore a high visibility tracksuit. He could see through his binocular sniper-scope that she had her mp3 player earphones on. She was partial to German classical music. The imperial sounds of Wagner's *Ride of the Valkyries* appeared to put an extra spring in her step.

Paresh activated the Doppler radar and adjusted the volume on his headset. The electronic voice announced, *target acquired* and commanded, *track target, track target...*

Paresh responded and placed the sniper-scope's crosshairs over Miss Bolly's head. Just then an eerie and yet familiar feeling overcame him. Oh no! He was having his flashbacks again. No, no, not now please he said to himself in desperation. In the past, when not in public view, he could overcome these painful flash backs by meditation. He rubbed his eyes, shook his head and got on with the business at hand. It only got him a temporary reprieve. He looked through the sniper-scope and saw that the system had already superimposed a faint outline of the target's ghost image. *Target approaching kill zone in 20 seconds* advised the system. Suddenly, the image cleared, and a scene from decades ago appeared in its place. It was Paresh's grandmother, who scolded him and his pre-teen friends about a fight they had gotten into over a disputed leg-before-wicket call. His grandmother wiped his bloodied nose with a towel, as Paresh boasted to his friends that the other guy got the worst of it. She gripped Paresh's upper arm and turned him to face Lord Shiva's statue in their living room.

"Shiva invites you to dance with him as he creates and destroys parts of the Universe. Haven't I told you to always dance on his creative side? Negotiate your quarrels. Be creative and never seek revenge. An eye for an eye will leave a world full of blind people," said the wise greying lady.

Paresh shook his head vigorously and said to himself. "Sorry grandma wherever you are, this woman took away everything I lived for. I am blind with rage already. Now she must pay the price."

With added determination, he looked through the sniper-scope again. *Ten seconds to kill zone* warned the Doppler radar unit. The ghost image had a stronger outline indicating an increase in signal strength and the accuracy of the offset prediction. Next, Cynthia appeared on the screen where the ghost image should have been.

Paresh blinked in annoyance. Is there no way to stop this madness? He asked himself. Cynthia was scolding him too, "Paresh what on earth are you up to? The kids and I need you. What you are about to do will ruin things for all of us."

Then Patelji entered the scene and reinforced her concerns, with his plea, "Please Uncle Paresh, please don't do this. You think it's easy to be a gifted kid? Some kids make fun of me; others steal my lunch money and beat me. My parents were killed by terrorists, and for a long time I thought of nothing else other than revenge or suicide. When I met Miss Cynthia and you, my whole world changed for the better. My telescope can only explore the solar system like the beautiful rings of Saturn. I want

to explore the Universe but I cannot do that without your help. Can you not move on to better things just like I have?"
Release safety instructed the unit. Paresh noticed that a bright red colour filled the ghost image, and it began to flash urgently. He could hear Miss Bolly's footsteps approach.
*Target in kill zone, target in kill zone, target in kill zone …*barked the unit.
Just then, an image of Lisa appeared to make a final plea, "Paresh, I need you more than ever now. Everyone other than Mom and you has deserted me. I was raped and abused as a foster child. The school board never gave me the support I needed. You guys helped me to forgive and forget. Can you not do the same for me?"
Shoot now, shoot now, shoot now... insisted the unit and then emitted a final continuous screech. Paresh squeezed the trigger. However, as the arrow sped away on its deadly flight, along a guide rail, he deliberately raised the stock.

Miss Bolly was oblivious to what was happening around her. She assumed she was alone and was enjoying the final crescendo of Wagner's Symphony and playfully conducted an imaginary orchestra with her arms. If the projectile had hit her, at least she would have died a happy person. Instead, it sailed past her harmlessly above her head. With Wagner blaring through her earphones, she neither saw nor heard anything.

Paresh rolled over on his back, lay still and looked at the rare cloudless English sky. As his eyes grew accustomed to the dark void beyond, thousands of tiny starlets and entire galaxies came out to greet him. He took in the expanse of the universe, and the promise it held for those that want to learn from it. For once, in over two years, he felt completely at ease and at peace with himself; no more awkward flash backs. He had cured himself. He met his nemesis head-on and proved that he could destroy her if he wanted to. There must be a better way to stop her without ruining it for Cynthia and the kids.

Paresh stood up and removed the cantankerous Doppler radar unit. He threw it into the wooded lot beyond the drive-in, leaving only the laser unit that was firmly screwed on to the crossbow's stock.

Patelji was in mortal danger but with the conference still two weeks away, he was convinced that Miss Bolly would not try anything until they got closer to the starting date. He had scheduled for a long awaited tête-á- tête with Cynthia that weekend. Together, he thought, they could plan an escape route for Patelji.

Chapter 29: Canadian Visitor Strikes Again

Michael paced the floor while he waited for Miss Bolly to arrive. He was convinced that he had witnessed a terrorist preparing for an assassination. He mused to himself that now he could kill two birds with one stone. He would finally win back Cynthia's respect, and if he played his cards right, he could even coerce sexual favours from Miss Bolly. His greed and total lack of professional integrity, in his business dealings that had resulted in serious illness, possible cancerous death and miscarriages for many expectant mothers, did not seem to bother his conscience.

Miss Bolly arrived and wore the same tracksuit in which, unbeknown to her, she had a close escape. Michael poured her a stiff drink and went on to relate what he had seen earlier that evening.

"What a coincidence." said Miss Bolly, "That lunatic played with his toys just before I went for a jog past Strawberry Fields."

"Yes indeed," said Michael. He still did not realize that Miss Bolly was the intended target.

"Well Michael, I must say you have surpassed yourself! If your narration were true, then this would make a spectacular story. Now, not a word to anyone while I snoop around and make a few enquiries," said Miss Bolly as she placed a finger on his lips.

Michael took her hand in his and kissed the top of her knuckles softly. He peered at her in the most Don Juan manner he could muster and said, "Would you like to come over to my place where we can celebrate this opportunity!"

"Dear Michael," said Miss Bolly, "You disserve a rich reward. However, since this is going to be our first time, I want it to be special for both of us. The ambiance has just got to be right."

"Absolutely, my dear," said Michael with his voice going hoarse with rising emotion. He kissed her forearm and continued kissing her upper arm. He negotiated her neck, when Miss Bolly diplomatically placed her hand on his forehead and stroked his hair.

"Save all your energy for later lover boy! You will need all your strength for what I have planned for you," said Miss Bolly as she fixed him with a coy smile.

"Anything, anything you say my love," said Michael with heated passion that rivalled any fever he ever had.

"Let's meet inside Lincoln Cathedral at 9 pm this Friday." she suggested, "I've always fantasized about doing something naughty in a holy place."

"What a great idea! The tourists and worshippers would have gone by then, and we will have the place to ourselves. What is more, we'll teach those hypocrites a lesson. For centuries they have been going to pray in

cathedrals like this then they colonized and exploited your people," said Michael as he tried to ingratiate himself to Miss Bolly.
"More significant is that Lincoln Cathedral owns the original Magna Carta manuscript that gave civil society it first taste of fundamental freedoms, colonized or otherwise. I think we should interpret this as giving us the freedom to do whatever we want in there. You would never have guessed, love conquers all!" said Miss Bolly and stopped to ask, "Do you have a set of realtor's skeleton keys that I could borrow?"
"I do have a set for Evergreen Estate. I won't ask what you intend to do with them," said Michael giving Miss Bolly a wink. He reached into his desk draw and retrieved a set of odd-looking thin keys and handed the bunch to Miss Bolly.
"One of these should open almost any residential front door lock in Lincoln. Happy snooping," he added.

Miss Bolly took the keys and hastened on her way.

That evening, Paresh returned to his flat and stored his crossbow and quiver of arrows under his bed. In the days that followed, he didn't give it a second thought. He spent long hours in the lab to finish Lisa's final dyslexia VR module. The future seemed uncertain for him, and now he needed to concentrate on getting Patelji out of harms way. He was unaware that Michael had just blown his cover. Miss Bolly realized that Paresh was a major threat to her mission and went about executing an ingenious plan to neutralize him.

Michael couldn't wait for Friday. The anticipation of making love with the most beautiful and smartest woman he had ever met was unbearable. He was blinded by passion and was so overwhelmed with a notion of male conquest that it had marred his judgment.

When Friday arrived, he drove uphill towards the cathedral and parked his Jaguar beside Miss Bolly's red SL 300. She was already in there waiting for him. His expectations added to his excitement and he found himself uncomfortably erect as he walked towards a side entrance. He entered hoping not to attract attention even though it was dark. He moved into the huge cavernous gothic cathedral and walked into the broad space between the front seats and the steps that led to the main alter. He retreated towards the shadows adjacent to the nearest wall as he surveyed the vast expanse of seats and adjacent passages. He looked everywhere, but could see no one.

Just as he began to feel a bit foolish and disappointed, music filled the entire cathedral. It was a melodious tune accompanied by a rhythmic and lively tabla beat. Miss Bolly stepped from behind a gothic pillar and broke into a choreographed dance sequence. She looked stunning in a blood red mini-skirt, with a saffron churidar and a pearled chocker. She spun in the air and even did a summersault much to Michael's delight. She displayed an excellent talent for fusion dance that comprised an even mix of classical Bharatanatyam and modern ballet. As she pirouetted and jumped through the air like a graceful gazelle, she moved closer and closer to Michael who stood his ground with open-mouthed amazement. Miss Bolly's physical prowess excited Michael as he yearned for intimacy with her.

Then the music stopped as suddenly as it started. Michael clapped enthusiastically. The sound of his applause echoed in the cathedral's towering heights. He removed his jacket, threw it on the nearest pew and walked towards her.

Miss Bolly held a black gloved hand up in the air and said, "Stay where you are! I have another surprise."

However, her voice sounded different as though someone else was speaking. It was a male voice with a pronounced Indian accent.

"What's up with your voice Bol? Got a sore throat?" asked Michael with genuine concern.

"This is what I really sound like," said Anil Godsé as he reached to pick up an object from an adjacent bench. It was the crossbow that he had stolen, unbeknown to Paresh, using the skeleton keys that Michael had given him.

Michael looked at the person in front of him. She looked identical to Miss Bolly. Then he noticed something different; her eyes. They were light blue and glistened like shiny marbles. He then noticed her chocker. This consisted of three rows of white pearls. Set within this backdrop of white pearls was a repeated pattern of black pearls. The pattern of nine black pearls resembled a band of Nazi swastikas round her neck.

A mechanical click resounded through the cathedral as Godsé flicked back the crossbow's safety latch. A thin ruby red laser beam produced a tiny red spot of light on the towering ceiling above him. Michael followed the beam to the spot where it reached the ceiling. He watched the spot race down the wall, over his head and momentarily dazzled him as it crossed his face and proceeded further down and pointed straight at his genitals.

Michael raised his hands in mock surrender and said, "Wait a minute Bol, don't shoot me there that would be bad for both of us!"

He assumed that the music, dance, the voice, the crossbow's laser beam and the cathedral's ambience were all part of Miss Bolly's seduction strategy. This excited him even further.

"Where do you want it then? Here?" asked the voice directing the laser spot at a position close to his navel.

"Put that thing down before it goes off by mistake and come over here Bol," reasoned Michael.

The red spot moved to the upper left region of his thorax.

The voice recited a verse in Sanskrit.

"What is it that you said?" asked Michael as he sensed that something was terribly wrong.

"Now I have become death, the destroyer of worlds," translated Godsé as he squeezed the trigger.

The arrow sliced through Michael. He was dead before his body fell to the floor.

Chapter 30: The Canadian Visitor is Nabbed

Sergeant Jim Paradis was rarely woken up at 2 am, in the call of duty. Lincoln, with its low crime rate seldom warranted such urgency. When Constable Watson called, he knew, even before he picked up his departmental cell phone, that something serious had occurred.
"Sorry to bother you guv," said the agitated young constable, "The janitor at Lincoln Cathedral just called to say that there is a man's body in the cathedral. He claims that the deceased was done in with an arrow."
"You must be joking!" exclaimed Jim, "First, someone strangled that Indian High Commission guy and now this. We have had more murders in the last two weeks than I have seen in twenty years!"
"But, you will never guess who it is," challenged the constable.
"Who is the deceased?" demanded Jim.
"It's Michael Caruthers, guv. He has been murdered!" said Watson in a grave tone.
"Oh Crikey!" exclaimed Paradis. He paused for a few moments and said, "I'll be there in fifteen minutes. Cordon off the cathedral. The whole place is now a crime scene."

Jim arranged for the transportation of Michael's body to the coroner's office, while he returned to his office with the crossbow, found at the scene. He waited until 8 am before he called Noby Clark, the local expert on all things to do with archery.

He first broke the news of Michael's death and eventually got around to asking Noby's opinion on the crossbow. Before Jim had a chance to complete its description, Noby said firmly, "That's Paresh Naik's crossbow. I am sure. There is only one of those in England. It's a custom built Canadian crossbow, with those mod cons that he has added to it."
"Thanks Noby. I am going to rely on you to inform Cynthia," said Jim Paradis.
"I didn't care too much for Michael. But, this is shocking! … shocking!" was Noby's response.

Paresh and Cynthia planned to get together, tell all and sort things out between themselves. Instead, Cynthia found herself with Murphy and Veronica, seated around her coffee table. She had a large pot of brewed tea. A freshly baked cake helped to ease the grim occasion. Murphy remarked at the homely aroma, as he walked in to join the impromptu condolence meeting of the three childhood friends. Their lives in Lincoln, a paragon of English serenity, were affected by world events. They did not associate the murder with the much talked about conference. This realization gradually dawned on them and the rest of Lincoln.

Cynthia wanted Paresh to join them, but he didn't answer his phone. He promised to be with her by this time but was inexplicably absent. Uncle Noby had left town with Lisa to attend a football match, as they had planned.

The trio realized the trouble Michael had got himself into, and the pain, illness and possibly death, he had caused amongst the Evergreen Estates residents. The scandal linked to Councillor MacMillan made its own way through the legal system. Over the months, each put a safe distance between themselves and Michael. Veronica ultimately acknowledged wisdom of Cynthia's earlier warnings. However, the atmosphere this afternoon was one of deep regret over a loss of a childhood friend.

"No one is perfect. Let's not be judgmental. Let's focus on who could have done this and see if any of this makes sense," said Cynthia as her friends leaned on her for comfort and strength.

"Michael cheated on me and deceived the Evergreen residents, but he didn't deserve this," said Veronica tearfully as she rested her head on Murphy's shoulder. He put his arm around her to comfort her and enquired, "Could it be an Evergreen Estate resident?"

"More likely one of his ex-lovers. He had others besides Veronica and me," offered Cynthia. The trio fell into a contemplative mood.

The telephone rang and broke the silence. The ring startled Veronica; on an edge. She spilled her tea over her dress. While Murphy helped her clear up the mess, Cynthia answered the phone.

"Hi Jim. What's up?" she asked, recognizing Jim Paradis's voice.

"Were you with Paresh Naik last night?" he asked.

"No, but I expected him to drop in this morning," replied Cynthia.

"We've had to bring Paresh in for questioning. I hoped you could provide him with an alibi. His crossbow was found near Michael's body with his finger prints all over it. There are no other finger prints on the weapon," said Jim.

"That's ridiculous! You must release him immediately. I don't know what trouble Michael got himself into, but it's got nothing to do with Paresh," said Cynthia angrily.

"I'm sorry, I can't do that. He does have a motive," said Jim.

"What would that be?" demanded Cynthia.

"Paresh and Michael were rivals for your affection," said Jim bluntly.

Cynthia blushed like a fifth former, on a first date, at the thought that someone would link her to Paresh romantically. She never felt like this before. She longed to see Paresh. She thought about their planned rendezvous all week. She would finally lift the mystery that separated them, and they would become united as a couple. His inaccessibility made her yearn for him. She put the phone down, sat with her head in her hands and tried to figure things out. She knew he disliked Miss Bolly, from his strange behaviour at Veronica's birthday party. That Paresh would want to harm Michael didn't make sense. Was all this linked to something he planned to reveal to her today?

Veronica and Murphy wanted to plan Michael's funeral although his body would still be retained at the coroner's. It helped to channel their grief into doing something. They, after all, were his only "family". They gave each other tasks to do and only turned to Cynthia occasionally to get her approval. Cynthia noticed a developing intimacy between them. She wondered why it took so long to realize that they had feelings for one another. Perhaps, Murphy's newfound self-confidence and assertiveness had caught Veronica's eye.

Cynthia waited all weekend hoping to get a call from Jim telling her to come over to the police station and drive Paresh home. Her calls were never returned.

Late Sunday evening, Lisa and Uncle Noby returned from their football weekend. They were inseparable when it came to football. Cynthia ignored their constant arguments and challenges regarding historical statistics of the English Premier League or past World Cup matches. The latest argument concerned who scored the winning goal for Manchester United in June of the previous year. She turned a deaf ear to the conversation and attended to some chores. Lisa went to the bathroom to prepare for bed while Uncle Noby explored backed up data on the family's multi-terabyte backup drive, in a folder that stored the recorded Premier League Games.

"That's another fiver you'll owe me luv," he shouted after Lisa. "At this rate you'll be handing over your entire first pay cheque."

"No way!" was Lisa's muffled good-humoured response.

Uncle Noby searched using a date range until he found what he wanted. He fast-forwarded the relevant match but he stopped when he came across something unrelated to football, which caught his eye.

"Hey Cynthia," he called out, "Come see, your Mr. Paresh was on TV." It turned out that during half-time, the TV station broadcasted the news and weather. This too got recorded.

Cynthia hurried over expecting to see the current news but soon realized it was news from over a year ago, about the time she first met Paresh.

The commentator described an anniversary gathering, at Cork, Ireland, of hundreds of relatives of the Air Kanishka disaster. They assembled at a newly erected memorial monument to the victims. A black glossy sundial monument stood in a coastal Park. It faced the open Irish Sea where portions of the aircraft, Flight 281, which exploded in mid-air, had come to rest. A paved patio that surrounded a stone circular sundial, led to a curved wall. The wall had polished black granite rectangular panels, embedded in it. The names of 529 victims were engraved, in gold, along each panel.

Loved ones scanned the memorial. Some lovingly caressed the names of their family members on the granite stone panels. Others stood by and reverently bowed their heads and some wept openly. There were widows who had lost their husbands, others that lost their husbands and children. There were widowers who had lost their wives and children. Friends who had lost friends and siblings that had lost siblings. The people appeared to be mostly of Indian origin but there were also many other nationalities represented.

Later the mourners reassembled on the beach. A choir from a neighbouring school had assembled and sang, “Abide with Me” and “Saving Grace”. Since the hymns' words were secular, Sikhs, Muslims, Hindus, Christians, Jews and other denominations and beliefs, appeared to mouth the chorus and some even sang whole-heartedly. After the hymns the local residents mingled with the mourners; some recognized each other, from their first visit during the fateful week of the air crash, a year earlier. Many shook hands and hugged. A bond of friendship and understanding existed between the visitors and the local residents. Children presented them with small bouquets. Many placed the bouquets of flowers on the waves of the out going tide. Lanterns were launched into the sea. These consisted of candles mounted on a floatation base surrounded by a protective cylindrical sidewall, about four inches in height. Soon hundreds of tiny lights seemed to float on a fortuitous current, in a procession going out to sea. The camera panned the beach and stopped to focus on one solitary male figure. He looked at the lights as they drifted away and then turned towards the mourners. The camera zoomed in. It was unmistakably Paresh Naik!

Cynthia covered her mouth as she let out a gentle scream. Lisa rushed to her side. They both knelt on the carpet before the TV screen. Uncle Noby reached for the remote and froze the frame that showed an enlarged image of Paresh.

Cynthia stood up but Lisa clung to her waist, to support her and looked up at her as if to ask – Are you, okay? The child could sense that Cynthia was going through a painful moment and needed help.

Cynthia’s complexion turned pale as the blood drained from her face. Her knees seemed to buckle, and Noby reached out to steady her on her feet and gently lowered her to the couch. Lisa fetched a glass of water.

Cynthia sipped the water and said, “Thanks, I feel better now.”

Her mind raced through the events over the past year that brought Paresh and her together, from the very first time they met, to his present incarceration at the local constabulary. Her logical and analytical mind started to put into place the pieces of the puzzle, which was the abiding mystery of Paresh Naik.

"I've been blind … we've been blind and unfair to expect so much from Paresh. All the time, he was a victim of the cruellest act of terrorism, which you could imagine. He needed our help to cope with his loss. He was just an ordinary person with a family then ... boom, suddenly it was all over. He is so traumatized by the murder of his wife and two beautiful kids that he still has painful flash backs and never wants to talk about his family. Some people think he is crazy. His flashbacks are symptomatic of PTSD. Our troops, who have returned from Iraq and Afghanistan, often suffer from PTSD, after being exposed to the carnage there. I still don't know why he came to Lincoln. When I first met him, he must have just participated in this memorial ceremony, in Cork. I recall that his station wagon had Irish number plates."

Cynthia's explanations seemed to go over Lisa's head. The previous uncertainty in her life made her feel anxious. She suddenly felt insecure and wondered whether it was going to fall apart, all over again, as it had done in the past.

"Is everything going to be alright?" she asked anxiously.

"Paresh is in trouble, but we will help him. Everything will be fine because Cynthia and I will always look out for you sweetie," said Uncle Noby giving Lisa a reassuring hug.

The next day, the Monday, following the worst weekend Cynthia could remember, armed with Uncle Noby's DVD, she went to see Jim Paradis at the constabulary. The local newspapers and radio stations were a buzz over the sensational murder of the controversial real estate developer. They claimed that a suspect was helping police with their enquiries, but mentioned no name. When Cynthia called the Rama Lab, Vivienne told her that someone called on behalf of Paresh and said that he had taken a week's sick leave to cope with nervous exhaustion. Since school was out, Cynthia decided to take Lisa and Patelji along to increase pressure on Jim Paradis. The children were distraught at the thought that Paresh might be in jail.

A rather sombre and tired looking Jim greeted them at the police station. He ushered the party into the interview room and shut the door.

"Where's Paresh? Could we see him now?" asked Lisa.

"Uncle Paresh has done nothing wrong. Why are you holding on to him?" demanded Patelji.

"Paresh Naik is safe and is well looked after," Jim assured the children. "He is helping us with our enquiries because his crossbow was used to kill Michael Caruthers."

"Is he being charged with anything?" asked Cynthia.
"No" said Jim.
"You should charge him or set him free. You have detained him for more than forty-eight hours," said Patelji.
Cynthia smiled to herself. The young lad, that Paresh had taught self-advocacy and to stand up to bullies, was now fighting for Paresh's rights!
"Forty-eight hours, that's two days isn't it mom?" asked Lisa.
"Good girl!" applauded Cynthia.
"I've been practising time periods with my language avatar. I know all about quarterly reports, 1st quarter, 2nd quarter, semi-annual, annual, fortnight, year end, fiscal year ..."
"Language avatar?" interrupted Jim, raising his eyebrows.
"Don't ask," said Cynthia shaking her head, "That's Paresh's latest virtual reality animation. I don't know why I am advocating for his release, he's going to put special ed. teachers out of business. Would he need a lawyer? "

Jim wore a frustrated expression as the he looked uneasily at the children and said, "Could you kids wait outside, please? I want to talk to Cynthia alone."
Once they had left the room, he whispered to Cynthia, "I can't release him because Special Branch came by and took over the file, saying that it was a matter of national security. They have transferred him to a detention centre. He has been detained under the UK Terrorism Act and has no access to lawyers."
"Well, in that case," said Cynthia, reaching into her handbag and handing Jim a copy of the Air Kanishka memorial ceremony, on a USB flash drive, "ask them to take a look at this. Paresh is not a terrorist, but a victim of terrorism."

She explained the significance of the evidence on the flash drive. Jim reflected momentarily and then said, "Thanks, this will help his cause. However, I should warn you, criminals have a nasty tendency of returning to the crime scene. This may not be enough to clear his name."

Cynthia stood up and walked towards the door. Before she opened it to leave, she turned to Jim and said, "Just think, while poor Paresh is languishing in a detention centre, the real terrorist is still at large and planning his next move."

To her surprise, Jim responded, "And just between you and me Cynthia, this is not an open and shut case. As far as I am concerned, regardless of the MIQ intervention, my investigation isn't over yet! The Indian High Commission is running a background check in Canada. This could be crucial towards clearing his name."

Chapter 31: Good Golly, It's Miss Bolly

Veronica and Murphy's careful planning of Michael's funeral paid off. Friends and business associates received email announcing Michael's funeral arrangements. The real estate office placed posters on the public notice boards, in the Evergreen Estate. An announcement appeared in the Lincoln Chronicle's Death Notices section.

Although Michael had not been forthright about the ground water contamination issues, many concluded that his ignorance of the carcinogenic nature of Agent Orange caused him to underestimate its effect on ground water and consequently its impact on the health and welfare of the estate's residents. Michael had hoped the problem would just go away. Other than that, Michael's popularity on the estate had not reduced.

Many tenants and property owners came to pay their respects. A few eulogies followed a simple church ceremony. The casket was transported to the local crematorium. The mourners gathered in the church basement where Veronica and Murphy had arranged for refreshments. They stood in small groups. The conversation divided between the lawsuit now directed towards the City, and rumours that a University professor might somehow be implicated in this crime. Some tenants singled Murphy out. They inquired about the Evergreen Estate Office and arrangements for the maintenance and rent collection. Murphy drew everybody's attention and announced that the Estate's residents would be contacted as soon as Michael's papers and Will were reviewed. The crowd gradually started to thin out. Veronica, Cynthia, Murphy and Inspector Jim Paradis were the largest group of people left.

"Jim," said Veronica, "Murphy has an interesting theory or concern."

"Is that true Murphy? What would this theory be?" asked Jim turning to face Murphy.

"It's plain speculation, and I rather speak to you in private if you don't mind," said Murphy clearly annoyed with Veronica for putting him on the spot.

"If there is anything you can say to help Paresh, speak up now!" demanded Cynthia.

"It's okay Murphy, I'll consider it off the record. You can always make a formal statement later. Right now, I'm just scratching around for clues. I am dumbfounded by these two murders. I'll be happy to accept anything from the best friend of the deceased."

"Well then here it is," whispered Murphy. "I never told anybody this because I was embarrassed by the whole incident. Michael and I bet against each other at Veronica's party that the first one to get Miss Bolly into bed would win a hundred pound. That night, I offered to drive Miss

Bolly home. Well …I must have had a lot to drink and shouldn't have been driving. I dropped Bolly off at her place and while I was saying a long goodbye, I decided to make my move and kiss her. She tried to push me a way and in the struggle my hand brushed passed her genitalia." Murphy stopped his narration and looked towards Veronica and said, "I wish you didn't have to hear this."

"Oh but I do Murphy. I really do. Your late friend cheated on me with the same woman. If we are to move forward with our relationship, I would expect you to be more honest with me," said Veronica firmly.

Murphy turned towards Jim and said, "Miss Bolly was furious and first punched me in the face and broke my nose. Then she gripped my throat, with a vice like grip and told me that if I didn't shut my mouth about this, I would be a dead man. When I finally came to, I found myself outside the Saracen's Head, but to save face, I lied to Constable Watson that I was mugged."

"Why would she want to kill you just for making a clumsy pass?" asked Jim.

"Because I found out that she's not …she's…" hesitated Murphy.

"Speak up man! This could be important!" demanded Jim.

"She's a bloke! She is a what-you-may-call-it ..."

"You mean to say she is a transvestite," prompted Cynthia.

Murphy gave and embarrassed nod. Veronica broke into a laugh, but checked herself and said, "So Michael left me to court a man?"

"Why didn't you at least take Michael, your best friend, into your confidence?" asked Jim.

"I wanted Michael, who always boasted about his prowess with women, to make a fool of himself. I didn't think it would come to this. She done it I tell you! That bitch murdered our Michael!" shouted Murphy.

"I guess, under the circumstances, all bets are off," asserted Jim with his eyes narrowed and brows furrowed, deep in thought.

He then continued, "But that's a serious allegation to make of such a fine and cultured lady who is well respected," and looked at Cynthia and said, "and her contribution to broadening our knowledge of South Asian culture is acknowledged by our school board.''

Nevertheless, Murphy's outburst gave the group much to ponder over as they stood together.

"What if it can be proved that Michael's death is some how linked to these rumours regarding a Canadian terrorist, hell bent on breaking up the CANDO Conference?" speculated Cynthia.

Jim didn't answer her immediately. He paced the floor as he struggled with a fresh lead, which he had never considered. Then, he got quite animated and said, waving his finger at Murphy, "You know lad, your

theory may not be that far fetched after all, and as Cynthia implied, there may be a linkage to the ongoing terrorist threat."
Jim then whipped out his smart phone and pressed a shortcut key that connected him straight to Watson.
"Watson, logon to the imaging software and load the picture of that Canadian Visitor chap, which the Yard sent us."
He paused as Constable Watson followed his orders.
"Okay, you got it? ...Now, I want you to modify some features. Work on his hair. Yes, same colour, but extend it from about chin length to about shoulder length. While you're on it, thin out the eyebrows a bit. Make them more feminine. Our boy has a unibrow. Got all that? Email it to me when you are finished. Also, send me a copy of Mr. Godsé's original picture. We'll soon see if there is any substance in this lead."
The group wandered off to the food table and stocked up on cake, shortcake biscuits and tea. They then sat together, drinking and eating, but not saying a word; each lost in their own thoughts and overwhelmed by the latest developments.
Ten minutes later, Constable Watson's email came through.
"Now," said Jim, "take a look. With the exception of Murphy, who may bear a grudge, I want the rest to tell me who you think this person looks like."
Everyone gathered behind Jim while he held his smart phone up.
"This is the enhanced image and here is the original image. What do you think?" he asked.
There were gasps all around.
"Admittedly, the modified image is a split image of Miss Bolly," said Cynthia and added, "However, there something that doesn't seem right ... It's her eyes. Bolly has beautiful doe like soft brown eyes. Your suspect has light blue eyes."
"Drat!" exclaimed Jim sounding disappointed, "That casts a doubt on the new lead."
Jim noticed Cynthia wore a puzzled and confused expression.
"A penny for your thoughts Cynthia," said Jim.
"Lisa told me the strangest thing, some months ago when she and Patelji returned from Miss Bolly's studio. She said that the girls noticed Bolly returning from the ladies washroom with one blue eye and one brown eye. They had a good laugh at her expense. Bolly went back into the washroom and fixed the problem. I presumed she was experimenting with blue contact lenses. But it never occurred to me that her natural eye colour could be blue and that she masked it with brown contact lenses."
A stunned silence followed.
"What now?" asked Murphy innocently.

"I need to find out more about Miss Bolly," said Jim. "What's her real name for God's sake?"
"It's Bina Apté," said Cynthia.
"Of all the Indian names, why does the name Apté ring a bell?" asked Jim.
"Well, does the name Godsé ring a bell?" asked the schoolteacher.
"Yes it does. It's my prime suspect's last name, Anil Godsé."
"Well then Inspector, Godsé and Apté were Mahatma Gandhi's assassins."
"No kidding! Is this a cruel joke or a strange coincidence? Is there any Gandhi around here that I should worry about?"
"Well, my special ed. student Patelji's last name is Gandhi. He is registered as Susheel Patel-Gandhi. But everyone just calls him Patel-G."
"Where is he now?" asked Jim getting increasingly agitated.
"Both Lisa and Patelji are at Miss Bolly's studio practising for a special Indian classical dance and music performance that the school board is organising for the conference delegates, on the opening day, next week. I am going to pick them up after we are done here."
"I have a bad feeling about all this," said Jim.
"As you said earlier Jim, you need to clear Bolly's name by doing your background check. As far as I am concerned, Miss Bolly is a wonderful person. She's beautiful, smart and cultured. I owe her a debt of gratitude for all the good work she has done for Lisa and Patelji as well as so many other students from our school board. They learned such a lot about dance and music from her that their self-esteem has gone through the roof. You won't find anything on our Miss Bolly," said Cynthia, stubbornly in Miss Bolly's defence.
"Based on Murphy's embarrassing encounter, I suspect that Godsé and Apté are the same person! That could explain things. Scotland Yard and the Indian Military attaché, who was murdered, couldn't track him down because they not only had the wrong name, more importantly, they had the wrong gender!" said Jim emphatically.
"For some reason, Paresh disliked her," said Cynthia.
"Perhaps he knew something about her, and that's why he blew up at my party and nearly attacked her," said Veronica.
"Paresh did say that Patelji was in grave danger, but he was given to these bouts of irrational behaviour that at that time I dismissed it as …" said Cynthia and stopped speaking suddenly.

Chapter 32: Not Just a Pretty Brain

Everyone looked at Cynthia while she read an incoming text message.
"I can't make sense of this. It's from Lisa. She's using the smart phone that Paresh gave her..."
"What's it say?" asked Veronica.
"Miss Bolly acting funny. She got Patelji. Help," read Cynthia. "At least her spelling has improved, but now we've got to work on her grammar," continued Cynthia shaking her head in disbelief.
"That's my queue!" said Jim leaping to his feet. Then he flicked opened his cell phone and said, "Watson! Open the armoury and bring out a Smith and Wesson with a packet of shells. Meet me at the Hugh's Church on Broadgate; arrange for backup."
Jim asked, "Where's this woman's studio?"
"It's on Church Lane. She has rented a bungalow with a large circular driveway. The Bollywood Song and Dance Studio signage is quite noticeable. Please be careful. My children are with her!" pleaded Cynthia.

Watson brought the unmarked car to a screeching halt outside Hughes Church. Jim jumped in, and they raced uphill towards Church Lane and drove until they came to the signage. They entered the driveway and saw man getting into Bolly's red Mercedes SL 300, parked diametrically opposite. He looked liked Anil Godsé.

Godsé was surprised to see them, but when he noticed Constable Watson's uniform, he reached for an Uzi sub-machine gun, from the passenger seat, and levelled it at the car.
"Duck," yelled Jim as Godsé fired two short bursts. The car slumped on to one side as both tires were riddled with bullets. Jim's experience made him appreciate the precision and deliberateness of the action. They were dealing with a professional gunman. Watson grabbed the handgun, but needed to wind the driver side window in order to return fire. When Godsé saw the handgun, he raised the Uzi again.
"Heads down!" shouted Jim.
Godsé sprayed their vehicle with a third burst of gunfire. He shot out the rear window. A glass shard cut Watson across the back of his head as he lowered it. It bled profusely.
"I'm a goner... he's got me head," cried the young constable, who panicked at the sight of his own blood.
Jim pulled Watson towards himself and held a handkerchief as a pressure bandage against the nasty gash.
"It's a flesh wound; you'll live. He could have killed us if he wanted to," said Jim.
"Hold this in place," he instructed as he placed the constable's quivering hand over the handkerchief.

Meanwhile, Godsé hopped into the 300 SL and accelerated down Church Lane. That's the last anyone ever saw of him.
Jim radioed the dispatcher a description of Godsé and his vehicle. Roadblocks were soon set up on all major highways around Lincoln City, but the red vintage sports car and its occupant appeared to have vanished without trace.

Jim rushed into Miss Bolly's studio. The door was wide open. He heard a muffled sound from the coat closet in the foyer. It had been jammed shut by a colourful telescopic umbrella, rammed through its handles. He opened the door. To his surprise, Lisa rolled out of the closet, bound wrists and feet with duct tape. There was a strip of duct tape across her mouth. Her wrists were bound in front of her. She held her smart phone by the tips of her fingers. In spite of her bound wrists, she had managed to tap a text message. Jim removed the duct tape from across her mouth, and Lisa immediately started to speak.
"Some man that looks like Miss Bolly, has got Patelji," said Lisa anxiously and nodded in the direction of the reception. Jim rushed over and found Patelji lying very still on a couch, similarly bound by duct tape around his feet and wrists. He was unconscious. On the floor, there were several empty vials of Insulin and a tell tale syringe. Miss Bolly had injected him with a potentially lethal overdose of her prescription Insulin.

It took Patelji a week to recover from his ordeal, with the first three days spent in intensive care. Aside from Mr. and Mrs. Patel, Cynthia and Lisa kept a constant vigil. Cynthia went home to attend to chores, but Lisa never left his side. He was the brooding intellectual who tackled everything from playing the tabla, scanning the night skies for the moons of distant planets or programming avatars like they were all part of a science project. She was just the opposite; flamboyant, extrovert, barely literate, but a popular, highly skilled football player. Secretly they each wanted to be like each other.

He would slip in and out of a consciousness, but Lisa kept talking to him. When Cynthia returned she would often find Lisa fallen asleep with a protective arm over him and her head on his chest. The bond of sibling love and dependency between the two children was much deeper than Cynthia had ever imagined.

Almost three days after he had been admitted, he woke up, but said nothing and stared into the ceiling and fell into a deep sleep again. The child trauma specialist pronounced that Patelji was well enough to be taken out of intensive care. In the general ward, he shared a semi-private room with another child. He recovered quickly from then on. Lisa would walk him around the ward. They discovered a playroom with computers and electronic games. They were soon absorbed in interactive computer games and frantically manipulating game controllers. Patelji was soon himself again, admonishing Lisa for the wrong moves that cost her the game.

A Paediatrician assured the Patels that Patelji would not suffer long-term physiological effects. The major concern centred on his psychological well-being. Counselling with a child psychologist was recommended. The Patels took their ward home, but were plagued by a sense of guilt. The move to take the child out of his native Gujarat and transport him to a safe haven in England had not worked. The Deccan Dhaku almost got to him as they did when they blew up his parents' car. The family were only very distant relatives of the famed Mahatma. The faintest connection to the personification of non-violence and peaceful co-existence was enough to gain the attention of the evil arms dealers who controlled the Deccan Dhaku.

The Patels consulted with Cynthia while they considered their next move to protect Patelji. He was in no immediate danger. The Deccan Dhaku retreated since by acting so visibly they had exposed their hand. RAG rounded up many suspects all over India including their headquarters in Puné. Their mission to stop the CANDO Conference had failed again.

Life for Patelji returned to normal, but he kept having nightmares and would cry out for Lisa. Cynthia offered to keep Patelji, and after much debate, the Patels agreed to allow Patelji to live with her. Uncle Noby had to sacrifice is archery workshop. The spares and tools were moved to a location in the archery clubhouse.

Patelji settled down well at Cynthia's place. The children continued to go to the Rama Lab where Vivienne worked with them. They were told that Paresh was away, being treated for his PTSD. The children couldn't get over the murder of Michael by their music and dance instructor, Miss Bolly. Why did she do this and where was she now? Why did she want to harm Patelji? On the day that she attempted to murder Patelji, why did she dress as a man and behave like a man? No adult offered any rational explanations for all these mysteries. The general belief was that more harm than good would result in a convoluted explanation, which included a global conspiracy by arms dealer funded terrorists in an attempt to disrupt the conference. The children, although adolescent in maturity, were resigned to accept that the passage of time and experience would provide better explanations, in the future.

Chapter 33: Parting is Such Sweet Sorrow

The red Mercedes was found in Paresh's garage. Godsé switched vehicles and drove off in Paresh's station wagon. It was suspected that he assumed his female "Bolly" persona and evaded the roadblocks, set up around Lincoln. He abandoned the vehicle near a ferry port at Hull. Scotland Yard concluded that he escaped via private ferry to the Continent and was on a devious route back to India.

The Scotland Yard soon issued a press release that stated that the terror suspect, code named Canadian Visitor, was part of a sleeper cell. She posed as a music and dance instructor and attempted to murder her music pupil, a distant relative of the Gandhi family and hence disrupt the forthcoming CANDO Conference.

Jim Paradis and Cynthia had much to exchange. They decided to meet over a round of Golf, away from Lincoln. During their game, Jim informed Cynthia of the latest developments. Scotland Yard reviewed Cynthia's flash drive and had no reason to detain Paresh, apart from his own safety. They concluded that Michael Caruthers's murder was a tactic used to direct attention on to Paresh; the only other blue eyed South Asian in Lincoln, while the Deccan Dhaku attempted its planned assassination.

The Yard's IT specialists examined Paresh's homemade mini-supercomputer. They were able to discern that Paresh used it to hack into the Deccan Dhaku's Internet Servers. Paresh intercepted and deciphered the encrypted Deccan Dhaku email to discover Miss Bolly's identity. However, the primary target, Patelji, remained a closely guarded secret. The encrypted email messages never referred to him by name.

Mavis provided Tiru with Paresh's background check, which he shared with Jim Paradis. It turned out that Paresh Naik was well know to the Aboriginal, Métis and First Nations communities, due to his pioneering satellite remote sensing work for resource management. His employers, a First Nations tribe in the Banff National Park of Alberta, were anxious to have their prime contractor back. They had worked out a witness protection scheme with the RCMP. He would be escorted back to Canada and placed in their protective care.

Cynthia was distraught to hear this news, since she had no way to contact him. The last time she saw him was when he hastily gave her Patelji's telescope, in the hospital lobby. Jim had anticipated her predicament and had arranged a rendezvous, prior to his departure.

After a long drive, Inspector Jim Paradis walked through security at the Midlands Regional Home Office Detention Centre. He was finally to a sparse, small 8 by 10 foot cell, where Paresh sat waiting. A single window, barred from the outside, let in a thin sliver of mild English late summer sunlight. Paresh greeted him with an unshaven smile.

Jim booked a hotel room and went to Paresh's residence. Based on instructions, given over the phone, he packed most of Paresh's belongings in a couple of suitcases. An overnight stay and a comfortable bed is what he needed. A shower and a chance to wear his own clothes followed by a wholesome English breakfast lifted his spirits.

Jim drove Paresh towards the rendezvous point. It started out as an overcast day. They drove along Penny Lane that skirted the Strawberry Fields drive-in. The former drive-in now swarmed with activity in preparation for the weekend's open-air concert for the conference attendees. On a raised platform, the technical staff, who worked for Mono's Tryst With Destiny (TWD) rock band, had set up huge loudspeakers and a complex array of lights. Jim had read Paresh's statement following his interrogation by Special Branch officers. He broke the silence and asked, "It must have required a great deal of self-control not to have killed Miss Bolly. What made you hold back?"

While Paresh contemplated a response, someone tested the sound system by giving a reasonable rendition of John Lennon's *Imagine*.

Paresh watched Penny Lane rush past him up to the location of the grassy knoll where he had aborted his assassination attempt. He pointed and said, "Right here, I had her in my sights. I could have killed her if I wanted to. It took the example of two orphaned special needs children and the love of their surrogate mother to show me what I really needed to do. I came face to face with her. However, instead of slaying her, I banished her from my life, by forgiving her and just moving on. I need to focus on the more important things. In the universal Dance of Shiva ..."

"Dance of what?" interrupted Jim.

"Some people believe that Lord Shiva, a deity, dances through the universe. As he traverses the universe, he creates and destroys parts of it. We are made from cosmic or more likely solar dust, and hence we appear to have inherited this creative and destructive tendency. We are citizens of the Sun. There is good and evil in all of us. Nevertheless, it is the awareness of our weaknesses that can make us better people since we see in ourselves the same imperfections that others display. The willingness to forgive comes from this realization. I interpreted the Dance of Shiva as an embodiment of the power of forgiveness."

"You did the right thing by sparing her however, you should have come clean when Commander Gill interviewed you," said the police officer.

"Special Branch has a copy of all the Deccan Dakhu email that I intercepted. That information could not incriminate Miss Bolly because all the emails were addressed to Godsé. She would be free to go, and the fiasco that occurred in Canada would have repeated itself. When religious figures and statesmen called for a non-violent response or passive resistance, they were concerned with the coercion of ordinary good people. A consequence of terrorism is the creation of the anti-terrorist. Revenge is blind, and these anti-terrorists must be equally feared. Their blind rage has killed and maimed almost as many innocent victims, often dismissed as collateral damage. This is equally a potent force of evil. I just made a personal choice to avoid this never-ending cycle of violence. In the Mahabharata, a galaxy of venerated and peaceful dancing transvestites celebrated the marriage of Lord Shiva to the Goddess Parvati. They are regarded as pure and virginal. Miss Bolly, alias Godsé, who is ironically a transvestite, chose a destructive path."

"Aahh well…" said Jim shaking his head "You academics can argue about the finer points of non-violence and the eternal Dance of Shiva, but blokes like me have to face real life issues. Out here, it is kill or be killed! You should have left your crossbow in Canada."

"I'm sorry about Michael Caruthers. That was an unexpected turn of events. I was about to have a heart to heart chat with Cynthia and then come to see you, regardless of the consequences. However, regarding Commander Gill, I had intercepted Deccan Dhaku email wherein they ordered his termination. I sent an anonymous email to warn him, but it was of no avail. I knew if he and Miss Bolly met, he would not stand a chance. The element of surprise would be in her favour," said Paresh.

The rendezvous was planned at a carpool lay by, off the south bound A57, not far from where Cynthia and Paresh met for the first time. The car park was empty save for two vehicles. Paresh recognized Cynthia's car, but the other vehicle was a black vehicle, with tinted windows and odd license plates.

Jim parked close to the dark vehicle. He turned to Paresh and said, "This is it mate. Take care. I don't think we'll see you again in these parts after the trouble you've got yourself into."

"Really," said Paresh, without regret or concern. He saw Cynthia step out of her car.

"I'll take your cases over. You've got a minute or two with Cynthia. The Yard folks are anxious to get you to Heathrow for your flight to … somewhere in Canada."

"Thanks," said Paresh as he shook Jim's hand and walked towards Cynthia. Just then the drizzle that they had experienced on the journey from the hotel, turned into torrential rain.

He stopped within a few feet of Cynthia and started to say, "I am sorry I dragged you into this mess. I should have made a clean breast of it …"

"No, no don't be," said Cynthia as she reached out and placed her palm on his cheek and then continued to say, "I saw a news clip that showed you and the rest of the folks at the memorial in Cork, Ireland. I figured out the rest for myself. I regret that I could have helped you, if I had only known."

"Oh you helped; you all have more than helped. You and the kids saved me from making the biggest mistake of my life," said Paresh hoarse with emotion.

"You wonderful, wonderful man, with your supercomputer, avatars and all that crazy stuff, you rescued those kids and gave them a purpose in life. Almost everyone else abandoned them," she said. Her voice shook with emotion. Her clothes were drenched. At a time when she would have liked to have looked her best for him, the rain had washed her makeup away and left her hair in a dark, bedraggled, clingy mess. This was of no consequence to Paresh as he put his arms around her and placed his cheek against hers in a deep embrace.

Just then, a voice from the dark car said, "Time to go guv!"

Paresh released her reluctantly and walked to the car. When he was near the open door, he turned and rushed back towards Cynthia. She ran towards him. He swept her off her feet as she clung to his neck. He kissed her face and rested his lips tenderly against her lips for a time that seemed like a pleasant eternity. The rapturous illusion evaporated in a flash as the black car tooted its horn. Paresh walked back to the car with his arm around Cynthia. As he got in, she grabbed his shirt and said, "How will we keep in touch?"

"Just watch Lisa's email on her smart phone," he said and after a hesitant pause, he added as he looked into her eyes, "I love you Cynthia … I have loved you from the first time we met."

"And I have always loved you," said Cynthia, never taking her eyes off him. Tears ran down her cheeks and the rest of her rain-washed face.

The door shut gently, and the car accelerated away. Cynthia felt as though her soul had left with it. The dark vehicle followed a U shaped road and merged into the highway traffic. She strained to catch a last glimpse of him as he looked back at her through the rear window.

The much-anticipated CANDO conference went off without a hitch. The attendees representing NGOs from North America and Europe converged on Lincoln. The weeklong event turned out to be a grand success. The keynote speakers came from CANDO, the UN and the UK government, as the host country. The UN representative drew attention to the linkage between carbon abatement funds and nuclear disarmament. He complimented the conference attendees for their foresight and flexibility to invest in global Green Industry. Corporations and NGOs from any funding country would be selected as vendors in proportion to their country's investment. The CANDO agreement ensured this process.

Mr. Tiru announced that the Indian parliament had voted to participate in the Escrow Agreement. The treaty would be signed after the conference, and once his government confirmed its commitment to match funds. Then, Mr. Tiru unleashed a surprise announcement. His government had also agreed to allow CANDO to monitor and audit the carbon abatement projects and the Nuclear Escrow Zone. The latter addressed the last unresolved issue and resulted in a standing ovation. More jobs would result from these audits! After the speeches were completed, the attendees awarded contracts to the proposals that had won.

Chapter 34: The Taj by Moonlight

The conference called for many volunteers. Cynthia relished the opportunity to chair the Education and Training committee. It helped to take her mind off the past month's events, and the fact that she and the children missed Paresh. The Subcontinent's painful progress toward carbon neutrality would require major training efforts. Universities worldwide hoped to collaborate with their Indian secondary and post-secondary counterparts.

After the conference, Cynthia started her late summer preparation for the new school year. The dinner conversations turned inevitably to news of Paresh or the lack of it. Lisa monitored her email but there was never anything. Cynthia suggested that Paresh needed time to settle down to his new life and new identity. Nevertheless, the kids were impatient and longed for even the smallest news about Paresh. Cynthia hid her disappointment but at least Lisa saw right through her.

Late one evening, Lisa rushed into the room to announce that a large email had arrived. Patelji looked at it and confirmed it had come from an email server somewhere in Canada, but the source was concealed. It had a huge video attachment. Everyone huddled around the small screen.

When it started to play, they were disappointed, as it revealed nothing about Paresh or his whereabouts. However, they had no doubt that he had sent it. It turned out to be a news item from an Indian TV station.

The reporter, speaking in Inglish, covered the Carbon Abatement and Nuclear Disarmament Treaty between the Indian Government and CANDO. The Escrow monitoring representatives from the European Union and the UN were also at hand. This was the final milestone that would enable many Carbon abatement projects to share over a billion dollars. More importantly, the first nuclear weapon would be placed into the Escrow Monitoring Zone.

The signing took place on the grounds of the Taj Mahal. The Heritage Protection Ministry only permitted the main signatories, their security staff and registered media personnel, to enter the grounds. Security was tight all around. The fear that the Deccan Dhaku, could try a last ditch effort to stop the proceedings, kept everyone on their toes. Many wanted to witness this significant event. The crowds, amounting to thousands, had to wait outside to watch the proceedings on large outdoor screens. They spilled out into the surrounding roads and laneways.

The moonlight made the Taj Mahal look more beautiful than ever. Its marble dome shone like an everlasting Islamic beacon of love, peace and tranquility. The decorative border adorned the dome's diameter resembled an enigmatic smile. It seemed to beckon to the world. Look, look at the wonderful thing that is happening below!

A young South Indian sat on the podium. UN and EU representatives sat on either side of him. In stark contrast, behind him stood his tall blonde Canadian bodyguard. They had come a long way together. The blonde took the Nuclear Escrow Agreement from the UN representative to the EU representative and then to the Indian. When he finished signing it, his colleagues urged him to say a few words. Tiru chose his words carefully, respecting many that had sacrificed their lives, including those on the Kashmir Princess and his friend Jeevan, before this agreement could be reached.

He said, "Some say, sometime in the 21st Century, India will become a major superpower. Today at least, it became a big country."

He handed Mavis the signed document. She turned to the crowds and held it up in the air for the media and TV cameras to see. A loud cheer went up from the crowds but this turned into gasps of wonder, for just at that moment, colourful starbursts lit the night sky behind the marble dome. They had almost forgotten. Devali had started. This season that celebrated the triumph of good over evil.

Cynthia, Uncle Noby and the kids stared at the little screen. The kids didn't grasp its far reaching significance. However, the video clip was an endearing link to Paresh. They played it repeatedly. He wasn't with them anymore but his video had arrived. Cynthia watched as the kids replayed the video. She felt proud in what had been achieved. No one would ever know the small and important role her kids had played in making all this happen. She reflected on the tremendous contributions people with challenges could make, if they were only given a chance.

Not long after the video arrived, another mysterious email arrived. However, this was directed to Patelji's attention. It gave him a series of puzzles. The collective solution would give him the password to a secret Internet server. He would need to use a secure Virtual Private Network (VPN) to get to the server. The VPN created a secure "tunnel" through the Internet. Patelji just loved the challenge and soon gained access to the server. He gave the downloaded information to Cynthia. This brightened her spirits.

Cynthia had discussed adopting Patelji, but the Patels had earlier wanted more time to make their minds up. When she informed them that she would be joining Paresh in Canada, they gave their consent to his adoption. Canada represented an opportunity, and its vastness would make it more difficult for the Deccan Dhaku to find Patelji.
Cynthia handed in her resignation to the school board and started preparing for the family's trip to Canada. Uncle Noby was not surprised with her decision and promised to visit when it was safe to do so. He was

busy planning a trip to India. British Aerospace was participating in an air show that featured vintage to modern combat aircraft, and they had asked him to represent them at the air show in Puné.

Chapter 35: Refuge by a Lake

Cynthia, the kids and Bandit arrived at Calgary International Airport in Alberta, Canada. An Attendant wheeled in Bandit's carrying cage. The family retrieved their bags from the luggage carousel. They had arrived during the quiet period between the summer holiday rush and the Thanksgiving travel crowds. Cynthia directed the children to wheel the luggage burdened trolley carts to a specific location outside the airport's Arrivals area. They waited by the curb, underneath a large poster for Air Kanishka. Bandit slept, thanks to a vet prescribed sedative.

"Will Uncle Paresh be meeting us here?" asked Patelji.

"I'm not sure what is going to happen. A taxi has been scheduled to pick us up from here, below this poster," assured Cynthia. The children looked at every taxi that hurried by.

Soon a nondescript minivan taxi pulled up beside them. The tinted windows made it difficult to see the driver.

The curb side rear sliding door slid open and Cynthia said, "Quick, get in and put on your seat belts," as she got into the front seat.

The driver, who happened to be a turbaned and bearded person, wore dark glasses. He opened the tailgate and loaded the luggage. However, as he handled Bandit's cage, Bandit appeared to spring to life and barked excitedly. He continued to bark and whine intermittently as they drove away, travelling West.

"Should I let him out of his cage," asked Lisa.

"No, I think I know what's got him all excited," said Cynthia, and to Lisa's surprise, smiled and winked at the driver.

Once on the highway, the taxi headed towards the setting sun. About twenty minutes later, the urban sprawl gave way to a breathtaking landscape. The forest thickened on either side. The Canadian Rockies loomed on the western horizon. The late sun caught the orange and gold of early autumn leaves. Banff National Park appeared on most subsequent road signs.

"Could we stop for a bit to give the dog a short walk?" asked Cynthia.

The driver nodded, but said nothing. They soon came to an exit marked Rest Area. He took it and drove into the parking lot.

"Look at those tall evergreen trees mom," remarked Lisa.

"Can you recall what they are called? Remember the Internet based research we did on Alberta?" challenged Cynthia.

"Err… Doug … Douglas ... something… Oh I remember, Douglas Firs!" said Lisa triumphantly.

"You are not just a pretty brain, you've got a face too!" said the driver, as he turned his head, took off his glare glasses and beamed at the kids with his marble blue eyes.

"Paresh!" screamed Lisa, as she threw her arms around him and almost knocked off his turban.
"Uncle Paresh! Is that really you?" shouted Patelji excitedly.

They got out of the minivan. There were many hugs and kisses. The sudden turn of events did not surprise the overjoyed Cynthia, thanks to the coded messages that Paresh had sent her earlier. The kids were overwhelmed and ecstatic at being united with Paresh again.

"Due to the bad things that have happened, the police advised me to change my name and appearance and live in seclusion. I've changed my family name to Singh," explained Paresh, talking directly to the kids.

"Great! Then I'm Lisa Singh" said Lisa.

"And I'm Patelji Singh" said Patelji not to be out done.

"And am I not your one and only Cynthia Singh?" pleaded Cynthia, batting her eyes at him.

"Of course you are!" assured Paresh.

He paused for a moment and continued to say, "In order to make ends meet, I drive this taxi part-time and have another job as a gardener at a tourist chalet. A First Nations tribe, my employers, own it."

"Uncle, aren't you embarrassed to drive a taxi and to do all this gardening stuff?" asked Patelji.

"Not at all," responded Paresh, "In fact I rather enjoy talking to other taxi drivers as we wait for our fares at the taxi stand. Most of them are graduates from some of the best Universities. Some have Ph.D.s and MBAs. I often get wrapped up in discussions from Brain Plasticity to Nanotechnology."

"It's such a waste of talent and experience," remarked Cynthia shaking her head.

"Well, in this country, becoming a cabby, for foreign trained professionals, is almost like a rite of passage before better prospects come our way," said Paresh with resignation.

Paresh and Cynthia walked hand in hand along the of the Rest Area's perimeter. Patelji wanted to walk behind them with Bandit on the leash, but Lisa pulled him in the opposite direction and scolded him saying, "Can't you see they want to be alone, silly! Haven't I taught you anything?"

As Cynthia and Paresh walked along, Cynthia brought him up to date on all the latest Lincoln news. Uncle Noby enjoyed his trip to India. His former squadron had arranged for him to fly in the back seat of a Puné based Sukhoi jet fighter.

A surprise revelation occurred during the reading of Michael Caruthers's will. He left the Saracen's Head to Murphy O'Neil. This allowed Murphy to raise money to buy a 50% partnership in Mr. Patel's printing business. The Patels were planning to go into semi-retirement.

They would spend their winters in warmer climes and leave the store in Murphy's care. Veronica resigned from her job at the University. She planned to help Murphy to manage his two businesses.

The family continued their journey westward past the Town of Banff and on towards Lake Louise. Paresh slowed the vehicle down to look for an exit.

"Not long to go now. We are entering a First Nation's reservation. It belongs to people who originally owned most of Canada!" he said to the kids who had dozed off at the back. Paresh took the required exit and drove on to a dirt road, which led to an evergreen forest. The ride was so bumpy that it prompted Cynthia to enquire, "I hope you know where you are going?"

"In a few months this road will be shut down for winter. I am told there would be about two feet of snow here," said Paresh.

The road emerged into a clearing. They drove along the bank of a lake. The dark, overcast skies prevented them from noticing the scenic splendour on the other side of the lake. Paresh entered the driveway to a mansion and turned left, to follow a lane, which led to a log cabin.

"Here we are at last," said Paresh as he led the way into the cabin. They entered a spacious but sparsely furnished area with three bedrooms that led away from a common kitchen and living area. The kids were tired and went straight to bed. Bandit followed Patelji. Ever since his episode with Miss Bolly, Bandit instinctively knew that Patelji needed to be protected.

"So, what are you going to do with me now Dr. Naik?" asked Cynthia as she grinned at him with her hands on her hips, almost defiant.

As long as Cynthia had known him, Paresh hadn't been a man of many words. True to form, he did not waste any time on verbiage. He lifted Cynthia off her feet, as she covered her mouth to suppress a gentle scream, and carried her across the threshold of their bedroom.

The next morning, when Cynthia woke up, she knew she had overslept. The kids watched TV with Bandit at their feet. Paresh was nowhere in sight. Cynthia looked around the kitchen to see what she could make for breakfast. As she opened the refrigerator, she heard a gentle knock. A lady, with tanned complexion, intricately platted long grey hair and a pleasant smile, greeted her at the front door.

"Hello there," said the lady cheerfully, "I'm Mary Lakekeeper. Welcome to our First Nation. Mr. Singh told us you folks have come all the way from the UK! Please join me on the patio out there," she said pointing towards the mansion, "I've made us some breakfast by the barbeque."

"Thanks very much. We'll be out there shortly," said Cynthia.

They hurriedly got ready and stepped into the autumn sunlight. The mansion and the log cabin overlooked a large emerald lake with a snow capped mountain in the background. They hadn't noticed it when they drove in, the previous night. Patelji held Cynthia's hand and Lisa walked behind with Bandit. Tall Douglas fir lined the lakeshore as far as the eye could see. The fresh, clean air made the children lively and alert, in a manner she hadn't noticed before.

Patelji asked, "Mom, does this lake have a lot of fish?"

"I don't know. We'll have to ask Mary," replied Cynthia. Finally, thought Cynthia, squeezing his hand for reassurance, a simple question from a normal child. Had he remained in England, he would have been sent up to Cambridge and would be expected to behave like an intellectual don and forfeit his childhood. He had been rescued from that cruel fate. Concerns about moving to Canada were melting away.

Directly opposite the mansion was a dock with a cabin cruiser and a rowboat moored alongside. Mary was clearly pleased to see the kids and reached out to give both of them a welcoming hug. They were greeted with a sumptuous breakfast. A large pile of pancakes and freshly grilled bacon, toast, orange juice, and a fruit basket were laid out around the table.

"Mmm ..." said Cynthia, "the bacon smells delicious. You've taken a lot of trouble on our account."

"Not at all," replied Mary, "A small token of our thanks for the great work your Mr. Singh has done around the house. My husband, Charlie, has been struggling with the electronic gadgetry that Mr. Singh fixed. They're both in the cabin cruiser messing around with the surround sound and wireless Internet connection. During the peak period in summer, the tourists are taken out to cruise and fish on the lake."

Cynthia noticed Patelji, who had never eaten pancakes, trying to eat it like a chapatti, by breaking off a bit and dipping it into maple syrup.

"Use a knife and fork sweetie or your fingers will get all sticky. Just watch your sister," suggested Cynthia. Which he promptly did, but she just stuck her tongue out at him and gobbled a piece of bacon saying, "You can't have any of this, you vegan!"

"Mom!" complained Patelji.

"It's okay, help yourself to some fruit," consoled Cynthia and turned to Mary to say,

"Sorry for my little British savages! They had better behave or they will be sent back. Right!"

"No problem, this feels like a family breakfast again. Our kids are at university now," smiled Mary.

Just then, Charlie called to them from the dock as he and Paresh emerged from the boat and walked towards them.

"Hi everyone," he said and holding his soiled hands in the air he said, "I won't shake hands or hug anyone, but welcome to you all."
"Does anyone fancy a ride in the row boat?" asked Paresh.
Both the kids jumped up and ran towards him.
"Excuse us," said Cynthia as she rose and ran after them.
"Not so fast young man," said Cynthia catching up to Patelji, "Remember what happened when you last went into a lake."
Patelji said nothing, but put on a long pleading expression.
"I'll ask Mary for a life vest for you, and we'll take you for a boat ride later," promised Cynthia.

She sat with her arm around Patelji with their bare feet dangling over the dock, touching the water while Paresh and Lisa got into the rowboat, followed by Bandit, who needed no invitation. Paresh splashed water on Lisa who squealed with delight. She urged him to row forward, but he teased her by rowing in wide circles instead. Bandit stood in the front and barked towards the open water.

Cynthia watched their playful antics with a widening smile. She then came to realize that the man who had learned to forgive, the man whom she loved, was finally rewarded with what he really wanted, a family of his own, by a peaceful lake, with a beautiful snow capped mountain reflected in it. The Canadian visitor had returned home.

Glossary

AGA Asian Global Alliance; a fictitious political party.

Ashoka Emblem Official emblem of the Government of India. It depicts four lions, facing in four directions, standing on a circular podium.

Asperger's Syndrome Asperger's is an Autism spectrum disorder, characterized by impaired social skills related to the lack of empathy and repetitive behaviour.

Autism or Autism Spectral Disorder Autism Spectral Disorder, or ASD, is also called Pervasive Developmental Disorder (PDD) because they involve delays in many areas of development. PDD or ASD is a category that includes five different disorders of development, each with differing severities and patterns.

Avatar In Sanskrit, Avatar refers to the descent of divinity to earth for the purpose of helping mortals. In the present context Avatars are simulated, using Virtual Reality technology, to represent elements of an instructional process to assist children with intellectual challenges.

Brahmin A caste associated with knowledgeable, highly educated people. The Brahmin priests are responsible for retaining and passing on information from generation to generation, religious tradition and knowledge.

CANDO Carbon Abatement and Nuclear Disarmament Organization (fictitious).

Chappati South Asian unleavened flatbread made of wheat flour and water.

Chikki A squared sweet that consists of layers of nuts of a single type or a mixed variety of nuts bonded together by a hard sweet resin.

Churidar tightly fitting trousers worn by both men and women in South Asia.

CISIA Canadian Inter Services Intelligence Agency; a fictitious Canadian Federal Intelligence Agency.

CPU Central Processing Unit in a computer.

Diet for a New America A non-fiction book by John Robbins How Your Food Choices Affect Your health, Happiness and the Future of Life on Earth, Stillpoint Publishing, (1987.)

Dhaku Translated literally from Hindi means dacoit.

Digs Accommodation provided for a paying guest.

Dubha Wallah A person that is employed to deliver home a cooked lunch to office workers.

Dyslexia A language processing disability associated with deficits in auditory processing. This condition, if not treated, could severely impede an individual's ability to read fluently and hence learn.

Escrow An accounting term used to specify a special account that is governed by rules or protocols that control who has debit and credit access to it. An Escrow account is usually used in real estate transactions to hold in trust deposits made by potential buyers.

Examination for Discovery A pre-trial process at which lawyers for each of the parties question other parties or their employees, under oath, about the matters involved in the lawsuit.

Fissile Material Fissile material is a material capable of sustaining a nuclear fission chain reaction. By definition, fissile material can sustain a chain reaction with neutrons of any energy.

Fusion Nuclear Reactor A Nuclear Reactor that uses Nuclear Fusion to generate energy. Nuclear Fusion is an atomic reaction in which multiple atoms combine to create a single, more massive atom. The resulting atom has a slightly smaller mass than the sum of the masses of the original atoms. The difference in mass is released in the form of energy during the reaction.

G-forces As a consequence of Isaac Newton's 'Laws of Motion,' any entity that is in a state of motion continues in that state unless a force or forces act on it causing it to change direction and or slow down or speed up. When this happens, an inertial force or forces, arise that resist this change and act on the entity in an equal and opposite direction to the applied force. This inertial force can be represented in terms of the gravitation constant “g” where the mass times g is the weight of the entity at rest. Hence the force per unit mass acting on the entity could be stated as say, “2 g” or twice its weight per unit mass.

GHG Green House Gases.

Glock 17 A brand name and model of a hand gun.

GPS Global Positioning System; a system of orbiting satellites that can be used to specify the location of a person or device using a GPS receiver. The receiver uses three of more satellites to calculate and display its longitude and latitude.

GPU Graphical Processing Unit.

Gross and fine sensory motor integration Sensory motor integration is the synergistic relationship between the sensory system and the motor system. Since the two communicate and coordinate with each other, if one is problematic, the other can suffer as a result. Gross motor implies large movement and actions as in walking and running. Fine motor motion implies movement associated with delicate and intricate skills such as writing and painting.

Helium 3 Helium 3 (He3) is a light, non-radioactive isotope of helium with two protons and one neutron, in contrast with two neutrons in common helium. He3 is proposed as a more attractive fuel in a fusion reactor because the by products are not radioactive and due to the elimination of high energy neutrons, are easier to contain.

Hijara A Hindi term for a transvestite.

Inglish A type of spoken English in India that consists of normal English but includes Hindi words that are used to emphasize a point or use an expression or term for which there is no accurate English translation.

Jeeves Jeeves is the name of a whimsical butler of an aristocratic 1930s era Englishman, created by British author, P. G. Woodhouse.

Kukri A short curved combat knife used by Gurkha soldiers from Nepal.

Lakh Indian term for 100,000.

Leg-before-wicket In the game of cricket, leg-before-wicket or lbw is an umpiring decision made to determine if the batsman's leg or any part of his/her body obstructed the path of the ball towards the wickets. If the batsman's bat touches the ball, then this ruling does not apply.

MAYDAY "Mayday, Mayday, Mayday" is an internationally recognized radio distress call used by mariners and aircraft pilots, in the event of a life threatening mishap or situation.

MIQ A fictitious UK Government intelligence agency.

Mountie Another name for a Royal Canadian Mounted Policeman or police woman.

Mumbaikar A resident of Mumbai city.

NGO Non-Governmental Organization

Niagara Escarpment The Niagara Escarpment is a geological landmark 450 million years in the making. It is a 750-kilometre ridge of fossil-filled rock, located in southern Ontario. It is home to many plant and animal species. It is a scenic wonder that is best accessed through the Bruce Trail.

Nuclear Escrow Zone A region, wherein nuclear warheads, entire ballistic missiles or highly enriched fissile and weapons grade material can be stored. This zone is created by one country or two or more nuclear adversaries and monitoring organizations, following the signing of a Nuclear Escrow Treaty. All items placed in escrow are subject to a strict treaty specified protocol that governs their placement, maintenance and disposal. Local electronic and remote satellite monitoring of items in the escrow zone is a joint responsibility of treaty signatories.

Orton-Gillingham method An intensive, sequential phonics-based system teaches the basics of word formation before whole meanings. The method accommodates and utilizes the three learning modalities, or pathways, through which people learn: visual, auditory and kinaesthetic.

Paki A racial slur usually directed to persons of South Asian descent.

PAN "Pan, Pan, Pan," Pay Attention Now; a first level of warning or notice issued by an airline pilot that indicates that the flight has encountered a serious safety or operational abnormality.

Pervasive Developmental Disorder (PDD) A form of autism.

Phoneme A phoneme is the smallest sound unit in a language that is capable of conveying a distinct meaning.

Pressure Transducer An electronic device that detects small changes in pressure.

Puja a religious offering.

RAG Research and Analysis Group; a fictitious Indian Central Government intelligence agency.

Ravana A mythological ten headed demon, featured in the Ramayana, which terrorized Sri-Lanka.

RCMP Royal Canadian Mounted Police.

RFID Radio Frequency Identifier - A miniature electronic device when attached to an item, radios information about it. This serves to identify it.

RSLI A fictitious Puné based company called, Roshni Sound and Light International.

Shaitan An Islamic term for the devil or in English and Hebrew better known as Satan.

Shalwar Kameez A combination shirt or tunic worn over tight pyjama like trousers. Typically a female attire in the Indian Sub-continent but a similar format of attire is also worn by boys and men.

Tata Nano A low priced, compact automobile made by the Tata company in India.

TGIF Thank God It's Friday.

UZI A submachine gun, manufactured in Israel, which can fire up to 32 rounds.

Virtual Reality A computer technology that simulates the physical presence of a user in a simulated environment that allows the user to interact with other simulated entities, including Avatars, in that environment, so as to create an experience that is close to reality.

VPN Virtual Private Network – an Internet transmission technique that uses an Internet tunnelling protocol, which allows information to be transmitted from one computer to another, in a secure manner.

WOG A racial slur that stands for Westernized Oriental Gentleman directed at people of colour of Asian decent.

51896309R00144

Made in the USA
Charleston, SC
06 February 2016